A. Alvarez

The Savage God

A Study of Suicide

W. W. Norton & Company
New York   London

First published as a Norton paperback 1990

Sections of this book have appeared in *New American Review,*
the *Atlantic Monthly, Partisan Review,* the *Listener,* the *Observer* and
Handbook for the Study of a Suicide, edited by Seymour Perlin.
First published by Weidenfeld & Nicolson 1971

The author and publishers are grateful to the copyright owners of
the following works for their permission to quote from them:
Ariel (published by Harper & Row) and *The Colossus* (published
by Alfred A. Knopf) by Sylvia Plath, copyright © Ted Hughes
1965 and 1960; *An Essay in Autobiography* by Boris Pasternak,
Collins Publishers; *The Less Deceived* by Philip Larkin,
copyright © The Marvell Press 1955, 1971; *The Collected Poems
of W. B. Yeats,* Macmillan.

Alvarez, A. (Alfred), 1929-
  The savage god : a study of suicide / A. Alverez.
      p.   cm.
  Reprint. Originally published: London: Penguin, © 1971.
  ISBN 0-393-30657-7 (pbk.) : $8.95
  1. Suicide. 2. Suicide in literature. I. Title.
[HV6545.A55 1990]
364.1'522—dc20   90-36405
                                                      CIP

ISBN 0-393-30657-7

W. W. Norton & Company, Inc.
500 Fifth Avenue, New York, N.Y. 10110
www.wwnorton.com

W. W. Norton & Company Ltd.
Castle House, 75/76 Wells Street, London W1T 3QT

7 8 9 0

Contents

After us the Savage God

The God Tezcatlipoca, he was considered a true god, invisible, able to enter everywhere, in the heavens, on earth and into the place of the dead. It was said that when he was upon earth he incited people to war, created enmity and discord and caused much anguish and disquiet. He set people against one another so that they made wars, and for this reason he was called 'the enemy on both sides'.

He alone understood how the world was governed, and alone gave prosperity and riches, and took them away at will; he gave riches, prosperity and fame, courage and command, dignities and honour, and took them away again as he willed. For this he was feared and reverenced, for it was within his power to raise up or cast down.

— SAHAGUN: *History of the Things of New Spain*

Preface

When I was at school there was an unusually sweet-tempered rather disorganized physics master who was continually talking, in a joky way, about suicide. He was a small man with a large red face, a large head covered with woolly grey curls and a permanently worried smile. He was said to have got a First in his subject at Cambridge, unlike most of his colleagues. One day at the end of a lesson, he remarked mildly that anyone cutting his throat should always be careful to put his head in a sack first, otherwise he would leave a terrible mess. Everyone laughed. Then the one o'clock bell rang and the boys all trooped off to lunch. The physics master cycled straight home, put his head in a sack and cut his throat. There wasn't much mess. I was tremendously impressed.

The master was much missed, since a good man was hard to find in that bleak, shut-in community. But in all the hush and buzz of scandal that followed, it never occurred to me that he had done anything wrong. Later, I had my own long run-in with depression and began to understand, I thought, why he had opted for such a desperate way out. Shortly after that, I got to know Sylvia Plath in that extraordinary creative period which preceded her death. We used to talk about suicide at times – but coolly, as a subject like any other. It was only after she took her life that I realized that I knew almost nothing about the act, despite the large claims to understanding I had been privately making to myself for so long. This book is an attempt to find out why these things happen.

It begins with a memoir of Sylvia Plath, not simply as a tribute to her, since I think she was one of the most gifted writers of our time, but also as a matter of emphasis. I want the book to start, as it ends, with a detailed case-history, so that whatever theories and abstractions follow can somehow be rooted in the human particular. No single theory will untangle an act as ambiguous and with such complex motives as suicide. The Prologue and Epilogue are there as reminders of how partial every explanation must always be. So I have tried to chart the shifts and confusions of feeling which led up to Sylvia's death as I understand them, and as objectively as I am able. From this one instance I have followed the subject where it has led into less personal areas.

It has proved a long trail. When I started I innocently thought that not much had been written about suicide: a beautiful philosophical essay by Camus, *The Myth of Sisyphus*, a great authoritative tome by Emile Durkheim, Erwin Stengel's invaluable Penguin handbook, and an excellent, but out of print historical survey by Giles Romilly Fedden. I soon found I was wrong. There is a huge mass of material on the topic and it grows larger every year. Yet little of it is of much interest to anyone except the specialist, and even less has to do with what the layman personally knows of suicide. The sociologists and clinical psychiatrists, in particular, have been peculiarly unstoppable. Yet it is possible – in fact, easy – to plough through almost any of their innumerable books and articles without once realizing that they are concerned with that shabby, confused, agonized crisis which is the common reality of suicide. Even the psycho-analysts seem to avoid the topic. It gets into their work mostly by the way, while discussing other things. There are a few notable exceptions – whom I duly acknowledge later – but to a large extent I have had to piece together the psycho-analytic theory of suicide as best I could, from the point of view of an interested outsider who is not in analysis. All that is in Part III. But anyone who wants a full survey of the facts and statistics of suicide and a résumé of the current state of play in theory and research should go to Professor Stengel's lucid and sympathetic study, *Suicide and Attempted Suicide*.

The more technical research I read, the more convinced I became that the best I could do would be to look at suicide from the perspective of literature to see how and why it colours the imaginative world of creative people. Not only is literature a subject I know something about, it is also a discipline which is concerned, above everything else, with what Pavese called 'this business of living'. Since the artist is, by vocation, more aware of his motives than most other people and better able to express himself, it seemed likely that he would offer illuminations which sociologists, psychiatrists and statisticians missed. In following this black thread I have arrived at a theory which, for me, in some way explains what the arts are about now. But in order to understand why suicide should seem so central to contemporary writing I have gone back a long way to see how the theme has developed imaginatively in the past five or six hundred years. This has involved a certain amount of, perhaps, dreary detail. But I am not writing for the literary specialist and if that is how the book comes across in the end, I have failed.

I offer no solutions. I don't, in fact, believe that solutions exist, since suicide means different things for different people at different times. For Petronius Arbiter it was a final stylish grace-note to a life devoted to high style. For Thomas Chatterton it was the alternative to a slow death by starvation. For Sylvia Plath it was an attempt to get herself out of a desperate corner her own poetry had boxed her into. For Cesare Pavese it was as inevitable as the next sunrise, an event which all the praise and success in the world could not put off. The only conceivable solution the suicide can hope for is help of one kind or another: sympathetic understanding of what he is going through from the Samaritans or the priest or from those few doctors who have the time and inclination to listen, trained help from the psycho-analyst or from what Professor Stengel hopefully calls a 'therapeutic community' specifically organized to cope with these emergencies. But then, he may not want help.

Instead of offering answers, I have simply tried to counterbalance two prejudices: the first is that high religiose tone – though now it is most often used by people who belong to no church they would care to mention – which dismisses suicide in horror as a moral crime or sickness beyond discussion. The second is the current scientific fashion which, in the very process of treating suicide as a topic for serious research, manages to deny it all serious meaning by reducing despair to the boniest statistics.

Nearly everybody has his own ideas about suicide and so more people than I could decently mention or thank have come up with references, details and suggestions. But I owe a great debt of gratitude to Tony Godwin whose conviction – against all the evidence – that I could produce this book made him arrange a generous advance which gave me the freedom to write it. My thanks, too, to the Arts Council of Great Britain for a grant which came mercifully and at a crucial moment. And to Diana Harte who struggled with the manuscript, typing and re-typing the thing meticulously. Thanks, above all, to my wife, Anne, who helped, criticised and, quite simply, got me through it.

A.A.

Part 1
Prologue: Sylvia Plath

Dying
Is an art, like everything else.
I do it exceptionally well.

I do it so it feels like hell.
I do it so it feels real.
I guess you could say I've a call.

— SYLVIA PLATH

The passion for destruction is also
a creative passion.

— MICHAEL BAKUNIN

As I remember it, I met Sylvia and her husband in London in the spring of 1960. My first wife and I were living near Swiss Cottage, on the unsmart edge of literary Hampstead, in a tall Edwardian building of particularly ugly red brick; it was the colour of some old boiler that had been left out to rust for so long that even the brightness of decay had worn off. When we moved in the place had just been converted by one of those grab-and-get-out property companies that did so well before the Rachman scandal made life harder for extortionist landlords. Naturally, they had made a shoddy job of it: the fittings were cheap and the finish awful; the window frames seemed too small for the brickwork around them and there were large, rough gaps at every joint. But we had sanded the floors and painted the place out in bright colours. Then we bought bits and pieces from the junk furniture dealers in Chalk Farm, and sanded and painted them, too. So in the end it seemed gay enough in a fragile, skin-deep way: just the place for the first baby, the first book, the first real unhappiness. By the time we left eighteen months later, there were gaping cracks in the outer wall where the new windows had been cut. But by that time there were gaping cracks in our lives, too, so it all seemed to fit.

Since I was the regular poetry critic for the *Observer* I saw few writers. To know whom I was reviewing seemed to make too many difficulties: nice men often write bad verse and good poets can be monsters; more often than not both the man and his work were unspeakable. It seemed easier all round not to be able to put a face to the name, and judge solely on the printed page. I kept to my rule even when I was told that Ted Hughes was living nearby, just across Primrose Hill, with an American wife and small baby. Three years before he had brought out *The Hawk in the Rain*, which I admired greatly. But there was something about the poems which made me suspect that he wouldn't care what I thought. They seemed to emerge from an absorbed, physical world that was wholly his own; for all the technical skill deployed, they gave the impression that literary goings-on were no concern of the author. 'Don't worry,' I was told, 'he never talks shop.' I was also told that he had a wife called Sylvia, who also wrote poetry, 'but' -- and this was said reassuringly - 'she's very sharp and intelligent'.

In 1960 came *Lupercal*. I thought it the best book by a young poet that I had read since I began my stint on the *Observer*. When I wrote a review to say so, the paper asked for a short piece about him for one of the more gossipy pages. I phoned him and we arranged to take our kids for a walk on Primrose Hill. It seemed like a nice, neutral idea.

They were living in a tiny flat not far from the Regent's Park Zoo. Their windows faced on to a run-down square: peeling houses around a scrappy wilderness of garden. Closer to the Hill gentility was advancing fast: smart Sunday newspaper house-agents had their boards up, the front doors were all fashionable colours – 'Cantaloup', 'Tangerine', 'Blueberry', 'Thames Green' – and everywhere was a sense of gleaming white interiors, the old houses writ large and rich with new conversions.

Their square, however, had not yet been taken over. It was dirty, cracked and rackety with children. The rows of houses that led off it were still occupied by the same kind of working-class families they had been built for eighty years before. No one, as yet, had made them chic and quadrupled their price – though that was to come soon enough. The Hughes's flat was one floor up a bedraggled staircase, past a pram in the hall and a bicycle. It was so small that everything seemed sideways on. You inserted yourself into a hallway so narrow and jammed that you could scarcely take off your coat. The kitchen seemed to fit one person at a time, who could span it with arms outstretched. In the living room you sat side by side, longways on, between a wall of books and a wall of pictures. The bedroom off it, with its flowered wallpaper, seemed to have room for nothing except a double bed. But the colours were cheerful, the bits and pieces pretty, and the whole place had a sense of liveliness about it, of things being done. A typewriter stood on a little table by the window, and they took turns at it, each working shifts while the other minded the baby. At night they cleared it away to make room for the child's cot. Later, they borrowed a room from another American poet, W. S. Merwin, where Sylvia worked the morning shift, Ted the afternoon.

This was Ted's time. He was on the edge of a considerable reputation. His first book had been well received and won all sorts of prizes in the States, which usually means that the second book will be an anticlimax. Instead, *Lupercal* effortlessly fulfilled and surpassed all the promises of *The Hawk in the Rain*. A figure had emerged on the drab scene of British poetry, powerful and undeniable. Whatever his natural hesitations and distrust of his own work, he must have had some sense of his own strength and achievement. God alone knew how far he was eventually going but in one essential way he had already arrived. He was a tall, strong-looking man in a black corduroy jacket, black trousers, black shoes; his dark hair hung untidily forward; he had a long, witty mouth. He was in command.

In those days Sylvia seemed effaced, the poet taking a back seat to the young mother and housewife. She had a long, rather flat body, a longish face, not pretty but alert and full of feeling, with a lively mouth and fine brown eyes. Her brownish hair was scraped severely into a bun. She wore jeans and a neat shirt, briskly American: bright, clean, competent, like a young woman in a cookery advertisement, friendly and yet rather distant.

Her background, of which I knew nothing then, belied her housewifely air. She had been a child prodigy – her first poem was published when she was eight – and then a brilliant student, winning every prize to be had, at Wellesley High School, then at Smith College: scholarships all the way, straight As, Phi Beta Kappa, president of this and that college society, and prizes for everything. A New York glossy magazine, *Mademoiselle*, had picked her as an outstanding possibility and wined her, dined her and photographed her all over Manhattan. Then, almost inevitably, she had won a Fulbright to Cambridge, where she met Ted Hughes. They were married in 1956, on Bloomsday. Behind Sylvia was a self-sacrificing, widowed mother, a schoolteacher who had worked herself into the ground so that her two children might flourish. Sylvia's father – ornithologist, entomologist, ichthyologist, international authority on bumble-bees and professor of biology at Boston University – had died when she was nine. Both parents were of German stock and were German speaking, academic and intellectual. When she and Ted went to the States after Cambridge, a glittering university career seemed both natural and assured.

On the surface it was a typical success story: the bril-

liant examination-passer driving forward so fast and relent-
lessly that nothing could ever catch up with her. And it can
last a lifetime, provided nothing checks the momentum,
and the vehicle of all those triumphs doesn't disintegrate
into sharp fragments from sheer speed and pressure. But
already her progress had twice lurched to a halt. Between
her month on *Mademoiselle* and her last year in college she
had had the nervous breakdown and desperately serious
suicide attempt, which became the theme of her novel, *The
Bell Jar*. Then, once re-established at Smith – 'an outstanding teacher,' said her colleagues – the academic prizes no
longer seemed worth the effort. So in 1958 she had thrown
over university life – Ted had never seriously contemplated
it – and gone freelance, trusting her luck and talent as a
poet. All this I learned much later. Now Sylvia had simply
slowed down; she was subdued, absorbed in her new baby
daughter, and friendly only in that rather formal, shallow,
transatlantic way that keeps you at your distance.

Ted went downstairs to get the pram ready while she
dressed the baby. I stayed behind a minute, zipping up my
son's coat. Sylvia turned to me, suddenly without gush.

'I'm so glad you picked *that* poem,' she said. 'It's one of
my favourites but no one else seemed to like it.'

For a moment I went completely blank; I didn't know
what she was talking about. She noticed and helped me out.

'The one you put in the *Observer* a year ago. About the
factory at night.'

'For Christ's sake, Sylvia *Plath*.' It was my turn to gush,
'I'm sorry. It was a lovely poem.

'Lovely' wasn't the right word, but what else do you say
to a bright young housewife? I had picked it from a sheaf
of poems which had arrived from America, immaculately
typed, with addressed envelope and international reply
coupon efficiently supplied. All of them were polished and

talented, but that in itself was not rare in those days. The late fifties was a period of particularly high style in American verse, when every campus worth its name had its own 'brilliant' poetic technician in residence. But at least one of these poems had more going for it than rhetorical elegance. It had no title, though later, in *The Colossus*, she called it 'Night Shift'. It was one of those poems which starts by saying what it is *not* about so strongly that you don't believe the explanations that follow:

> It was not a heart, beating,
> That muted boom, that clangour
> Far off, not blood in the ears
> Drumming up any fever
>
> To impose on the evening.
> The noise came from outside:
> A metal detonating
> Native, evidently, to
>
> These stilled suburbs: nobody
> Startled at it, though the sound
> Shook the ground with its pounding.
> It took root at my coming . . .

It seemed to me more than a piece of good description, to be used and moralized upon as the fashion of that decade dictated. The note was aroused and all the details of the scene seemed continually to be turning inwards. It is a poem, I suppose, about fear, and although in the course of it the fear is rationalized and explained (that pounding in the night is caused by machines turning), it ends by re-asserting precisely the threatening masculine forces there were to be afraid of. It had its moments of awkwardness — for example, the prissy, pausing flourish in the manner of Wallace Stevens: 'Native, evidently, to . . .' But compared with most of the stuff that thudded unsolicited through my letter-box every morning, it was that rare thing: the always unexpected, wholly genuine article.

I was embarrassed not to have known who she was. She seemed embarrassed to have reminded me, and also depressed.

After that I saw Ted occasionally, Sylvia more rarely. He and I would meet for a beer in one of the pubs near Primrose Hill or the Heath, and sometimes we would walk our children together. We almost never talked shop; without mentioning it, we wanted to keep things unprofessional. At some point during the summer Ted and I did a broadcast together. Afterwards we collected Sylvia from the flat and went across to their local. The recording had been a success and we stood outside the pub, round the baby's pram, drinking our beers and pleased with ourselves. Sylvia, too, seemed easier, wittier, less constrained than I had seen her before. For the first time I understood something of the real charm and speed of the girl.

About that time my wife and I moved from our flat near Swiss Cottage to a house higher up in Hampstead, near the Heath. A couple of days before we were due to move I broke my leg in a climbing accident, and that put out everything and everyone, since the house had to be decorated, broken leg or not. I remember sticking black and white tiles to floor after endless floor, a filthy dark brown glue coating my fingers and clothes and gumming up my hair, the great, inert plaster cast dragging behind me like a coffin as I crawled. There wasn't much time for friends. Ted occasionally dropped in and I would hobble with him briefly to the pub. But I saw Sylvia not at all. In the autumn I went to teach for a term in the States.

While I was there the *Observer* sent me her first book of poems to review. It seemed to fit the image I had of her:

serious, gifted, withheld, and still partly under the massive shadow of her husband. There were poems that had been influenced by him, others which echoed Theodore Roethke and Wallace Stevens; clearly, she was still casting about for her own style. Yet the technical ability was great, and beneath most of the poems was a sense of resources and disturbances not yet tapped. 'Her poems,' I wrote, 'rest secure in a mass of experience that is never quite brought out into the daylight . . . It is this sense of threat, as though she were continually menaced by something she could see only out of the corners of her eyes, that gives her work its distinction.'

I still stand by that judgement. In the light of her subsequent work and, more persuasively, her subsequent death, *The Colossus* has been overrated. 'Anyone can see,' the doctrine now runs, 'that it's all there in crystalline form.' There are even academic critics who prefer these elegant early poems to the more naked and brutal frontal attacks of her mature work, although when the book first appeared their reviews were cool enough. Meanwhile, hindsight can alter the historical importance but not the quality of the verse. *The Colossus* established her credentials: it contained a handful of beautiful poems, but more important was the sheer ability of the work, the precision and concentration with which she handled language, the unemphatic range of vocabulary, her ear for subtle rhythms, and her assurance in handling and subduing rhymes and half-rhymes. Obviously, she had now developed the craft to cope with anything that arrived. My mistake was to imply that at that stage she hadn't, or wouldn't, recognize the forces that shook her. It turned out that she knew them all too well: they had driven her to the thin near edge of suicide when she was nineteen, and already in the last piece in the book, the long 'Poem for a Birthday', she was turning to face them. But the echoes of Roethke in the poem obscured that for me, and I couldn't see it.

When I got back from the States in February 1961, I saw the Hugheses again, but briefly and not often. Ted had fallen out of love with London and was fretting to get away; Sylvia had been ill – first a miscarriage, then an appendicitis – and I had my own problems, a divorce. I remember her thanking me for the review of *The Colossus*, adding disarmingly that she agreed with the qualifications. I also remember her enthusing about the beautiful house they had found in Devon – old, thatched, flagstoned, and with a large orchard. They moved, I moved, something was finished.

Both of them continued to send poems to the *Observer*. In May 1961 we published Sylvia's poem about her daughter, 'Morning Song'; in November of that year, 'Mojave Desert', which remained uncollected for some years; two months later, 'The Rival'. The current was deepening, its flow becoming easier.

I didn't see her again until June 1962 when I dropped in on them on my way down to Cornwall for the long Whitsun week-end. They were living a few miles north-west of Exeter. By Devon standards it wasn't a pretty village: more grey stone and gloom than timber, thatch and flowers. Where the most perfect English villages give the impression of never having been properly awakened, theirs seemed to have retired into sleep. Once it might have been a centre for the surrounding countryside, a place of some presence where things happened. But not any more. Exeter had taken over, and the life of this village had drained slowly away, like a family that has come down in the world.

The Hughes's house had once been the local manor. It was set slightly above the rest of the village, up a steep lane next to a twelfth century church, and seemed important. It was large and thatched, with a cobbled courtyard and a front door of carved oak, the walls and passages were stone, the rooms gleamed with new paint. We sat out in the big wild garden drinking tea while little Frieda, now aged two, teetered among the flowers. There was a small army of apple and cherry trees, a vivid laburnum swaying with blossom, a vegetable patch and, off to one side, a little hillock. Sylvia called it a prehistoric burial mound. Given the Hughes's flair and tastes, it could hardly have been anything else. Flowers glowed everywhere, the grass was long and unkempt, and the whole luxuriant place seemed to be overflowing with summer.

They had had a new baby in January, a boy, and Sylvia had changed. No longer quiet and withheld, a housewifely appendage to a powerful husband, she seemed made solid and complete, her own woman again. Perhaps the birth of a son had something to do with this new confident air. But there was a sharpness and clarity about her that seemed to go beyond that. It was she who showed me round the house and the garden; the electric gadgets, the freshly painted rooms, the orchard and the burial mound – above all, the burial mound, 'the wall of old corpses'*, she called it later in a poem – were *her* property. Ted, meanwhile, seemed content to sit back and play with little Frieda, who clung to him dependently. Since it appeared to be a strong, close marriage, I supposed he was unconcerned that the balance of power had shifted for the time being to her.

I understood why as I was leaving. 'I'm writing again,' she said. 'Really writing. I'd like you to see some of the new poems.' Her manner was warm and open, as though she had decided I could be trusted.

* The 'burial mound' was in fact, a prehistoric fort, and I am told that the 'wall of old corpses' probably refers to the wall between the Hughes garden and the adjacent churchyard.

Some time before, the *Observer* had accepted a poem by her called 'Finisterre'. We finally published it that August. In the meantime she sent a beautiful short poem, 'Crossing the Water', which was not in *Ariel*, although it is as good as many that are. It arrived with a formal note and a meticulously stamped-addressed envelope. She seemed to be functioning as efficiently as ever. Yet when I saw Ted some time later in London, he was tense and preoccupied. Driving on her own, Sylvia had had some kind of accident; apparently, she had blacked out and run off the road on to an old airfield, though mercifully without damaging herself or their old Morris station-wagon. His dark presence, as he spoke, darkened an even deeper shade of gloom.

When August came, I went abroad for a few weeks, and by the time I got back autumn had already started. Although it was not yet mid-September, the leaves had begun to blow about the streets and the rain came down. That first morning, when I woke up to a drowning London sky, summer seemed as far away as the Mediterranean itself. Automatically, I found myself huddling into my clothes; the London crouch. We were in for a long winter.

At the end of September the *Observer* published 'Crossing the Water'. One afternoon soon after, when I was working and the charlady was banging around upstairs, the bell rang. It was Sylvia, smartly dressed, determinedly bright and cheerful.

'I was just passing, so I thought I'd drop in,' she said. With her formal town clothes and prim bun of hair, she had the air of an Edwardian lady performing a delicate but necessary social duty.

The little studio I rented had been converted from an old stable. It lay down a long passage, behind a garage, and was beautiful, in its crumbling way, but uncomfortable; there was nothing to lounge on – only spidery Windsor chairs and a couple of rugs on the blood-red uncarpeted lino. I poured her a drink and she settled in front of the coal stove on one of the rugs, like a student, very much at her ease, sipping whisky and making the ice clink in her glass.

'That sound makes me homesick for the States,' she said. 'It's the only thing that does.'

We talked about her poem in the *Observer*, then chatted about nothing in particular. Finally, I asked her why she was in town. She replied, with a kind of polished cheerfulness, that she was flat-hunting, and then added casually that she and the children were living on their own for the time being. I remembered the last time I had seen her, in that overflowing Devon garden, and it seemed impossible that anything could have disrupted the idyll. But I asked no questions and she offered no explanations. Instead, she began to talk about the new drive to write that was upon her. At least a poem a day, she said, and often more. She made it sound like demonic possession. And it occurred to me that maybe this was why she and her husband had, however temporarily, parted: it was a question not of differences but of intolerable similarities. When two genuinely original, ambitious, full-time poets join in one marriage, and both are productive, every poem one writes probably feels to the other as though it had been dug out of his, or her, own skull. At a certain pitch of creative intensity it must be more unbearable for the Muse to be unfaithful to you with your partner than for him, or her, to betray you with a whole army of seducers.

'I'd like to read you some of the new poems,' she said, and pulled a sheaf of typescripts from her shoulder-bag on the floor beside her.

'Gladly,' I said, reaching over for them, 'Let's see.'

She shook her head: 'No. I don't want you to read them

to yourself. They've got to be read out loud. I want you to *hear* them.'

So sitting cross-legged on the uncomfortable floor, with the charlady clanking away upstairs, she read me 'Berck-Plage':

This is the sea, then, this great abeyance . . .

She read fast, in a hard, slightly nasal accent, rapping it out as though she were angry. Even now I find it a difficult poem to follow, the development indirect, the images concentrated and eliding thickly together. I had a vague impression of something injurious and faintly obscene, but I don't think I understood much. So when she finished I asked her to read it again. This time I heard it a little more clearly and could make some remarks about details. In some way, this seemed to satisfy her. We argued a bit and she read me more poems: one of them was 'The Moon and the Yew Tree'; 'Elm', I think, was another; there were six or eight in all. She would let me read none to myself, so I didn't get much, if anything, of their subtlety. But I did at least recognize that I was hearing something strong and new and hard to come to terms with. I suppose I picked on whatever details and slight signs of weakness I could as a kind of protection. She, in her turn, seemed happy to read, argue and be heard sympathetically.

'She's a poet, isn't she?' asked my charlady the next day.

'Yes.'

'I thought so,' she said with grim satisfaction.

After that, Sylvia dropped in fairly often on her visits to London, always with a batch of new poems to read. This way I first heard, among others, the 'Bee' poems, 'A Birthday Present', 'The Applicant', 'Getting There', 'Fever 103°',

'Letter in November', and 'Ariel', which I thought extraordinary. I told her it was the best thing she had done and a
few days later she sent me a fair copy of it, carefully written out in her heavy, rounded script, and illuminated like a
medieval manuscript with flowers and ornamental
squiggles.

One day – I'm not sure when – she read me what she
called 'some light verse'. She meant 'Daddy' and 'Lady
Lazarus'. Her voice, as she read them, was hot and full of
venom. By this time I could hear the poetry fairly clearly,
without too great a time-lag and sense of inadequacy. I was
appalled. At first hearing, the things seemed to be not so
much poetry as assault and battery. And because I now
knew something about her life, there was no avoiding how
much she was part of the action. But to have commented
on that would have been to imply that the poems had failed
as poetry, which they clearly had not. As always, my defence was to nag her about details. There was one line I
picked on in particular:

Gentlemen, ladies

These are my hands
My knees.
I may be skin and bone,
I may be Japanese ...

'Why *Japanese*?' I niggled away at her. 'Do you just need
the rhyme? Or are you trying to hitch an easy lift by dragging in the atomic victims? If you're going to use this kind
of violent material, you've got to play it cool....' She
argued back sharply but later, when the poem was finally
published after her death, the line had gone. And that, I
think, is a pity: she did need the rhyme; the tone is quite
controlled enough to support the apparently not quite rele-

vant allusion; and I was over-reacting to the initial brutality of the verse without understanding its weird elegance.

In all this time the evidence of the poems and the evidence of the person were utterly different. There was no trace of the poetry's despair and unforgiving destructiveness in her social manner. She remained remorselessly bright and energetic: busy with her children and her bee-keeping in Devon, busy flat-hunting in London, busy seeing *The Bell Jar* through the press, busy typing and sending off her poems to largely unreceptive editors (just before she died she sent a sheaf of her best poems, most of them now classics, to one of the national British weeklies; none was accepted). She had also taken up horse-riding again, teaching herself to ride on a powerful stallion called Ariel, and was elated by this new excitement.

Cross-legged on the red floor, after reading her poems, she would talk about her riding in her twanging, New England voice. And perhaps because I was also a member of the club, she talked, too, about suicide in much the same way: about her attempt ten years before which, I suppose, must have been very much on her mind as she corrected the proofs of her novel, and about her recent incident with the car. It had been no accident; she had gone off the road deliberately, seriously, wanting to die. But she hadn't, and all that was now in the past. For this reason, I am convinced that at this time she was not contemplating suicide. On the contrary, she was able to write about the act so freely because it was already behind her. The car crash was a death she had survived, the death she sardonically felt herself fated to undergo once every decade:

> I have done it again.
> One year in every ten
> I manage it –

> A sort of walking miracle ...
> I am only thirty.
> And like the cat I have nine times to die.

> This is Number Three ...

In life, as in the poem, there was neither hysteria in her voice, nor any appeal for sympathy. She talked about suicide in much the same tone as she talked about any other risky, testing activity : urgently, even fiercely, but altogether without self-pity. She seemed to view death as a physical challenge she had, once again, overcome. It was an experience of much the same quality as riding Ariel or mastering a bolting horse – which she had done as a Cambridge undergraduate – or careering down a dangerous snow slope without properly knowing how to ski – an incident, also from life, which is one of the best things in *The Bell Jar*. Suicide, in short, was not a swoon into death, an attempt 'to cease upon the midnight with no pain'; it was something to be felt in the nerve-ends and fought against, an initiation rite qualifying her for a *life* of her own.

God knows what wound the death of her father had inflicted on her in her childhood, but over the years this had been transformed into the conviction that to be an adult meant to be a survivor. So, for her, death was a debt to be met once every decade : in order to stay alive as a grown woman, a mother and a poet, she had to pay – in some partial, magical way – with her life. But because this impossible payment involved also the fantasy of joining or regaining her beloved dead father, it was a passionate act, instinct as much with love as with hatred and despair. Thus in that strange, upsetting poem 'The Bee Meeting', the detailed, doubtless accurate description of a gathering of local bee-keepers in her Devon village gradually becomes an invocation of some deadly ritual in which she is the sacrificial virgin whose coffin, finally, waits in the sacred grove. Why this should happen becomes, perhaps, slightly less mysterious when you remember that her father was an authority on bees; so her bee-keeping becomes a way of symbolically allying herself to him, and reclaiming him from the dead.

The tone of all these late poems is hard, factual and, despite the intensity, understated. In some strange way, I suspect she thought of herself as a realist: the deaths and resurrections of 'Lady Lazarus', the nightmares of 'Daddy' and the rest had all been proved on her pulses. That she brought to them an extraordinary inner wealth of imagery and associations was almost beside the point, however essential it is for the poetry itself. Because she felt she was simply describing the facts as they had happened, she was able to tap in the coolest possible way all her large reserves of skill: those subtle rhymes and half-rhymes, the flexible, echoing rhythms and off-hand colloquialisms by which she preserved, even in her most anguished probing, complete artistic control. Her internal horrors were as factual and precisely sensed as the barely controllable stallion on which she was learning to ride or the car she had tried to smash up.

So she spoke of suicide with a wry detachment, and without any mention of the suffering or drama of the act. It was obviously a matter of self-respect that her first attempt had been serious and nearly successful, instead of a mere hysterical gesture. That seemed to entitle her to speak of suicide as a subject, not as an obsession. It was an act she felt she had a right to as a grown woman and a free agent, in the same way as she felt it to be necessary to her development, given her queer conception of the adult as a survivor, an imaginary Jew from the concentration camps of the mind. Because of this there was never any question of motives: you do it because you do it, just as an artist always knows what he knows.

Perhaps this is why she scarcely mentioned her father, however clearly and deeply her fantasies of death were involved with him. The autobiographical heroine of *The Bell Jar* goes to weep at her father's grave immediately before she holes up in a cellar and swallows fifty sleeping pills. In 'Daddy', describing the same episode, she hammers home her reasons with repetitions:

> At twenty I tried to die
> And get back, back, back to you.
> I thought even the bones would do.

I suspect that finding herself alone again now, whatever her pretence of indifference, all the anguish she had experienced at her father's death was reactivated: despite herself, she felt abandoned, injured, enraged and bereaved as purely and defencelessly as she had as a child twenty years before. As a result, the pain that had built up steadily inside her all that time came flooding out. There was no need to discuss motives because the poems did that for her.

These months were an amazingly creative period, comparable, I think, to the 'marvellous year' in which Keats produced nearly all the poetry on which his reputation finally rests. Earlier she had written carefully, more or less painfully, with much rewriting and, according to her husband, with constant recourse to *Roget's Thesaurus*. Now, although she abandoned none of her hard-earned skills and discipline, and still rewrote and rewrote, the poems flowed effortlessly until, at the end, she occasionally produced as many as three a day. She also told me that she was deep into a new novel. *The Bell Jar* was finished, proof-read and with her publishers; she spoke of it with some embarrassment as an autobiographical apprentice-work which she had to write in order to free herself from the past. But this new book, she implied, was the genuine article. Considering the conditions in which she worked, her productivity was phenomenal. She was a full-time mother with a two-year-old daughter, a baby of a few months, and a house to look after. By the time the children were in bed at night she was too tired for anything more strenuous than 'music and brandy and water'. So she got up very early each morning and worked until the children woke. 'These new poems of mine have one thing in common,' she wrote in a note for a reading she prepared, but never broadcast, for the BBC, 'they were all written at about four in the morning – that still blue, almost eternal hour before the baby's cry, before the glassy music of the milkman, settling his bottles.' In those dead hours between night and day, she was able to gather herself into herself in silence and isolation, almost as though she were reclaiming some past innocence and freedom before life got a grip on her. Then she could write. For the rest of the day she was shared among the children, the housework, the shopping, efficient, bustling, harassed, like every other housewife.

But this dawn sense of paradise temporarily regained does not explain the sudden flowering and change in her work. Technically, the clue is in her insistence that she herself should always read the poems out loud. In the early sixties this was a rare procedure. It was, after all, still a period of high formalism, of Stevensesque cadences and Empsonian ambiguities at which she herself was, as her earlier work proved, particularly adept. Essentially, this was the style of the academies, of self-imposed limitations of feeling and narrow devotion to the duties of craftsmanship which were echoed in thumping iambics and painfully analysable imagery. But in 1958 she had made the vital decision to abandon the university career for which she had so carefully prepared herself all through her adolescence and early twenties. Only gradually over the next four years did that total commitment to her own creative life emerge in the fabric of her verse, breaking down the old, inert moulds, quickening the rhythms, broadening the emotional range. The decision to abandon teaching was the first critical step towards achieving her identity as a poet, just as the birth of her children seemed, as she described it, to vindicate her as a woman. In these last poems the process was complete: the poet and the poems became one. What she wrote depended on her voice in the same way as her children depended on her love.

The other crucial element in her poetic maturity was the example of Robert Lowell's *Life Studies*. I say 'example' rather than 'influence' because, although Sylvia had attended Lowell's classes at Boston University in the company of Anne Sexton and George Starbuck, she never picked up his peculiarly contagious style. Instead of a style, she took from him a freedom. She told a British Council interviewer:

'I've been very excited by what I feel is the new breakthrough that came with, say, Robert Lowell's *Life Studies*. This intense breakthrough into very serious, very personal emotional experience, which I feel has been partly taboo. Robert Lowell's poems about his experiences in a mental hospital, for example, interest me very much. These peculiar private and taboo subjects I feel have been explored in recent American poetry ...'

Lowell provided her with an example of the quality she most admired outside poetry and had herself in profusion: courage. In its way, *Life Studies* was as brave and revolutionary as *The Waste Land*. After all, it appeared at the height of the tight-lipped fifties, the era of doctrinaire New Criticism, of the Intentional Fallacy, and the whole elaborate, iron dogma by which poetry was separated utterly from the man who made it. In his time, Lowell had been the darling of the school with his complex Catholic symbolism, thickly textured Eliot-Elizabethan language, and his unwavering ability to stamp every line with his own individual rhythm. Then, after nearly ten years' silence, he turned his back on it all. The symbols disappeared, the language clarified and became colloquial, the subject-matter became intensely, insistently personal. He wrote as a man who had had breakdowns and was haunted at every crisis by family ghosts; and he wrote without evasions. All that was left of the former young master of Alexandrian complexity was the still unanswerable skill and originality. Even more strongly than before, it was impossible to avoid the troubled presence of Lowell himself, but now he was speaking out in a way that violated all the principles of New Criticism: there was immediacy instead of impersonality, vulnerability in place of exquisitely dandified irony.

Sylvia derived from all this, above all, a vast sense of release. It was as though Lowell had opened a door which had previously been bolted against her. At a critical moment in her development there was no longer any need to be imprisoned in her old poetic habits, which despite their elegance – or maybe because of it – she now felt to be intolerably constricting. 'My first book, *The Colossus*,' she told the man from the British Council – 'I can't read any of the poems aloud now. I didn't write them to be read aloud. In fact, they quite privately bore me.' *The Colossus* was the culmination of her apprenticeship in the craft of poetry. It completed the training she began as an eight-year-old and continued through the tensely stylish verse of her undergraduate days, when each poem seemed built up grudgingly, word by word, like a mosaic. Now all that was behind her. She had outgrown the style; more important, she had outgrown the person who had written in that oblique, reticent way. A combination of forces, some chosen deliberately, others chosen for her, had brought her to the point where she was able to write as from her true centre about the forces that really moved her: destructive, volatile, demanding, a world apart from everything she had been trained to admire. 'What,' asked Coleridge, 'is the height and ideal of mere association? Delirium.' For years Sylvia had apparently agreed, pursuing formal virtues and finger-tip detachment, contemptuous of the self-pity, self-advertisement and self-indulgence of the Beatniks. Now, right on cue, came *Life Studies* to prove that the violence of the self could be written about with control, subtlety and a dispassionate but undefended imagination.

I suspect that this is why she had first come to me with the new poems, although she knew me only glancingly. It helped that I had reviewed *The Colossus* sympathetically and had got the *Observer* to publish some of her more recent things. But more important was the introduction to my Penguin anthology, *The New Poetry*, which had been published the previous spring. In it I had attacked the British poets' nervous preference for gentility above all else, and their avoidance of the uncomfortable, destructive truths both of the inner life and of the present time. Apparently, this essay said something she wanted to hear; she spoke of it often and with approval, and was disappointed not to have been included among the poets in the book. (She was later, since her work, more than anyone else's, vindicates my argument. But in the first edition I had stuck to British poets, with the exception of two older Americans, Lowell and Berryman who, I felt, set the tone for the postwar, post-Eliot period.) Perhaps it made things easier for her to know that someone was making a critical case for what she was now trying to do. And perhaps it made her feel less lonely.

Yet lonely she was, touchingly and without much disguise, despite her buoyant manner. Despite, too, the energy of her poems, which are, by any standards, subtly ambiguous performances. In them she faced her private horrors steadily and without looking aside, but the effort and risk involved in doing so acted on her like a stimulant: the worse things got and the more directly she wrote about them, the more fertile her imagination became. Just as disaster, when it finally arrives, is never as bad as it seems in expectation, so she now wrote almost with relief, swiftly as though to forestall further horrors. In a way, this is what she had been waiting for all her life, and now it had come she knew she must use it. 'The passion for destruction is also a creative passion,' said Michael Bakunin, and for Sylvia also this was true. She turned anger, implacability and her roused, needle-sharp sense of trouble into a kind of celebration.

I have suggested that her cool tone depends a great deal on her realism, her sense of fact. As the months went by and her poetry became progressively more extreme, this gift of transforming every detail grew steadily until, in the last weeks, each trivial event became the occasion for poetry: a cut finger, a fever, a bruise. Her drab domestic life fused with her imagination richly and without hesitation. Around this time, for example, her husband produced a curious radio play in which the hero, driving to town, runs over a hare, sells the dead animal for five shillings, and with the blood money buys his girl two roses. Sylvia pounced on this, isolating its core, interpreting and adjusting it according to her own needs. The result was the poem 'Kindness', which ends:

> The blood-jet is poetry,
> There is no stopping it.
> You hand me two children, two roses.

There was, indeed, no stopping it. Her poetry acted as a strange, powerful lens through which her ordinary life was filtered and refigured with extraordinary intensity. Perhaps the elation that comes of writing well and often helped her to preserve that bright American façade she unfailingly presented to the world. In common with her other friends of that period, I chose to believe in this cheerfulness against all the evidence of the poems. Or rather, I believed in it and I didn't believe. But what could one do? I felt sorry for her, but she clearly didn't want that. Her jauntiness forestalled all sympathy and, if only by her blank refusal to discuss them otherwise, she insisted that her poems were purely poems, autonomous. If attempted suicide is, as some psychiatrists believe, a cry for help, then Sylvia at this time was not suicidal. What she wanted was not help but confirmation: she needed someone to acknowledge that she was coping exceptionally well with her difficult routine life of children, nappies, shopping and writing. She needed, even more, to know that the poems worked and were good, for although she had gone through a gate Lowell had opened, she was now far along a peculiarly solitary road on which not many would risk following her. So it was important for her to know that her messages were coming back clear and strong. Yet not even her determinedly bright self-reliance could disguise the loneliness that came from her almost palpably, like a heat haze. She asked for neither sympathy nor help but, like a bereaved widow at a wake, she simply wanted company in her mourning. I suppose it provided confirmation that, despite the odds and the internal evidence, she still existed.

One gloomy November afternoon she arrived at my studio greatly excited. As usual, she had been trudging the chill streets, house-hunting despondently and more or less aimlessly. A block away from the square near Primrose Hill where she and Ted had lived when they first came to London, she saw a 'To Let' notice up in front of a newly refurbished house. That in itself was something of a miracle in those impossible, overcrowded days. But more important, the house bore a blue plaque announcing that Yeats had once lived there. It was a sign, the confirmation she had been looking for. That summer she had visited Yeats's Tower at Ballylee and wrote to a friend that she thought it 'the most beautiful and peaceful place in the world'. Now there was a possibility of finding another Yeats tower in her favourite part of London which she could in some way share with the great poet. She hurried to the agent's and found, improbably, that she was the first to apply. Another sign. On the spot she took a five-year lease of the flat, although the rent was more than she could afford. Then she walked across dark, blowy Primrose Hill to tell me the news.

She was elated not just because she had at last found a flat, but because the place and its associations seemed to her somehow preordained. In varying degrees, both she and her husband seemed to believe in the occult. As artists, I suppose, they had to, since both were intent on finding voices for their unquiet, buried selves. But there was, I think, something more to their belief than that. Ted has written that 'her psychic gifts, at almost any time, were strong enough to make her frequently wish to be rid of them'. That could simply have been her poet's knack of sensing the unspoken content of every situation and, later, her easy, instinctive access to her own unconscious. Yet although both of them talked often enough about astrology, dreams and magic – enough, anyway, to imply that these were not just casually interesting subjects – I had the impression that at heart their attitudes were utterly different. Ted constantly and carefully mocked himself and deflated his pretensions, yet there was always a sense of his being in touch with some primitive area, some dark side of the self which had nothing to do with the young literary man. This, after all, was what his poems were about: an immediate, physical apprehension of the violence both of animal life and of the self – of the animality of the self. It was also part of his physical presence, a quality of threat beneath his shrewd, laconic manner. It was almost as though, despite all the reading and polish and craftsmanship, he had never properly been civilized – or had, at least, never properly believed in his civilization. It was simply a shell he sardonically put up with for the sake of convenience. So all that astrology, primitive religion and black magic he talked about, however ironically, was a kind of metaphor for the shaking but obscure creative powers he knew himself to possess. For this reason those dubious topics took on for him an immediacy which may not have implied any belief but which certainly transformed them into something beyond mere fad. Perhaps all I am describing is, quite simply, a touch of genius. But it is a genius that has little to do with the tradional Romantic concept of the word: with Shelley's canny other-worldliness or Byron's equally canny sense of his own drama. Ted too, is canny and practical, like most Yorkshiremen, unwillingly fooled and with a fine, racing-mechanic's ear for the rumblings of the literary machine. But he is also, in a curiously complete way, an original: his reactions are unpredictable, his frame of reference different. I imagine the most extreme example of this style of genius was Blake. But there are also many people of genius – perhaps the majority – who have almost nothing of that dislocating and dislocated quality: T. S. Eliot, for example, the Polish poet Zbigniew Herbert, John Donne and Keats – all men whose unusual creative intelligence and awareness seem not essentially at odds with the reality of their everyday worlds. Instead, their particular gift is to clarify and intensify the received world.

Sylvia, I think, belonged with these latter. Her intensity was of the nerves, something urban and near screaming-point. It was also, in its way, more intellectual than Ted's. It was part of the fierceness with which she had worked as a student, passing exam after exam brilliantly, effortlessly, hungrily. With the same intensity she immersed herself in her children, her riding, her bee-keeping, even her cooking; everything had to be done well and to the fullest. Since her husband was interested in the occult – for whatever clouded personal reasons – she threw herself into that, too, almost out of the desire to excel. And because her natural talents were very great, she discovered she had 'psychic gifts'. No doubt the results were genuine and even uncanny, but I suspect they were a triumph of mind over ectoplasm. It is the same in the poems: Ted's gain their effect by expressing his sense of menace and violence immediately, unanswerably; in Sylvia's the expression, though often more powerful, is a by-product of a compulsive need to understand.

On Christmas Eve 1962, Sylvia telephoned me: she and the children had finally settled into their new apartment; could I come round that evening to see the place, have a meal and hear some new poems? As it happened, I couldn't, since I had already been invited to dinner by some friends who lived a few streets away from her. I said I'd drop in for a drink on my way.

She seemed different. Her hair, which she usually wore in

a tight, school-mistressy bun, was loose. It hung straight to her waist like a tent, giving her pale face and gaunt figure a curiously desolate, rapt air, like a priestess emptied out by the rites of her cult. When she walked in front of me down the hall passage and up the stairs of her apartment – she had the top two floors of the house – her hair gave off a strong smell, sharp as an animal's. The children were already in bed upstairs and the flat was silent. It was newly painted, white and chill. There were, as I remember, no curtains up yet and the night pressed in coldly on the windows. She had deliberately kept the place bare: rush matting on the floor, a few books, bits of Victoriana and cloudy blue glass on the shelves, a couple of small Leon Baskin woodcuts. It was rather beautiful, in its chaste, stripped-down way, but cold, very cold, and the oddments of flimsy Christmas decoration made it seem doubly forlorn, each seeming to repeat that she and the children would be alone over Christmas. For the unhappy, Christmas is always a bad time: the terrible false jollity that comes at you from every side, braying about goodwill and peace and family fun, makes loneliness and depression particularly hard to bear. I had never seen her so strained.

We drank wine and, as usual, she read me some poems. One of them was 'Death & Co.'. This time there was no escaping the meaning. When she had written about death before it was as something survived, even surpassed: 'Lady Lazarus' ends with a resurrection and a threat, and even in 'Daddy' she manages finally to turn her back on the grinning, beckoning figure – 'Daddy, daddy, you bastard, I'm through'. Hence, perhaps, the energy of these poems, their weird jollity in the teeth of everything, their recklessness. But now, as though poetry really were a form of black magic, the figure she had invoked so often, only to dismiss triumphantly, had risen before her, dank, final and not so be denied. He appeared to her in both his usual shapes: like her father, elderly, unforgiving and very dead, and also younger, more seductive, a creature of her own generation and choice.* This time there was no way out for her; she could only sit still and pretend they hadn't noticed her:

> I do not stir.
> The frost makes a flower,
> The dew makes a star,
> The dead bell,
> The dead bell.

> Somebody's done for.

Perhaps the bell was tolling for 'somebody' other than herself; but she didn't seem to believe so.

I didn't know what to say. The earlier poems had all insisted, in their different ways, that she wanted nobody's help – although I suddenly realized that maybe they had insisted in such a manner as to make you understand that help might be acceptable, if you were willing to make the effort. But now she was beyond the reach of anyone. In the beginning she had called up these horrors partly in the hope of exorcizing them, partly to demonstrate her omnipotence and invulnerability. Now she was shut in with them and knew she was defenceless.

I remember arguing inanely about the phrase 'The nude/Verdigris of the condor'. I said it was exaggerated, morbid. On the contrary, she replied, that was exactly how a condor's legs looked. She was right, of course. I was only

*In her own note on the poem which she wrote for the BBC, she said: 'This poem – "Death & Co." – is about the double or schizophrenic nature of death – the marmoreal coldness of Blake's death mask, say, hand in glove with the fearful softness of worms, water and other katabolists. I imagine these two aspects of death as two men, two business friends, who have come to call.'

trying, in a futile way, to reduce the tension and take her mind momentarily off her private horrors – as though that could be done by argument and literary criticism! She must have felt I was stupid and insensitive. Which I was. But to have been otherwise would have meant accepting responsibilities I didn't want and couldn't, in my own depression, have coped with. When I left about eight o'clock to go on to my dinner-party, I knew I had let her down in some final and unforgivable way. And I knew she knew. I never again saw her alive.

It was an unspeakable winter, the worst, they said, in 150 years. The snow began just after Christmas and would not let up. By New Year the whole country had ground to a halt. The trains froze on the tracks, the abandoned trucks froze on the roads. The power stations, overloaded by million upon pathetic million of hopeless electric fires, broke down continually; not that the fires mattered, since the electricians were mostly out on strike. Water pipes froze solid; for a bath you had to scheme and cajole those rare friends with centrally heated houses, who became rarer and less friendly as the weeks dragged on. Doing the dishes became a major operation. The gastric rumble of water in outdated plumbing was sweeter than the sound of mandolins. Weight for weight, plumbers were as expensive as smoked salmon and harder to find. The gas failed and Sunday joints were raw. The lights failed and candles, of course, were unobtainable. Nerves failed and marriages crumbled. Finally, the heart failed. It seemed the cold would never end. Nag, nag, nag.

In December the *Observer* had published a long-uncollected poem by Sylvia called 'Event'; in mid-January we published another, 'Winter Trees'. Sylvia wrote me a note about it, adding that maybe we should take our children to the Zoo and she would show me 'the nude verdigris of the condor'. But she no longer dropped into my studio with poems. Later that month I met a literary editor of one of the big weeklies. He asked me if I had seen Sylvia recently.

'No. Why?'

'I was just wondering. She sent us some poems. Very strange.'

'Did you like them?'

'No,' he replied, 'too extreme for my taste. I sent them all back. But she sounds in a bad state. I think she needs help.'

Her doctor, a sensitive, overworked man, thought the same. He prescribed sedatives and arranged for her to see a psychotherapist. Having been bitten once by American psychiatry, she hesitated for some time before writing for an appointment. But her depression did not lift and finally the letter was sent. It did no good. Either her letter or that of the therapist arranging a consultation went astray; apparently the postman delivered it to the wrong address. The therapist's reply arrived a day or two after she died. This was one of several links in the chain of accidents, coincidences and mistakes that ended in her death.

I am convinced by what I know of the facts that this time she did not intend to die. Her suicide attempt ten years before had been, in every sense, deadly serious. She had carefully disguised the theft of the sleeping pills, left a misleading note to cover her tracks, and hidden herself in the darkest, most unused corner of a cellar, rearranging behind her the old firelogs she had disturbed, burying herself away like a skeleton in the nethermost family closet. Then she had swallowed a bottle of fifty sleeping pills. She was found late and by accident, and survived only by a miracle. The flow of life in her was too strong even for the violence she had done it. This, anyway, is her description of the act in *The Bell Jar*; there is no reason to believe it false. So she had learned the hard way the odds against successful suicide; she had learned that despair must be counterpoised by an almost obsessional attention to detail and disguise.

By these lights she seemed, in her last attempt, to be taking care not to succeed. But this time everything conspired to destroy her. An employment agency had found her an *au pair* girl to help with the children and housework while Sylvia got on with her writing. The girl, an Australian, was due to arrive at nine o'clock on the morning of Monday 11 February. Meanwhile, a recurrent trouble, her sinuses were bad; the pipes in her newly converted flat froze solid; there was still no telephone and no word from the psychotherapist; the weather continued monstrous. Illness, loneliness, depression and cold, combined with the demands of two small children, were too much for her. So when the week-end came she went off with the babies to stay with friends in another part of London. The plan was, I think, that she would leave early enough on Monday morning to be back in time to welcome the Australian girl. Instead, she decided to go back on the Sunday. The friends were against it but she was insistent, made a great show of her old competence and seemed more cheerful than she had done for some time. So they let her go. About eleven o'clock that night she knocked on the door of the elderly painter who lived below her, asking to borrow some stamps. But she lingered in the doorway, drawing out the conversation until he told her that he got up well before nine in the morning. Then she said good night and went back upstairs.

God knows what kind of a sleepless night she spent or if she wrote any poetry. Certainly, within the last few days of her life she wrote one of her most beautiful poems, 'Edge', which is specifically about the act she was about to perform :

> The woman is perfected.
> Her dead
>
> Body wears the smile of accomplishment,
> The illusion of a Greek necessity
>
> Flows in the scrolls of her toga,
> Her bare
>
> Feet seem to be saying :
> We have come so far, it is over.
>
> Each dead child coiled, a white serpent,
> One at each little
>
> Pitcher of milk, now empty.
> She has folded
>
> Them back into her body as petals
> Of a rose close when the garden
>
> Stiffens and odours bleed
> From the sweet, deep throats of the night flowers.
>
> The moon has nothing to be sad about,
> Staring from her hood of bone.
>
> She is used to this sort of thing.
> Her blacks crackle and drag.

It is a poem of great peace and resignation, utterly without self-pity. Even with a subject so appallingly close she remains an artist, absorbed in the practical task of letting each image develop a full, still life of its own. That she is writing about her own death is almost irrelevant. There is another poem, 'Words', also very late, which is about the way language remains and echoes long after the turmoil of life has passed; like 'Edge', it has the same translucent calm. If these were among the last things she wrote, I think she must in the end have accepted the logic of the life she had been leading and come to terms with its terrible necessities.

Around 6 a.m. she went up to the children's room and left a plate of bread and butter and two mugs of milk, in case they should wake hungry before the *au pair* girl arrived. Then she went back down to the kitchen, sealed the door and window as best she could with towels, opened the oven, laid her head in it and turned on the gas.

The Australian girl arrived punctually at 9 a.m. She rang and knocked a long time but could get no answer. So she went off to search for a telephone kiosk in order to phone the agency and make sure she had the right address. Sylvia's name, incidentally, was not on either of the doorbells. Had everything been normal, the neighbour below would have been up by then; even if he had overslept, the girl's knocking would have aroused him. But as it happened, the neighbour was very deaf and slept without his hearing aid. More important, his bedroom was immediately below Sylvia's kitchen. The gas seeped down and knocked him out cold. So he slept on through all the noise. The girl returned and tried again, still without success. Again she went off to telephone the agency and ask what to do; they told her to go back. It was now about eleven o'clock. This time she was lucky: some builders had arrived to work in the frozen-up house, and they let her in. When she knocked on Sylvia's door there was no answer and the smell of gas was overpowering. The builders forced the lock and found

Sylvia sprawled in the kitchen. She was still warm. She had left a note saying, 'Please call Dr—', and giving his telephone number. But it was too late.

Had everything worked out as it should – had the gas not drugged the man downstairs, preventing him from opening the front door to the *au pair* girl – there is no doubt she would have been saved. I think she wanted to be; why else leave her doctor's telephone number? This time, unlike the occasion ten years before, there was too much holding her to life. Above all, there were the children: she was too passionate a mother to want to lose them or them to lose her. There were also the extraordinary creative powers she now unequivocally knew she possessed: the poems came daily, unbidden and unstoppable, and she was again working on a novel about which, at last, she had no reservations.

Why, then, did she kill herself? In part, I suppose, it was 'a cry for help' which fatally misfired. But it was also a last desperate attempt to exorcize the death she had summoned up in her poems. I have already suggested that perhaps she had begun to write obsessively about death for two reasons. First, when she and her husband separated, whether she was willing or not, she went through again the same piercing grief and bereavement she had felt as a child when her father, by his death, seemed to abandon her. Second, I believe she thought her car crash the previous summer had set her free; she had paid her dues, qualified as a survivor and could now write about it. But, as I have written elsewhere, for the artist himself art is not necessarily therapeutic; he is not automatically relieved of his fantasies by expressing them. Instead, by some perverse logic of creation, the act of formal expression may simply make the dredged-up material more readily available to him. The result of handling it in his work may well be that he finds himself living it out. For the artist, in short, nature often imitates art. Or, to change the cliché, when an artist holds a mirror up to nature he finds out who and what he is; but the knowledge may change him irredeemably so that he becomes that image.

I think Sylvia, in one way or another, sensed this. In an introductory note she wrote to 'Daddy' for the BBC, she said of the poem's narrator, 'She has to act out the awful little allegory once over before she is free of it.' The allegory in question was, as she saw it, the struggle in her between a fantasy Nazi father and a Jewish mother. But perhaps it was also a fantasy of containing in herself her own dead father, like a woman possessed by a demon (in the poem she actually calls him a vampire). In order for her to be free of him, he has to be released like a genie from a bottle. And this is precisely what the poems did: they bodied forth the death within her. But they also did so in an intensely living and creative way. The more she wrote about death, the stronger and more fertile her imaginative world became. And this gave her everything to live for.

I suspect that in the end she wanted to have done with the theme once and for all. But the only way she could find was 'to act out the awful little allegory once over'. She had always been a bit of a gambler, used to taking risks. The authority of her poetry was in part due to her brave persistence in following the thread of her inspiration right down to the ~~Minotaur~~'s lair. And this psychic courage had its parallel in her physical arrogance and carelessness. Risks didn't frighten her; on the contrary, she found them stimulating. Freud has written, 'Life loses in interest, when the highest stake in the game of living, life itself, may not be risked.' Finally, Sylvia took that risk. She gambled for the last time, having worked out that the odds were in her favour, but perhaps, in her depression, not much caring whether she won or lost. Her calculations went wrong and she lost.

It was a mistake, then, and out of it a whole myth has grown. I don't think she would have found it much to her taste, since it is a myth of the poet as a sacrificial victim, offering herself up for the sake of her art, having been dragged by the Muses to that final altar through every kind of distress. In these terms, her suicide becomes the whole point of the story, the act which validates her poems, gives them their interest and proves her seriousness. So people are drawn to her work in much the same spirit as *Time* featured her at length: not for the poetry but for the gossipy, extra-literary 'human interest'. Yet just as the suicide adds nothing at all to the poetry, so the myth of Sylvia as a passive victim is a total perversion of the woman she was. It misses altogether her liveliness, her intellectual appetite and harsh wit, her great imaginative resourcefulness and vehemence of feeling, her control. Above all, it misses the courage with which she was able to turn disaster into art. The pity is not that there is a myth of Sylvia Plath but that the myth is not simply that of an enormously gifted poet whose death came carelessly, by mistake, and too soon.

I used to think of her brightness as a façade, as though she were able, in a rather schizoid way, to turn her back on her suffering for the sake of appearances, and pretend it didn't exist. But maybe she was also able to keep her unhappiness in check because she could write about it, because she knew she was salvaging from all those horrors something rather marvellous. The end came when she felt she could stand the subject no longer. She had written it out and was ready for something new.

> The blood-jet is poetry,
> There is no stopping it.

The only method of stopping it she could see, her vision by then blinkered by depression and illness, was that last gamble. So having, as she thought, arranged to be saved, she lay down in front of the gas-oven almost hopefully, almost with relief, as though she were saying, 'Perhaps this will set me free.

On Friday 15 February, there was an inquest in the drab, damp coroner's court behind Camden Town: muttered evidence, long silences, the Australian girl in tears. Earlier that morning I had gone with Ted to the undertaker in Mornington Crescent. The coffin was at the far end of a bare, draped room. She lay stiffly, a ludicrous ruff at her neck. Only her face showed. It was grey and slightly trans-parent, like wax. I had never before seen a dead person and I hardly recognized her; her features seemed too thin and sharp. The room smelled of apples, faint, sweet but some-how unclean, as though the apples were beginning to rot. I was glad to get out into the cold and noise of the dingy streets. It seemed impossible that she was dead.

Even now I find it hard to believe. There was too much life in her long, flat, strongly boned body, and her longish face with its fine brown eyes, shrewd and full of feeling. She was practical and candid, passionate and compassion-ate. I believe she was a genius. I sometimes catch myself childishly thinking I'll run into her walking on Primrose Hill or the Heath, and we'll pick up the conversation where we left off. But perhaps that is because her poems still speak so distinctly in her accents: quick, sardonic, unpre-dictable, effortlessly inventive, a bit angry, and always utterly her own.

This is just one example. According to the official statistics, there would have been at least ninety-nine other suicides in Great Britain the week Sylvia died. Another twenty-five to fifty people would also have taken their own lives in the same period without ever making the official lists. In the United States the figures would have been four times greater. The suicide-rate per hundred thousand population is roughly the same in both countries. In Hungary it is over twice as high. Throughout the world, says a W.H.O. report, at least one thousand people take their own lives each day.

Why do these things happen? Is there any way in which such waste can be explained, since it can hardly ever be justified? Is there, for someone creative like Sylvia, a tradition of suicide, or were there quasi-literary forces leading her to it? These are questions which I shall try to answer in the rest of this book. But first there is a question of background, of the history of the act and its strange transformations in western culture.

Part 2
The Background

Nor dread nor hope attend
A dying animal;
A man awaits his end
Dreading and hoping all;
Many times he died,
Many times rose again.
A great man in his pride
Confronting murderous men
Casts derision upon
Supersession of breath;
He knows death to the bone —
Man has created death.

— W. B. YEATS

                      Then is it sin
To rush into the secret house of death,
Ere death dare come to us?

— WILLIAM SHAKESPEARE

If you can't stand a giggle, you shouldn't
have joined the club.

— OLD SAYING

A man was hanged who had cut his throat, but who had been brought back to life. They hanged him for suicide. The doctor had warned them that it was impossible to hang him as the throat would burst open and he would breathe through the aperture. They did not listen to his advice and hanged their man. The wound in the neck immediately opened and the man came back to life again although he was hanged. It took time to convoke the aldermen to decide the question of what was to be done. At length aldermen assembled and bound up the neck below the wound *until he died*. Oh my Mary, what a crazy society and what a stupid civilization.[1]

So Nicholas Ogarev writing to his mistress Mary Sutherland around 1860, with news from the London papers. Ogarev was an alcoholic Russian exile of mildly revolutionary politics, the son of a wealthy landowner and close friend of Alexander Herzen; his mistress was a good-natured prostitute whom he had reformed and was slowly educating. I suspect that it took two complete outsiders, one of them an enlightened and political foreigner, to notice the barbarity of a situation which the newspaper had reported simply as an unexpected twist to a public execution, odd enough to be newsworthy but not otherwise sufficiently shocking or remarkable to require comment.

Yet by pursuing their poor suicide with such weird vindictiveness – condemning a man to death for the crime of having condemned himself to death – the London aldermen were acting according to a venerable tradition sanctified by both Church and State. The history of suicide in Christian Europe is the history of official outrage and unofficial despair. Both can be measured by the dry, matter-of-fact tone in which the accepted enormities were described. Writing in 1601, the Elizabethan lawyer Fulbecke says that the suicide 'is drawn by a horse to the place of the punishment and shame, where he is hanged on a gibbet, and none may take the body down but by the authority of a magistrate'. In other words, the suicide was as low as the lowest criminal. Later another great legal authority, Blackstone, wrote that the burial was 'in the highway, with a stake driven through the body',[2] as though there was no difference between a suicide and a vampire. The chosen site was usually a crossroads, which was also the place of public execution, and a stone was placed over the dead man's face; like the stake, it would prevent him rising as a ghost to haunt the living. Apparently, the terror of suicides lasted longer than the fear of vampires and witches: the last recorded degradation of the corpse of a suicide in England took place in 1823, when a man called Griffiths was buried at the intersection of Grosvenor Place and the King's Road, Chelsea. But even then self-murderers were not left in peace: for the next fifty years the bodies of unclaimed and destitute suicides went to the schools of anatomy for dissection.

With variations, similar degradations were used all through Europe. In France, varying with local ground rules, the corpse was hanged by the feet, dragged through the street on a hurdle, burned, thrown on the public garbage heap. At Metz, each suicide was put in a barrel and floated down the Moselle away from the places he might wish to haunt. In Danzig, the corpse was not allowed to leave by the door; instead it was lowered by pulleys from the win-

dow; the window-frame was subsequently burnt. Even in
the civilized Athens of Plato, the suicide was buried outside
the city and away from other graves; his self-murdering
hand was cut off and buried apart. So, too, with minor
variations, in Thebes and Cyprus. Sparta, true to form, was
so severe in its ruling that Aristodemus was punished pos-
thumously for deliberately seeking death in the battle of
Plataea.[3]

In Europe these primitive revenges were duly dignified
and made economically profitable to the State by law. As
late as 1670 *le roi soleil* himself incorporated into the
official legal code all the most brutal practices concerning
the degradation of the corpse of a suicide, adding that his
name was to be defamed *ad perpetuam rei memoriam;*
nobles lost their nobility and were declared commoners;
their escutcheons were broken, their woods cut, their
castles demolished. In England a suicide was declared a
felon (*felo de se*). In both countries his property reverted to
the crown. In practice, Voltaire sourly noted, this meant:
'*On donne son bien au Roi qui en accorde presque toujours
la moitié à la première fille de l'opéra qui le fait demander
par un de ses amants; l'autre moitié appartient de droit à
Messieurs les Fermiers généraux.*'[4]*

In France, despite the derision of Voltaire and Montesquieu, these laws lasted at least until 1770 and, indeed, were
twice reinforced in the eighteenth century. The confiscation
of the suicide's property and defamation of his memory
finally disappeared with the Revolution; suicide is not mentioned in the new penal code of 1791.[5] Not so in England,
where the laws concerning the confiscation of property were

---

*'His goods are given to the King who almost always grants half
of them to the leading lady of the Opera who prevails on one of her
lovers to ask for it; the other half belongs by law to the Inland
Revenue.'

not changed until 1870, and an unsuccessful suicide could still be sent to prison as late as 1961.* Thus the phrase 'suicide while the balance of his mind was disturbed' was evolved by lawyers as a protection against the inanities of the law, since a verdict of *felo de se* would deprive the dead man of a religious burial and his inheritors of his estate. An eighteenth century satirist put it this way:

From reading the public prints a foreigner might naturally be led to imagine, that we are the most lunatic people in the world. Almost every day informs us, that the coroner's inquest has sate on the body of some miserable suicide and brought in their verdict lunacy. But it is very well known, that the inquiry has not been made into the state of mind of the deceased, but into his fortune and family. The law has indeed provided, that the deliberate self-murderer should be treated like a brute and denied the rites of burial. But of hundreds of lunatics by purchase, I never knew this sentence executed but on one poor cobler, who hanged himself in his own stall. A penniless poor dog, who has not left enough money to defray the funeral charges, may perhaps be excluded the church-yard; but self-murder by a pistol genteelly mounted, or the Paris-hilted sword, qualifies the polite owner for a sudden death, and entitles him to a pompous burial and a monument setting forth his virtues in Westminster-Abbey.[6]

Whence Professor Joad's aphorism that in England you must not commit suicide, on pain of being regarded as a criminal if you fail and a lunatic if you succeed.

These official, legal idiocies were, mercifully, the last pale flourishing of prejudices which had once been infinitely more virulent and profound. Since the savagery of any punishment is proportional to the fear of the act, why should a gesture so essentially private inspire such primitive terror and superstition? Fedden produces evidence to

Plus ça change . . . In 1969 an Isle of Man court ordered a teenager to be birched for attempting suicide.

suggest that Christian revenges repeat, with suitable modifications, the taboos and purification rituals of the most primitive tribes. The learned jurists who decreed that a suicide should be buried at a crossroads had at least that prejudice in common with the witch-doctors of Baganda.[7] They were also harking back to a pre-Christian Europe where victims were sacrificed on altars at these same crossroads. Like the stake and the stone, the site had been chosen in the hope that the constant traffic above would prevent the restless spirit from rising; should that fail the number of roads would, hopefully, confuse the ghost and so hinder his return home. After the introduction of Christianity, the cross formed by the roads became a symbol which would disperse the evil energy concentrated in the dead body.[8] It was a question, in short, of an archaic fear of blood wrongly spilt crying out for revenge. That is, it was a question of that peculiarly baffled terror which is produced by guilt. Freud's early theory that suicide is transposed murder, an act of hostility turned away from the object back on to the self, seems to be borne out by Christian superstition and law.

In primitive societies, the mechanics of revenge are simple: either the suicide's ghost will destroy his persecutor for him, or his act will force his relatives to carry out the task, or the iron laws of the tribe will compel the suicide's enemy to kill himself in the same manner. It depends on the customs of the country. In any case, suicide under these conditions is curiously unreal; it is as though it were committed in the certain belief that the suicide himself would not really die. Instead, he is performing a magical act which will initiate a complex but equally magic ritual ending in the death of his enemy.*

* The same magical thinking still prevails in some modern political suicides. In January 1969, Jan Palach burned himself to death in the

The primitive horror of suicide, which survived so long in Europe, was then a horror of blood evilly spilt and unappeased. In practice, this meant that suicide was equated with murder. Hence, presumably, the custom of punishing the body of a suicide as though he were guilty of a capital crime, by hanging it from a gibbet. Hence, too, the terminology of the act. 'Suicide', which is a Latinate and relatively abstract word, appeared late. The OED dates the first use as 1651; I found the word a little earlier in Sir Thomas Browne's *Religio Medici*, written in 1635, published in 1642.† But it was still sufficiently rare not to appear in the 1755 edition of Dr Johnson's Dictionary. Instead, the phrases used were 'self-murder', 'self destruction', 'self-killing', 'self-homicide', self-slaughter' – all expressions reflecting the associations with murder.

They also reflect the difficulty the Church had in ration-

desperate belief that nothing less than his own self-immolation could effectively protest against the Russian invasion of Czechoslovakia. About a year later, when the first anniversary of Palach's death coincided with the end of the Biafran affair, seven people took their own lives in France in the space of ten days, mostly in the same terrible way. The second victim, a nineteen-year-old student from Lille, left a message saying he was 'against war, violence, and the destructive folly of men. . . . If I die, do not weep. I have done it because I could not adapt myself to this world. I did it as a protest against violence and to draw the attention of the world of which a very small part is dealt with here. Death is a form of protest on condition that it is desired by a human being for himself. One can very well refuse it.'9 Behind these horrors, and behind the boy's confusion of altruism and egoism, is a certain residue of primitive magic: it is as though the suicide believes, despite all the evidence to the contrary, that he will finally have his posthumous way, provided his death is sufficiently terrible.

There seems to me to be nothing to justify such optimism.

†'Herein are they in extremes, that can allow a man to be his own assassin, and so highly extol the end and suicide of Cato.' (*Religio Medici*, Sect. XLIV.)

alizing its ban on suicide, since neither the Old nor New Testament directly prohibits it. There are four suicides recorded in the Old Testament – Samson, Saul, Abimelech and Achitophel – and none of them earns adverse comment. In fact, they are scarcely commented on at all. In the New Testament, the suicide of even the greatest criminal, Judas Iscariot, is recorded as blankly; instead of being added to his crimes, it seems a measure of his repentance. Only much later did the theologians reverse the implicit judgement of St Matthew and suggest that Judas was more damned by his suicide than by his betrayal of Christ. In the first years of the Church, suicide was such a neutral subject that even the death of Jesus was regarded by Tertullian, one of the most fiery of the Early Fathers, as a kind of suicide. He pointed out, and Origen agreed, that He voluntarily gave up the ghost, since it was unthinkable that the Godhead should be at the mercy of the flesh. Whence John Donne's comment in *Biathanatos*, the first formal defence of suicide in English : 'Our blessed Saviour . . . chose that way for our Redemption to sacrifice his life, and profuse his blood.'[10]

The idea of suicide as a crime comes late in Christian doctrine and as an afterthought. It was not until the sixth century AD that the Church finally legislated against it, and then the only biblical authority was a special interpretation of the sixth commandment: 'Thou shalt not kill.' The bishops were urged into action by St Augustine; but he, as Rousseau remarked, took his arguments from Plato's *Phaedo*, not from the Bible. Augustine's arguments were sharpened by the suicide-mania which was, above all, the distinguishing mark of the early Christians. I will return to this. But ultimately his reasons were impeccably moral. Christianity was founded on the belief that each human body is the vehicle of an immortal soul which will be judged not in this world but the next. And because each soul is immortal, every life is equally valuable. Since life itself is the gift of God, to reject it is to reject Him and to frustrate His will; to kill His image is to kill Him – which means a one-way ticket to eternal damnation.

The Christian ban on suicide, like its ban on infanticide and abortion, was, then, founded on a respect for life utterly foreign to the indifference and casual murderousness of the Romans. But there is a paradox involved: as David Hume pointed out, monotheism is the only form of religion that can be taken seriously, because only monotheism treats the universe as a single, systematic, intelligible whole; yet its consequences are dogmatism, fanaticism and persecution; whereas polytheism, which is intellectually absurd and a positive obstacle to scientific understanding, produces tolerance, a respect for individual freedom, a civilized breathing space. So with suicide: when the bishops decided it was a crime, they were in some way emphasizing the moral distance travelled from pagan Rome, where the act was habitual and even honoured. Yet what began as moral tenderness and enlightenment finished as the legalized and sanctified atrocities by which the body of the suicide was degraded, his memory defamed, his family persecuted. So although the idea of suicide as a crime was a late, relatively sophisticated invention of Christianity, more or less foreign to the Judeo-Hellenic tradition, it spread like a fog across Europe because its strength came from primitive fears, prejudices and superstitions which had survived despite Christianity, Judaism and Hellenism. Given the barbarity of the Dark Ages and early Middle Ages, it was no doubt inevitable that the savage mind should once again have its day. The process was much the same as that by which the Christian calendar took over the pagan festivals, and the first Spanish missionaries in Mexico invented saints to whom they could dedicate the churches they built on the altar of each Aztec and Mayan god. In the modern business world this process is called 'buying the goodwill' of a defunct firm. As far as suicide is concerned, Christianity bought up the pagan badwill.

Yet there is evidence that, even to the savage mind, the horror of suicide did not always come naturally. The primitive fear of the dead may have been overpowering, particularly the terror of the spirits of those who had died unnaturally and wilfully, murdered or by their own hand. It was largely as a protection against these restless and unappeased ghosts that the whole ornate complex of taboos was elaborated.[11] But to be afraid of the vengeful dead is something rather different from being afraid of death itself.*

---

*We should beware of projecting our own anxieties on to other periods. The idea of death as an unmentionable, almost unnatural, subject is a peculiarly twentieth-century invention. What was once public, simple and commonplace has now become private, abstract and shocking, a fact almost as furtive and secret as sex once was to the Victorians. Yet we are constantly told that the violence of our societies is preternatural and is augmented by the violence served up, continually and inescapably, to entertain our leisure on film, on television, in pulp fiction, even on the news. Perhaps. But I wonder if all this is not now remote and antiseptic compared with habits not long passed. A Roman holiday involved the slaughter of, literally, thousands in gladiatorial shows. After Spartacus' uprising, the crucified bodies of six thousand slaves lined the road from Rome to Capua like lamp-posts. In Christian Europe executions replaced the Roman circuses. Criminals were beheaded publicly, they were hanged, cut down while still alive, their intestines drawn out and their bodies quartered; they were guillotined and elaborately tortured in front of festive crowds; their severed heads were exposed on pikes, their bodies hung in chains from gibbets. The public was amused, excited, more delighted than shocked. An execution was like a funfair, and for the more spectacular occasions even apprentices got the day off. This casual bloodthirstiness continued long after the last suicide had been buried at the crossroads. Executions were public

Thus in some warrior societies, whose gods were those of violence and whose ideal was bravery, suicide was often looked on as a great good. For example, the paradise of the Vikings was Valhalla, 'the Hall of those who died by violence', where the Feast of Heroes was presided over by the god Odin. Only those who had died violently could enter and partake of the banquet. The greatest honour and the surest qualification was death in battle; next best was suicide. Those who died peacefully in their beds, of old age or disease, were excluded from Valhalla through all eternity. Odin himself was the supreme God of War, but, according to Frazer, he was also called the Lord of the Gallows or the God of the Hanged, and men and animals were hanged in his honour from the sacred trees of the holy grove at Upsala. The weird, beautiful lines of the *Havamal* suggest that the god also died in the same ritual, as a sacrifice to himself:

> I know that I hung in the windy tree
> For nine whole nights,
> Wounded with the spear, dedicated to Odin,
> Myself to myself.[12]

in England until 1868. In Paris the Morgue was a tourist attraction where the corpses were displayed like the waxworks at Madame Tussaud's; it was even rebuilt to improve the facilities in 1865 and was not closed to the public until the 1920s. In wars, hand-to-hand fighting with swords, daggers, axes and primitive guns left battlefields looking like butchers' shops. Our own massacres may be infinitely greater but they often take place by remote control and at a distance; in comparison with the great pitched battles of the past, they seem almost abstract. Of course, there is a difference. Unlike our ancestors who, at best, read about them later, we actually see the results. But in the eye of television, as in the eye of God, all things are equal; a real atrocity on the screen in our own home seems neither more nor less genuine than some fantasy acted out in a studio for our amusement. In these circumstances, death is a kind of pornography, at once exciting and unreal: 'Death is something that we fear/But it titillates the ear.'

According to another tradition, Odin wounded himself with his sword before being ritually burnt.[13] Either way, he was a suicide and his worshippers acted according to his divine example. Similarly, there was a Druid maxim promoting suicide as a religious principle: 'There is another world, and they who kill themselves to accompany their friends thither, will live with them there.'[14] That, in turn, links with the custom common among African tribes: that the warriors and slaves put themselves to death when their king dies, in order to live with him in Paradise. Whence, with more sophistication, Hindu *suttee*. The ritual in which the bereaved wife burnt herself to death on the funeral pyre of her husband.

Elsewhere, tribes as far apart as the Iglulik Eskimos and the inhabitants of the Marquesas Islands believed that a violent death was a passport to Paradise, which the Iglulik called the Land of Day. In contrast, those who died peacefully from natural causes were consigned to eternal claustrophobia in the Narrow Land. In the Marquesas they went to the lower depths of Hawaiki.[15] Even the victims of the terrible Aztec rites, the youths who became gods for a period on the understanding that they would eventually have their living hearts cut out, went to the altar with a kind of perverse optimism.

Obviously, to promote the idea of violent death as glorious was an efficient way of preserving a properly warlike spirit; the Americans might have been spared some of their embarrassment in Vietnam had they been able to instil into their conscripts the same primitive virtues. Thus the ancient Scythians regarded it as the greatest honour to take their own lives when they became too old for their nomadic way of life; thereby saving the younger members of the tribe both the trouble and the guilt of killing them. Quintus Curtius described them graphically:

Among them exists a sort of wild and bestial men to whom they give the name of sages. The anticipation of the time of death is a glory in their eyes, and they have themselves burned alive as soon as age or sickness begins to trouble them. According to them, death, passively awaited, is a dishonour to life; thus no honours are rendered those bodies which old age has destroyed. Fire would be contaminated if it did not receive the human sacrifice still breathing.[16]

Durkheim called this style of suicide 'altruistic'; one of the supreme examples is Captain Oates, who walked out to his death in the Antarctic snow in order to help Scott and his other doomed companions. But where the whole of a tribe's morality and mythology made it seem that suicide was a way to a better life, the motives of those who took their own lives were evidently not altogether pure and self-sacrificing. They were, instead, intensely narcissistic: '. . . dedicated to Odin,/Myself to myself.' 'Through the primitive act of suicide,' writes Gregory Zilboorg, 'man achieved a *fantasied* immortality, i.e. uninterrupted fulfilment of the hedonistic ideal through mere fantasy and not through actual living.'[17] Since death was both inevitable and relatively unimportant, suicide ultimately became more a matter of pleasure than of principle: one sacrificed a few days or years on this earth in order to feast with the gods eternally in the next. It was, essentially, a frivolous act.

In contrast, a serious suicide is an act of choice, the terms of which are entirely those of this world; a man dies by his own hand because he thinks the life he has not worth living. Suicides of this kind are usually thought to be an index of high civilization – as who should say, tell me your suicide-rate and I will tell you your cultural sophistication – for the simple reason that the act goes against the most basic of instincts, that of self-preservation. But it is not necessarily so. For example, the Tasmanian aborigines died out not just because they were hunted like kangaroos for an afternoon's sport, but also because a world in which this could happen was intolerable to them; so they committed suicide as a race by refusing to breed. Ironically perhaps, and as though to confirm the aborigines' judgement, the mummified remains of the old lady who was the last to survive have been preserved by the Australian Government as a museum curiosity. Similarly, hundreds of Jews put themselves to death at Masada, rather than submit to the Roman legions. More extreme still, the history of the Spanish conquest of the New World is one of deliberate genocide in which the native inhabitants themselves co-operated. Their treatment at the hands of the Spaniards was so cruel that the Indians killed themselves by the thousand rather than endure it. Of forty natives from the Gulf of Mexico who were brought to work in a mine of the Emperor Charles V, thirty-nine starved themselves to death. A whole cargo of slaves contrived to strangle themselves in the hold of a Spanish galleon, although the head room was so limited by the heavy ballast of stones that they were forced to hang themselves in a squatting or kneeling position. In the West Indies, according to the Spanish historian, Girolamo Benzoni, four thousand men and countless women and children died by jumping from cliffs or by killing each other. He adds that, out of the two million original inhabitants of Haiti, less than 150 survived as a result of the suicides and slaughter.[18] In the end the Spaniards, faced with an embarrassing labour shortage, put a stop to the epidemic of suicides by persuading the Indians that they, too, would kill themselves in order to pursue them in the next world with even harsher cruelties.

The despair which ends with racial suicide is a peculiarly pure phenomenon and proportionately rare. Only under the most extreme conditions does the psychic mechanism of self-preservation go into reverse for a whole nation, un-sanctioned by morality or belief and unswayed by zealotry. In a less pure, more complex culture, where death is accepted casually but beliefs are no longer simple and morality fluctuates, within limits, according to the individual, the question of suicide becomes urgent in another way. The supreme example is that of the Romans who turned the ancient world's toleration of suicide into a high fashion.

The toleration began with the Greeks. The taboos against the act which obtained even in Athens – the corpse buried outside the city, its hand cut off and buried separately – were linked with the more profound Greek horror of killing one's own kin. By inference, suicide was an extreme case of this, and the language barely distinguishes between self-murder and murder of kindred. Yet in literature and philosophy the act passes more or less without comment, certainly without blame. The first of all literary suicides, that of Oedipus's mother Jocasta, is made to seem praiseworthy, an honourable way out of an insufferable situation. Homer records self-murder without comment, as something natural and usually heroic. The legends bear him out. Aegeus threw himself into the sea – which thereafter bore his name – when he mistakenly thought his son Theseus had been slain by the ~~Minotaur~~. Erigone hanged herself from grief when she discovered the murdered body of her father Ikarios – thereby, incidentally, causing an epidemic of suicide by hanging among the Athenian women, which lasted until the blood was wiped out by the institution of the Aiora festival in honour of Erigone. Leukakas jumped off a rock in order to avoid being raped by Apollo. When the Delphic oracle announced that the Lacedaemonians would capture Athens if they did not kill the Athenian king, the reigning monarch Codrus entered the enemy camp in disguise, picked a quarrel with a soldier and allowed himself to be slaughtered. Charondas, the law-giver of Catana, a Greek colony in Sicily, took his life when he broke one of his own laws. Another law-giver, Lycurgus of Sparta, extracted an oath from his people that they would keep his laws until he returned from Delphi, where he went to consult the oracle about his new legal code. The oracle gave a favourable answer, which he sent back in writing. He then starved himself to death so that the Spartans should never be absolved from their oath. And so on.[19] They all had one quality in common: a certain nobility of motive. So far as the records go, the ancient Greeks took their own lives only for the best possible reasons: grief, high patriotic principle or to avoid dishonour.

Their philosophical discussion of the subject is proportionately detached and balanced. The keys were moderation and high principle. Suicide was not to be tolerated if it seemed like an act of wanton disrespect to the gods. For this reason, the Pythagoreans rejected suicide out of hand since, for them as for the later Christians, life itself was the discipline of the gods. In the *Phaedo*, Plato made Socrates repeat this Orphic doctrine approvingly before he drank the hemlock. He used the simile – often to be repeated later – of the soldier on guard duty who must not desert his post, and also that of man as the property of the gods, who are as angry at our suicide as we would be if our chattels destroyed themselves. Aristotle used much the same argument, though in a more austere way: suicide was 'an offence against the State' because, on religious grounds, it polluted the city and, economically, weakened it by destroying a useful citizen. It was an act, that is, of social irresponsibility. Logically, this is no doubt impeccable. But it also seems curiously irrelevant to the act of suicide. It is not, I mean, a style of argument likely to impinge on the

state of mind of a man about to take his own life. The fact
that it was considered to be so cogent – Aristotle's huge
authority apart – implies a curiously cool and detached
attitude to the problem of suicide.

In contrast, Plato's arguments are less simple, more
subtle. Socrates' sweetly reasonable tone repudiates suicide,
yet at the same time he makes death seem infinitely desirable; it is the entry to the world of ideal presences of
which earthly reality is a mere shadow. In the end, Socrates
drinks the hemlock so cheerfully and has argued so
eloquently for the benefits of death that he has set an example to others to come. The Greek philosopher Cleombrotus is said to have been inspired by the *Phaedo* to drown
himself, and Cato read the book through twice the night
before he fell on his own sword.

Plato also allowed for moderation in the other sense. He
suggested that if life itself became immoderate, then suicide
became a rational, justifiable act. Painful disease or intolerable constraint were sufficient reasons to depart. And this,
when the religious superstitions faded, was philosophical
justification enough. Within a hundred years of Socrates'
death, the Stoics had made suicide into the most reasonable
and desirable of all ways out. Both they and the Epicureans
claimed to be as indifferent to death as to life. For the Epicureans the principle was pleasure; whatever promoted
that was good, whatever produced pain was evil. For the
Stoics the ideal was vaguer, more dignified: that of life in
accordance with nature. When it no longer seemed to be so,
then death came as a rational choice befitting a rational
nature. Thus Zeno, the founder of the school, is said to have
hanged himself out of sheer irritation when he stumbled
and wrenched his finger; he was ninety-eight at the time.
His successor Cleanthes died with equally philosophical
aplomb. As a cure for a gumboil he was ordered to starve

himself. Within two days the gumboil was better and his doctor put him back on to an ordinary diet. But Cleanthes refused, 'as he had advanced so far on his journey towards death, he would not now retreat'; he duly starved himself to death.

Classical Greek suicide, then, was dictated by a calm, though slightly excessive, reasonableness. In Athens, as in the Greek colonies of Marseilles and Ceos, where hemlock was developed and whose customs inspired Montaigne to his eloquent defence of noble suicide, the magistrates kept a supply of poison for those who wished to die. All that was required was that they should first plead their cause before the senate and obtain official permission. The precepts were clear:

Whoever no longer wishes to live shall state his reasons to the Senate, and after having received permission shall abandon life. If your existence is hateful to you, die; if you are overwhelmed by fate, drink the hemlock. If you are bowed with grief, abandon life. Let the unhappy man recount his misfortune, let the magistrate supply him with the remedy, and his wretchedness will come to an end.[20]

These early Stoics brought to the subject of their own death the same degree of nicety that Henry James reserved for morals. And this was appropriate since the question of how they died became for them the final measure of discrimination. Plato had justified suicide when external circumstances became intolerable. The Greek Stoics developed and rationalized this attitude according to their ideal of life in accordance with nature. The advanced Stoicism of the later Roman Empire was a further development of Plato; the argument was essentially the same but now the circumstances were internalized. When the inner compulsion became intolerable the question was no longer whether or not one should kill oneself but how to do so with the greatest dignity, bravery and style. To put it another way, it was an achievement of the Greeks to empty suicide of all the primitive horrors and then gradually to discuss the subject more or less rationally, as though it were not invested with much feeling, one way or another. The Romans, on the other hand, reinvested it with emotion but, in doing so, turned the emotions upside down. In their eyes suicide was no longer morally evil; on the contrary, one's manner of going became a practical test of excellence and virtue. On the night the Emperor Antoninus Pius died, the password, by his command, was '*aequanimitas*'.[21]

I mentioned the belief that the more sophisticated and rational a society becomes, the further it travels from superstitious fears and the more easily suicide is tolerated. Roman Stoicism would seem to be the ultimate example of this. Stoic writing is full of exhortations to suicide, all of which embroider more or less elegantly on those Athenian precepts quoted above from Libanius. The most famous is Seneca's:

Foolish man, what do you bemoan, and what do you fear? Wherever you look there is an end of evils. You see that yawning precipice? It leads to liberty. You see that flood, that river, that well? Liberty houses within them. You see that stunted, parched, and sorry tree? From each branch liberty hangs. Your neck, your throat, your heart are all so many ways of escape from slavery ... Do you enquire the road to freedom? You shall find it in every vein of your body.

It is a beautiful and cadenced piece of rhetoric. But where most rhetoric is a protection from reality, a verbal armour the writer puts between himself and the world, Seneca finally practised his precepts: he stabbed himself to avoid the vengeance of Nero, who had once been his pupil. His wife Paulina, no less Stoic, attempted to die with him in the same way, but was saved.

One other example is enough to set the tone of the times. It is the advice of Seneca's ascetic friend Attalus to one Marcellinus, who was suffering from an incurable disease and was contemplating suicide:

Be not tormented, my Marcellinus, as if you were deliberating any great matter. Life is a thing of no dignity or importance. Your very slaves, your animals, possess it in common with yourself: but it is a great thing to die honourably, prudently, bravely. Think how long you have been engaged in the same dull course: eating, sleeping, and indulging your appetites. This has been the circle. Not only a prudent, brave, or a wretched man may wish to die, but even a fastidious one.[22]

Again there is no gap between rhetoric and reality. Marcellinus took his friend's advice and starved himself to death, a 'fastidious' answer to the wild indulgence of Tiberius's Rome.

In doing so, he also joined the company of the most distinguished men of the ancient world. I have already mentioned Socrates, Codrus, Charondas, Lycurgus, Cleombrotus, Cato, Zeno, Cleanthes, Seneca and Paulina. Among many others were the Greek orators Isocrates and Demosthenes; the Roman poets Lucretius, Lucan and Labienus, the dramatist Terence, the critic Aristarchus, and Petronius Arbiter, who was the most fastidious of them all; Hannibal, Boadicea, Brutus, Cassius, Mark Antony and Cleopatra, Cocceius Nerva, Statius, Nero, Otho, King Ptolemy of Cyprus and King Sardanapalus of Persia. There was also Mithridates who, to protect himself from his enemies, had immunized himself by years of swallowing small doses of poison. As a result, when he finally tried to take his own life by poison he failed. And so on. John Donne's list of notable suicides of the classical world runs to three pages, including witty comments; Montaigne produced a host of others. Both chose more or less at random from many hundreds of possibilities; and these, in turn, were only a fraction of those who died in the Roman fashion.

The evidence is, then, that the Romans looked on suicide neither with fear nor revulsion, but as a carefully considered and chosen validation of the way they had lived and the principles they had lived by. The supreme, and supremely perverse, example is that of Corellius Rufus, a nobleman who, according to Fedden, 'put off committing suicide throughout the reign of Domitian, saying that he did not wish to die under a tyrant. Once this powerful Emperor was dead he took his own life with an easy mind, and as a free Roman.'[23] To live nobly also meant to die nobly and at the right moment. Everything depended on the dominant will and a rational choice.

This attitude was reinforced by Roman law. There were no revenges, no degradation, no evidence of fear or horror. Instead, the law was the law – practical. According to Justinian's *Digest*, suicide of a private citizen was not punishable if it was caused by 'impatience of pain or sickness, or by another cause', or by 'weariness of life ... lunacy, or fear of dishonour'. Since this covered every rational cause, all that was left was the utterly irrational suicide 'without cause', and that was punishable on the grounds that 'whoever does not spare himself would much less spare another'.[24] In other words, it was punished because it was irrational, not because it was a crime. There were other exceptions but they were even more strictly practical: it was a crime for a slave to kill himself for the simple reason that he represented to his master a certain capital investment. Like a car, a slave was guaranteed against faults: hidden physical blemishes, a suicidal or criminal nature. If he killed himself, or attempted to, within six months of his purchase he could be returned – alive or dead – to his old master and the deal was declared invalid.[25] In the same way, a soldier was considered to be the property of the State and his suicide was tantamount to desertion. Roman law, that is, took literally the two similes – the soldier and the chattel – which Socrates had used so eloquently. Finally, it was also an offence for a criminal to take his own life in order to avoid trial for a crime for which the punishment would be forfeiture of his estate. In this case, a suicide was declared to be without legal heirs. The relatives, however, were allowed to defend the accused as though he were still alive; if he were found innocent, they then retained their inheritance; if not, it went to the State. In short, in Roman law the crime of suicide was strictly economic. It was an offence neither against morality nor religion, only against the capital investments of the slave-owning class or the treasury of the State.

The icy heroism of all this is admirable, even enviable, but it also seems, at least from our perspective, curiously unreal. It seems impossible that life and behaviour could ever be quite so rational and the will, at the moment of crisis, quite so dependable. That the Romans were able to act as though they were indicates an extraordinary inner discipline – a discipline of the soul they did not believe in. But it also says something about the monstrous civilization of which they were part. I suggested earlier that only comparatively recently has death ceased to be casual and public. In Imperial Rome this casualness reached that point of lunacy where the crowd, for its entertainment, would be satisfied with nothing less than death. Donne quotes a learned source who says that in one month thirty thousand men died in gladiatorial shows.[26] Frazer says that at one time people would offer themselves for execution to amuse the public at five *minae* a time (about £120), the money to be paid to their heirs; he adds that the market was so competitive that the candidates would offer to be beaten to death rather than beheaded, since that was slower, more painful and so more spectacular.*[27] Perhaps, then, Stoic dignity was a last defence against the murderous squalor of Rome itself. When those calm heroes looked around them they saw a life so unspeakable, cruel, wanton, corrupt and apparently unvalued, that they clung to their ideals of reason much as the Christian poor used to cling to their belief in Paradise and the goodness of God despite, or because of, the misery of their lives on this earth. Stoicism, in short, was a philosophy of despair. It was not for nothing that Seneca, who was its most powerful and influential spokesman, was also the teacher of the most vicious of all Roman emperors, Nero.

Perhaps this is why Stoic calm was so easily assimilated to the religious hysteria of the early Christians. Rational suicide was a kind of aristocratic corollary of vulgar bloodlust. Christianity, which began as a religion for the poor and rejected, took that bloodlust, combined it with the habit of suicide, and transferred both into a lust for martyrdom. The Romans may have fed Christians to the lions for sport, but they were not prepared for the fact that the Christians welcomed the animals as instruments of glory and salvation. 'Let me enjoy those beasts,' said Ignatius, 'whom I wish much more cruell than they are; and if they will not attempt me, I will provoke and draw them by force.'[28] The persecution of the early Christians

*There is a case in the late eighteenth century of a man who advertised that he would commit suicide publicly in Covent Garden in order to raise money for his poverty-stricken family — provided he could find enough spectators willing to pay one pound each. By this time brutal amusement was qualified by an even stronger taste for 'the Pathetick'. Nowadays, someone making a similar offer would qualify only for the nearest psychiatric ward, or as a suitable case for treatment in the Theatre of the Absurd.

was less religious and political than a perversion of their own seeking. For the sophisticated Roman magistrates Christian obstinacy was mostly an embarrassment: as when the Christians refused to make the token gestures towards established religion which would save their lives or, failing that, refused to avail themselves of the convenient pause between judgement and execution in which to escape. Embarrassment moved into irritation when the would-be martyrs, student revolutionary tacticians before their day, responded to clemency with provocation. And it finished with boredom: an African proconsul surrounded by a mob of Christians baying for martyrdom shouted to them: 'Goe hang and drown your selves and ease the Magistrate.'[29] Others, no less bored, were less forbearing. The glorious company of martyrs came to number thousands of men, women and children who were beheaded, burned alive, flung from cliffs, roasted on gridirons and hacked to pieces – all more or less gratuitously, of their own free will, as so many deliberate acts of provocation. Martyrdom was a Christian creation as much as a Roman persecution.

Just as the early Christians took over the Roman religious festivals, so they also took over the Roman attitudes to death and suicide, and in doing so magnified them theologically, distorted them and finally turned them upside-down. To the Romans of every class death itself was unimportant. But the way of dying – decently, rationally, with dignity and at the right time – mattered intensely. Their way of death, that is, it was the measure of their final value of life. The early Christians showed this same indifference to death but changed the perspective. Viewed from the Christian Heaven, life itself was at best unimportant, at worst, evil: the fuller the life the greater the temptation to sin. Death, therefore, was a release awaited or sought out with impatience. In other words, the more powerfully the Church instilled in believers the idea that this world was a vale of tears and sin and temptation, where they waited uneasily until death released them into eternal glory, the more irresistible the temptation to suicide became. Even the most stoical Romans committed suicide only as a last resort; they at least waited until their lives had become intolerable. But for the primitive Church life was intolerable whatever its conditions. Why, then, live unredeemed when heavenly bliss is only a knife stroke away? Christian teaching was at first a powerful incitement to suicide.

The early Fathers had another inducement, almost as powerful as heavenly bliss. They offered posthumous glory: the martyrs' names celebrated annually in the Church calendar, their passing officially recorded, their relics worshipped. Tertullian, the most bloodthirsty of the Fathers, who explicitly forbade his flock even to attempt to escape persecution, also proffered them the sweetest of recompenses, revenge: 'No City escaped the punishment, which had shed Christian blood.'[30] The martyrs would peer down from Paradise and see their enemies tortured eternally in Hell.

But above all, martyrdom afforded certain redemption. Just as baptism purged away original sin, so martyrdom wiped out all subsequent transgressions. It was as much a guarantee of Paradise to the Christians as violent death was to the Vikings and the Iglukik Eskimos. The only difference was that the martyrs died not as warriors but as passive victims; the war they fought was not of this world and all their victories were Pyrrhic. We are back, by another route, with frivolous suicide.

Theologically, the argument was irresistible, but to respond to it required a zealotry which touched on madness.

Donne remarked, unwillingly and with some embarrassment, 'that those times were affected with a disease of this
naturall desire of such a death. . . . For that age was growne
so hungry and ravenous of it [martyrdom], that many
were baptized onely because they would be burnt, and children taught to vexe and provoke Executioners, that they
might be thrown into the fire.'[31] It culminated in the genuine lunacy of the Donatists, whose lust for martyrdom
was so extreme that the Church eventually declared them
heretics. Gibbon elegantly described their weird and ambiguous glory:

The rage of the Donatists was enflamed by a phrensy of a
very extraordinary kind: and which, if it really prevailed
among them in so extravagant a degree, cannot surely be paral-
leled in any country or in any age. Many of these fanatics were
possessed with the horror of life and the desire of martyrdom;
and they deemed it of little moment by what means or by what
hands they perished, if their conduct was sanctified by the
intention of devoting themselves to the glory of·the true faith
and the hope of eternal happiness. Sometimes they rudely disturbed the festivals and profaned the temples of paganism with
the design of exciting the most zealous of the idolators to
revenge the insulted honour of their Gods. They sometimes
forced their way into the courts of justice and compelled the
affrighted judge to give orders for their execution. They frequently stopped travellers on the public highways and obliged
them to inflict the stroke of martyrdom by promise of a re-
ward, if they consented – and by the threat of instant death, if
they refused to grant so very singular a favour. When they
were disappointed of every other resource, they announced the
day on which, in the presence of their friends and brethren,
they should cast themselves headlong from some lofty rock;
and many precipices were shown, which had acquired fame by
the number of these religious suicides.[32]

The Donatists flourished – if that is the word – in the fourth and fifth centuries AD and inspired their contemporary, St Augustine, to comment, 'to kill themselves out of respect for martyrdom is their daily sport'. But Augustine also recognized the logical dilemma of Christian teaching if suicide were allowed in order to avoid sin, then it became the logical course for all those fresh from baptism That sophistry, combined with the suicide mania of the martyrs, provoked him into arguments to prove suicide to be 'a detestable and damnable· wickedness', a mortal sin greater than any that could be committed between baptism and a divinely ordained death. I have already mentioned that the first of the arguments he used was derived from the sixth commandment, 'Thou shalt not kill'. Thus the man who killed himself broke this commandment and became a murderer.* Moreover, if a man killed himself to atone for his sins, he was usurping the function of the State and the Church; and if he died innocent in order to avoid sin, then he had his own innocent blood on his hands – a worse sin than any he might commit, since it was impossible for him to repent. Finally, Augustine took over Plato's and the Pythagoreans' argument that life is the gift of God and our sufferings, being divinely ordained, are not to be foreshortened by our own actions; to bear them patiently is a measure of

---

*It was this argument which was assimilated into civil law: 'Up to this day, we do not know what crime suicide constituted, whether a crime *sui generis* or a particular instance of murder, the better view being that it was the latter. Another interesting feature of that crime is the manner in which it was formulated. In the case of all other offenses, the common law defines the crime itself ("larceny is the felonious taking"; "murder is the unlawful killing"). But in suicide, not the crime but the criminal is defined: *"felo de se* is *he who kills".* Obviously, as was Christian doctrine, so was the common law struggling with the dilemma of a crime in which the aggressor and the object of aggression are united in one person.'[33]

one's greatness of soul. Thus to take one's own life proved only that one did not accept the divine will.

Augustine's large authority and the excesses of the presumptive martyrs finally swung opinion against suicide. In AD 533 the Council of Orleans denied funeral rites to anyone who killed himself while accused of a crime. And in doing so, they were not merely following Roman law which had been formulated to safeguard the State's rights to the suicide's inheritance. Instead, they were condemning suicide both as a crime in itself and also a crime more serious than others, since ordinary criminals were still allowed a properly Christian burial. Thirty years later this seriousness was recognized without qualification by Canon Law. In 562 at the Council of Braga funeral rites were refused to *all* suicides regardless of social position, reason or method. The final step was taken in 693 by the Council of Toledo, which ordained that even the attempted suicide should be excommunicated.

The door had slammed shut. The decent alternative of the Romans, the key to paradise of the early Christians, had become the most deadly of mortal sins. Where St Matthew recorded the suicide of Judas Iscariot without comment – implying by his silence that it in some way atoned for his other crimes – later theologians asserted that he was more damned for killing himself than for betraying Christ. St Bruno, in the eleventh century, called suicides 'martyrs for Satan' and two centuries later St Thomas Aquinas sealed up the whole question in the *Summa*: suicide, he said, is a mortal sin against God who has given life; it is also a sin against justice and against charity. Yet even there, in what was to be the centre of Christian doctrine, Aquinas takes his arguments from non-Christian sources. The sin against God derives ultimately, like Augustine's similar argument, from Plato. The sin against justice – by which he means the

individual's responsibilities to his community – harks back
to Aristotle. As for the sin against charity, Aquinas means
that instinctive charity each man bears towards himself –
that is, the instinct of self-preservation which man has in
common with the lower animals; to go against that is a
mortal sin since it is to go against nature.* That reason was
first used by the Hebrew general Josephus to dissuade his
soldiers from killing themselves after they had been defeated
by the Romans. (He also used Plato's argument.)

But however un-Christian the sources of the arguments,
suicide became, in the long, superstitious centuries between
Augustine and Aquinas, the most mortal of Christian sins.
Augustine had attacked suicide as a preventive measure:
the cult of martyrdom had got out of hand and was, anyway, no longer relevant to the situation of the Church in
the fourth century AD. Moreover, it was an offence against
that respect for life as the vehicle of the soul which was the
essence of Christ's teaching; to love one's neighbour as oneself makes no sense if to kill oneself is also permitted. Yet
the fact remained that suicide, thinly disguised as martyrdom, was the rock on which the Church had first been
founded. So perhaps the absoluteness with which the sin
was condemned and the horrors of the vengeance visited on
the dead bodies of the suicides were directly proportional
to the power the act exerted on the Christian imagination,
and to the lingering temptation to escape the snares of the
flesh by the shortest, most certain way. Thus when the
Albigensians, in the early thirteenth century, followed

---

* It isn't. Glanville Williams quotes a learned source to show that
dogs sometimes commit suicide, 'usually by drowning or by refusing food, for a number of reasons – generally when the animal is
cast out from the household, but also from regret or remorse or even
from sheer ennui. Animal suicide of these kinds is capable of being
regarded as a manifestation of intelligence.'[34]

the example of the early saints and suicidally sought martyrdom, they were thought only to have compounded the
damnation their other heresies had already earned them. In
doing so, they justified the terrible savagery with which they
were butchered.

Fedden believes that Augustine's teaching and Canon
Law acted together as a catalyst which released all those
primitive terrors of suicide which are repressed in more
rational periods. Perhaps. But what also occurred was
somehow more profound: what began as a preventive
measure finished as a kind of universal character-change.
An act which, during the first flowering of western civilization, had been tolerated, later admired, and later still sought
as the supreme mark of zealotry, became finally the object
of intense moral revulsion. When, in the late Renaissance,
the question of the individual's right to take his own life
once more arose, it seemed to be challenging the whole
structure of Christian belief and morals. Hence the deviousness with which men like John Donne began once again to
argue the case for suicide after a gap of more than a thousand years. Hence, too, the note of hoarse moral rectitude
of their detractors, that earnest certainty which could dispense with argument because it had behind it the whole
massive weight of the Church's authority. The increasingly
outspoken and rational arguments of the philosophers –
Voltaire, Hume, Schopenhauer – did more or less nothing to
shake this moral certainty, although as time went on the
pious denunciations became shriller, less assured, more outraged.

It took the counter-revolution of science to change all
this. Henry Morselli, an Italian professor of psychological
medicine and Durkheim's most distinguished predecessor in
the use of statistics to analyse the problem of suicide, wrote
in 1879: 'The old philosophy of individualism had given to

suicide the character of liberty and spontaneity, but now it became necessary to study it no longer as the expression of individual and independent faculties, but certainly as a social phenomenon allied with all the other racial forces.'[35]

The shift is from the individual to society, from morals to problems. Socially, the gains were enormous: the legal penalties gradually dropped away; the families of successful suicides no longer found themselves disinherited and tainted with the suspicion of inherited insanity; they could bury their dead and grieve for them in much the same way as any other bereaved. As for the unsuccessful suicide, he faced neither the gallows nor prison but, at worst, a period of observation in a psychiatric ward; more often, he faced nothing more piercing than his own continuing depression.

Existentially, however, there were also losses. The Church's condemnation of self-murder, however brutal, was based at least on concern for the suicide's soul. In contrast, a great deal of modern scientific tolerance appears to be founded on human indifference. The act is removed from the realm of damnation only at the price of being transformed into an interesting but purely intellectual problem, beyond obloquy but also beyond tragedy and morality. There seems to me remarkably little gap between the idea of death as a fascinating, slightly erotic happening on a television screen and that of suicide as an abstract sociological problem. Despite all the talk of prevention, it may be that the suicide is rejected by the social scientist as utterly as he was by the most dogmatic Christian theologians. Thus even the author of the entry on suicide in the *Encyclopaedia of Religion and Ethics* writes, with unconcealed relief: 'Perhaps the greatest contribution of modern times to the rational treatment of the matter is the consideration ... that many suicides are non-moral and entirely the affair of the specialist in mental diseases.' The implication is clear: modern suicide has been removed from the vulnerable, volatile world of human beings and hidden safely away in the isolation wards of science. I doubt if Ogarev and his prostitute mistress would have found much in the change to be grateful for.

Part 3
The Closed World
of Suicide

Every man is the greatest enemy unto himself . . . We study many times to undo ourselves, abusing those good things which God hath bestowed upon us, health, wealth, strength, wit, learning, art, memory, to our own destruction . . . we arm ourselves to our own overthrows; and use reason, art judgement, all that should help us, as so many instruments to undo us.

— ROBERT BURTON

Everywhere there were people living out their lives using aspects of suicide against themselves. They did not even have the authenticity of the final act to speak for them. Suicide is, in short, the one continuous, every-day, ever-present problem of living. It is a question of degree. I'd seen them in all varying stages of development and despair. The failed lawyer, the cynical doctor, the depressed housewife, the angry teen-ager . . . all of mankind engaged in the massive conspiracy against their own lives that is their daily activity. The meaning of suicide, the true meaning, had yet to be defined, had yet to be created in the broad dimensions it deserved.

— DANIEL STERN

1. Fallacies

No one ever lacks a good reason for suicide.

CESARE PAVESE

Suicide is still suspect but in the last eighty odd years a change of tone has taken place: odium, like patriotism, is no longer enough. The suicide prejudice continues but the religious principles by which it was once dignified now seem altogether less self-evident. As a result, the note of righteous denunciation has been modified. What was once a mortal sin has now become a private vice, another 'dirty little secret', something shameful to be avoided and tidied away, unmentionable and faintly salacious, less self-slaughter than self-abuse.

One reason for this odd shift of emphasis is that suicide, while remaining humanly shocking, has at the same time become respectable; that is, it has become the subject of intensive scientific research – and science makes anything respectable. The change began in 1897 with the publication of Emile Durkheim's classic *Suicide: a Study in Sociology*. The sub-title made the point unequivocally; the question was no longer the morality of the act but the social conditions which produce such despair. 'To be or not to be' had given way to 'the reason why'. After Durkheim there was no hesitation. Scientific studies of suicide have multiplied like flies, particularly since the 1920s: clinical investigations, statistical analyses, aspects of this and that, theories of every colour by psycho-analysts, psychiatrists and clinical psychologists, sociologists and social workers, statisticians and medical men; even the insurance companies are in on the act. The contributions to learned journals are unceasing, each year there are new specialized books, most years see another fat volume of essays. As a research subject, suicide has, as they say, come big; it even has its own name, 'suicidology'. There is a high-powered and thriving suicidological unit attached to the famous medical school at Johns Hopkins University in Baltimore; the United States Government's Department of Health, Education and Welfare sponsors a magazine called *Bulletin of Suicidology*. Allied to all this research has been a steady growth in public concern. The Samaritans – who, in their practical way, probably do more in a month to prevent suicide than the scientists manage in a decade – set up their first emergency centre in London in 1953. Beleaguered and faintly condescended to in the beginning, much like the Marie Stopes Clinics, there are now about one hundred branches in England, others in the Commonwealth, and similar services throughout most of northern Europe. The United States has its own Suicide Prevention Centres organized from Los Angeles. Each year there is an international conference on the subject, part scientific, part practical.

How much the potential suicide has been helped by all this activity is often not obvious. But at least most of the old fallacies have been demolished. It used to be thought, for example, that suicide was inextricably mixed with young love. The paradigm was Romeo and Juliet – youthful, idealistic and passionate. Yet statistically, the chances of Romeo and Juliet succeeding in taking their own lives are far smaller than those of King Lear, who died of natural causes, or of Gloucester, who only attempted the act. The incidence of successful suicide rises with age and reaches its peak between the ages of fifty-five and sixty-five. In comparison, the young are great attempters; their peak is between twenty-five and forty-four. It may be that the old succeed because they are more knowing and more careful, whereas the young act impetuously, on the wave of emotion. But I suspect that something more radical is involved: if, as Professor Erwin Stengel believes, attempted suicide is a cry for help, then the young, even in their self-destruction, remain optimistic. Although they may be more vulnerable than their elders, they still believe, like Mr Micawber, that something or someone will turn up. In plot, *Romeo and Juliet* is a misfired comedy, just as *The Winter's Tale* is a misfired and redeemed tragedy. The old who, like Lear, are often without friends or family or employment, and may be suffering from an incurable disease, are under no such illusion.* In short, the real fallacy, which science

---

* Two extreme examples, both British, both recent.

First, a ninety-five-year-old ex-army officer who had lived for years in a hotel on his small pension. Eventually, the hotel changed hands and the new management raised the rent of his room to a price he could not afford. He knew he must disrupt the pattern of his life and move out. For some time before this, he had complained to his doctor of stomach pains and asked if he might possibly have 'a growth'. The doctor examined him and pooh-poohed his anxiety as hypochondria. The post-mortem showed he had advanced cancer of the stomach. Maybe his sense of life was still strong enough, even at ninety-five, to enable him to recognize death when it was in him − despite what his doctor said. This underlying physical unease combined with the intolerable aggravation of the threatened move: he put his head in a plastic bag and suffocated.

Second, in the same area an old lady took her life in the same way. She was eighty-five years old, healthy, vigorous, seemingly cheerful. But her husband was dead, her children had gone off. One morning she took a large plastic bag full of Brussels sprouts, carefully piled the sprouts on the table − the reflex, presumably, of a lifetime of careful housekeeping − put the bag over her head and suffocated. When she was found, there was a sprout leaf over each eye.

Writing of a similar case, K. R. Eissler remarks: 'I noticed that the suicide of an old man, who had been fatally sick for a long time and whose natural death would have been taken as a matter of

is unlikely to disprove, is that of the serenity of old age.

Romeo and Juliet also embody another popular misconception: that of the suicidal great passion. It seems that those who die for love usually do so by mistake and ill-luck. It is said that the London police can always distinguish, among the corpses fished out of the Thames, between those who have drowned themselves because of unhappy love affairs and those drowned for debt. The fingers of the lovers are almost invariably lacerated by their attempts to save themselves by clinging to the piers of the bridges. In contrast, the debtors apparently go down like slabs of concrete, without struggle and without afterthought.

The third popular fallacy is that suicide is produced by bad weather. An early eighteenth-century French novel begins: 'In the gloomy month of November, when the people of England hang and drown themselves. . . .' The belief that suicide is somehow connected with winter is, presumably, a remnant of our superstitious fear of the act as a deed of darkness, and also of a vague, childish omnipotence which says that the weather of the soul is reflected in the

course, provoked unusually strong emotions in others. Some spoke of him as if he had accomplished a great deed; others reproached him for the exhibitionistic way in which he had proceeded. But there was a general agreement that he must have suffered severely, and everyone felt far greater pity for him than if the proximate cause of his death had been the fatal disease because of which he ostensibly committed suicide. Here society's ambivalent attitude is well demonstrated. The person who commits suicide becomes a hero and therefore arouses ambivalent reactions – veneration and anger. Because he defied death he is revered like Empedocles, but he is censured because he took flight.'[1] There is no disputing the pity these cases arouse but the admiration has, I think, little to do with defying death. It is, instead, for the extraordinary realism of these old people, who were willing to face and judge the unacceptable terms of the life they were living, without taking refuge in the delusions, self-pity and crotchety egoism of old age.

skies. In fact, in the gloomy month of November the suicide-rate is approaching its annual low. The cycle of self-destruction follows precisely that of nature : it declines in autumn, reaches its low in mid-winter and then begins to rise slowly with the sap; its climax is in early summer, May and June; in July it gradually begins once more to drop. Even Professor Stengel, a most humane and sensitive authority, is puzzled by this phenomenon. He suggests that it may be linked with 'the rhythmical biological changes which play an important part in animal life although they are much less conspicuous in man'.[2] It seems to me more likely that the opposite is true : the impulse to take one's life increases in the spring not because of any mysterious biological changes but because of the lack of them. Instead of change, there is stasis:

> Birds build – but not I build; no, but strain,
> Time's eunuch, and not breed one work that wakes.
> Mine, O thou lord of life, send my roots rain.

A suicidal depression is a kind of spiritual winter, frozen, sterile, unmoving. The richer, softer and more delectable nature becomes, the deeper that internal winter seems, and the wider and more intolerable the abyss which separates the inner world from the outer. Thus suicide becomes a natural reaction to an unnatural condition. Perhaps this is why, for the depressed, Christmas is so hard to bear. In theory it is an oasis of warmth and light in an unforgiving season, like a lighted window in a storm. For those who have to stay outside, it accentuates, like spring, the disjunction between public warmth and festivity, and cold, private despair.

The fourth popular fallacy is that of suicide as a national habit. Two hundred years ago, self-murder was regarded as an English sickness. The French adopted the word '*suicide*' into their language as an Anglicism, just as they have recently adopted Americanisms like *le hot dog* and *le drug store*. An eighteenth-century French essayist wrote of the English :

> They die by their own hands with as much indifference as by another's ... Last year in the space of fifteen days, three girls hanged themselves for some uneasiness in their *amours*; and the people that told me of it, did not seem so much concerned at the thing as that two of them should do it for the sake of Irishmen, whom they despise much and looked upon as incapable of love.[3]

Even the great Montesquieu thought well enough of this fairy-tale to enshrine it in *The Spirit of the Laws* :

> We do not find that the Romans ever killed themselves without a cause; but the English destroy themselves most unaccountably; they destroy themselves often in the very bosom of happiness. This action among the Romans was the effect of education; it was connected with their principles and customs; among the English it is the effect of a distemper. It may be complicated with the scurvy.[4]

A country credited with suicide as a kind of national reflex action is automatically made ridiculous. In the eighteenth century, Europe's clownish spiritual scapegoats were the British, perched on the edge of continental civilization in an impossible climate, cutting their own throats, shooting and hanging themselves on the least provocation. As Lawrence Sterne noted ironically, 'They order this matter better in France.'

In our own century, the blame has been shifted on to the Swedes, whom President Eisenhower singled out as a terrible warning of what too much social welfare can do. He seems to have been more than usually badly briefed. The present suicide-rate in Sweden is about the same as it was in 1910, before the social welfare schemes began. It is lower even than that of Switzerland, that haven of private enter-

prise and tax inducements, and is in fact ranked ninth on
the most recent national suicide league table published by
the World Health Organization.[5] The Swedes, perhaps because their steady neutrality has kept them out of the insane wars in which the rest of the world has so long been
embroiled, have inherited an international prejudice which
was once bestowed on the English. Like their weather, they
are thought to be gloomy, frigid and unpredictable. Yet it
turns out that these characteristics do little to encourage
the suicide-rate. The Norwegians, who have much the same
weather as the Swedes, have a particularly low rate, while
the Finns – whom everyone, except the Russians, admires,
and whom even the Swedes think of as an imaginative, out-
going lot – have the second highest suicide-rate in the
world. The real storm-centre seems to have shifted to the
relatively temperate and culturally sophisticated countries
of Central Europe: Hungary has the highest national rate;
Austria and Czechoslovakia are third and fourth.* Maybe
some culture-hating spokesman of the silent majority will
yet make political capital out of that phenomenon.

The statistics, in short, say less about national characteristics than about the way facts are gathered or covered up.
Norway, for example, has a suicide-rate less than half that
of Sweden; but its accident-rate is almost twice as large.
Devout, backward countries, like Ireland and Egypt, where
suicide is considered a mortal sin, have correspondingly
pleasing figures – among the lowest in the world. And so on.
Stengel remarks that 'it is obvious that highly industrialized

* On the non-national chart, the highest suicide-rate in the world
is that of the thriving mini-democracy of West Berlin. Its rate is
more than twice that of West Germany as a whole. The city is a
model of what Durkheim called 'anomie' – moral, cultural, spiritual,
political and geographical alienation. Added to that, a high proportion of its population is middle-aged and elderly.

and prosperous countries tend to have comparatively high suicide-rates'. But they also tend to have comparatively sophisticated methods of collecting the information on which the statistics will be based, and comparatively fewer prejudices against doing so.

Only one generalization is wholly certain and generally agreed : that the official statistics reflect at best only a fraction of the real figures, which various authorities reckon to be anything between a quarter and half as large again. Religious and bureaucratic prejudices, family sensitivity, the vagaries and differences in the proceedings of coroners' courts and post-mortem examinations, the shadowy distinctions between suicides and accidents – in short, personal, official and traditional unwillingness to recognize the act for what it is – all help to pervert and diminish our knowledge of the extent to which suicide pervades society. A man smashes up his car while driving alone and dies either on the spot or later of his injuries, a woman takes an overdose but has been drinking heavily beforehand, an old-age pensioner steps in front of a lorry, a sportsman blows his brains out 'while cleaning his gun': invariably the verdict will be 'accidental death' or 'death by misadventure'. Mary Holland, writing on suicide in the *Observer* in 1967, mentioned the famous, probably legendary West of Ireland coroner who returned a verdict of accidental death on a man who had shot himself, with the words: 'Sure, he was only cleaning the muzzle of the gun with his tongue.'

For suicide to be recognized for what it is, there must be an unequivocal note or a setting so unambiguous as to leave the survivors no alternatives : all the windows sealed and a cushion under the dead head in front of the unlit gas-fire. Without these signs the corpse is always given the benefit of the doubt, probably for the first time, almost certainly for the first time he would not have wanted it. For suicide is, after all, the result of a choice. However impulsive the action and confused the motives, at the moment when a man finally decides to take his own life he achieves a certain temporary clarity. Suicide may be a declaration of bankruptcy which passes judgement on a life as one long history of failures. But it is a history which also amounts at least to this one decision which, by its very finality, is not wholly a failure. Some kind of minimal freedom – the freedom to die in one's own way and in one's own time – has been salvaged from the wreck of all those unwanted necessities. Perhaps this is why totalitarian states feel cheated when their victims take their own lives. 'Is it conceivable,' asked Pavese, 'to murder someone in order to count for something in his life? Then it is conceivable to kill oneself so as to count for something in one's own life. Here's the difficulty about suicide: it is an act of ambition that can be committed only when one has passed beyond ambition.'[6] To have that last, partial and lop-sided triumph turned, for reasons of decency and bureaucracy, into a malicious accident is to compound failures with final failure.

Those whom the suicide leaves behind want it that way, of course, since self-destruction, among its many other attributes, is deeply distasteful to them – if for no other reason than that it so effortlessly promotes guilt. Every child knows this instinctively when, in a tantrum, he yells, 'I'll die and then you'll be sorry.' In the end, the popular beliefs about suicide all tend to reduce the act to childishness. The most hardy of all the techniques of denial and dismissal are those of bluff health and common sense. In 1840 a Victorian doctor wrote of a suicidal patient:

After trying various remedies without effecting much relief, a cold shower was recommended every morning. In the course of ten days, the desire to commit self-destruction was entirely removed and never afterwards returned.

A timely administered purge has been known to dispel the desire of self-destruction. Esquirol knew a man who was decidedly insane whenever he allowed his bowels to be in an inactive condition.[7]

The Cold-Bath-Laxative-and-Prayer School is with us still in the shape of the two most sturdy fallacies: that those who threaten to kill themselves never do; that those who have attempted once never try again. Both beliefs are false. Stengel estimates that seventy-five per cent of successful and would-be suicides give clear warning of their intentions beforehand, and are often driven to the act because their warnings are ignored or brushed aside or, like Mayakovsky's, treated as mere bravado. At a certain point of despair a man will kill himself in order to show he is serious. It is also estimated that a person who has once been to the brink is perhaps three times more likely to go there again than someone who has not. Suicide is like diving off a high board: the first time is the worst.

All these six fallacies still prevail, despite experience, despite statistics, despite our increased sensitivity to the deviousness of human behaviour and our awareness of the psyche's defences. They prevail because they are cheering: they reduce the suicide's anguish to hysterical self-pity, to an attention-seeking device – jejune, ostentatious, disproportionate.

In the end, the suicide is rejected because he is so completely rejecting. All the traditional fallacies are ways of denying his sour Pyrrhic victory and robbing it of meaning. Thus suicide is said to be the prerogative of the young, who don't know any better and are, anyway, drunk with their own feelings; or it is the product of bad weather and national quirks – both circumstances, as they say, beyond our control; or those who really do it are never those who talk, and therefore think, about it – which implies that it comes out of nowhere like an act of God, a thunderbolt striking down its unwitting victim suddenly and without warning, 'while the balance of mind was disturbed'. And like thunder, where it has struck once it never strikes again. Each fallacy is a strategy for devaluing an act that cannot be denied or reversed.

That which befalleth the sons of men befalleth
beasts; even one thing befalleth them : as the one
dieth, so dieth the other; yea, they have all one
breath; so that a man hath no preeminence above a
beast : for all is vanity.
All go to one place; all are of the dust, and all turn
to dust again.
Who knoweth the spirit of man that goeth upward,
and the spirit of the beast that goeth downward to
the earth?
— ECCLESIASTES

Death is nature's way of telling us to slow down.
— AMERICAN INSURANCE PROVERB

2. Theories

All these comforting fallacies have been disproved patiently and meticulously, by research. But in the process other distortions have taken their place. It is as though the procedures necessary to a scientific understanding of suicide had made the subject unreal.

In part, this is the doing of the great sociologist, Emile Durkheim. In his battle to pierce the defences of moral indignation which surrounded suicide, making it irrational and undiscussable, he insisted that every suicide could be classified scientifically as one of three general types – egoistic, altruistic, anomic – and that each type was the product of a specific social situation. Thus egoistic suicide occurs when the individual is not properly integrated into society but is, instead, thrown on to his own resources. Hence Protestantism, with its emphasis on free will and grace, tends to encourage suicide more than the Catholic Church, which insists on a greater subservience to its rituals and doctrines and so involves each believer in its circumscribed, collective religious life. Similarly, the rise of science, which undercut the simple belief in the origin and structure of a natural world presided over by a more or less benevolent and omniscient God, brought with it a rise in the suicide-rate. Hence, too, the old pattern of family life – grandparents, parents and children all living intensely together under one roof – protected each member from his impulses to self-destruction, whereas the modern disintegration of family life – children scattered, parents divorced – encourages them. This also explains the drop in the suicide-rate during wars and other national crises when everyone, literally, rallies round the flag.

The exact opposite of all this is 'altruistic suicide'. It occurs when an individual is so completely absorbed in the group that its goals and its identity become his. The tribe or religion or group has such 'massive cohesion' that each member is willing to sacrifice his life for the sake of his beliefs – like the Hindus who threw themselves under the wheels of the Juggernaut; or for the good of the cause – like the Communists who confessed to imaginary crimes during the Moscow show trials of the late thirties; or simply to help his friends survive – like Captain Oates. Altruistic suicide, Durkheim thought, was a characteristic of primitive societies and such primitive, rigidly structured groups as survive today, like the Army. Camus summed it up neatly in a parenthesis: 'What is called a reason for living is also an excellent reason for dying.'

Both egoistic and altruistic suicide are related to the degree to which the individual is integrated into his society, too little or too much. Anomic suicide, on the other hand, is the result of a change in a man's social position so sudden that he is unable to cope with his new situation. Great, unexpected wealth or great, unexpected poverty – a big win on the pools or a stock market crash – a searing divorce or even a death in the family can thrust a man into a world where his old habits are no longer adequate, his old needs no longer satisfied. Instead of his society being too slackly or harshly structured, it seems no longer structured at all. He kills himself because, for better or worse, his accustomed world has been destroyed and he is lost. T. S. Eliot once talked of 'dislocating language into meaning'. But a process which, with words, can produce poetry, when applied to the habits of a lifetime may result in chaos and death.

In other words, egoistic and altruistic suicide differ much as the world of *Catch 22* differs from that of the *kamakaze* pilots. Beyond them both is the anomie of, say, Kafka's *Metamorphosis*.

The broad effect of Durkheim's masterpiece was to insist that suicide was not an irredeemable moral crime but a fact of society, like the birth-rate or the rate of productivity; it had social causes which were subject to discernible laws and could be discussed and analysed rationally. At the pessimistic worst, it was a social disease, like unemployment, which could be cured by social means. Granted, Durkheim wrote before Freud. Granted, too, his range and interests were large enough and subtle enough to have ensured that he would have used the insights of psycho-analysis had they been available to him at the time. Yet his influence on the lesser men who have followed him has been curiously deadening. Perhaps because his authority was so massive, they seem to have accepted the letter of his law, rather than its spirit. As a result, the more that has been written, the narrower the field has become. To wade through even the shallow end of the mass of books and articles on the sociology of suicide is an odd experience. Clearly, the researchers are serious men, well-trained and well-informed, sometimes gifted and perceptive. Yet what they actually write seems somehow to be not wholly real. Or rather, by the time they have put their observations into discreetly scientific prose a weird transformation has taken place: they seem no longer concerned with human beings, only with anonymous case-histories and statistics, with odd facts and facets on which theories can be based. The amount of information is prodigious, yet it tells you almost nothing. Consider, for example, this comparatively relaxed and chatty passage from an exhaustive study by an American sociologist:

> To say that a suicidal action has a general dimension of meaning to the effect that something is wrong with the situation of the actor at the time he commits the suicidal action is almost humorous. This is such a fundamental meaning of just about any suicidal action that it is hard to seriously consider it. But it is precisely this taking of the obvious for granted that has, presumably, led to the general failure to see the many implications of the fundamental meaning of suicidal actions.
>
> It is the *reflexive dimension of the meaning of suicidal actions* which make suicidal actions such effective social weapons.[8]

He means, I take it, 'no man kills himself unless there is something wrong with his life. This fact is so obvious that it is often ignored. So one vital meaning of the act is missed: the suicide wishes to show those who survive him how bad things are.' Fancy that. And he takes ten lines, six repetitions of the phrase 'suicidal action', and one split infinitive to say so.

Neither the professor nor his Byzantine prose are in any way unusual; indeed, he is better read and wider-ranging than most of his fellow sociologists. I can only conclude from the evidence that, as he no doubt would put it, 'the reflexive dimension of the meanings of sociological prose is to reduce the communication level of sociological prose, thereby depriving the subject under discussion of all meanings, reflexive and otherwise'. In other words, some space-explorer from another planet, even if he were miraculously able to penetrate the jargon, would never guess from the welter of abstractions, theories and figures that a suicide was a man who took his own life. All that anguish, the slow tensing of the self to that final, irreversible act, and for what? In order to become a statistic. It is a dubious immortality. Obviously controls, calculations and an objective concern with observable facts are essential to a proper scientific procedure. Without them there are only fallacies, prejudices, chaos. Yet with them something is also missed, perhaps as much as was ever lost in the moral distortions of the earlier discussions of suicide.

Much of this sometimes disproportionate objectivity is vindicated by the fact that the researchers, like Durkheim, are interested in suicide as, above all, a symptom of what is wrong with society: the higher the suicide-rate, the greater the social tension and unease. Suicide, that is, interests them only in as much as it teaches them about the nature of society. By implication, it is a problem that can be solved by social engineering, social conscience, social concern and genuinely enlightened social services. Yet the example of maligned Sweden proves, if nothing else, that even the most enlightened social welfare in the world makes more or less no difference to the national suicide-rate. In short, the nature of society, which can hopefully be transformed, however painfully and slowly, is continually brought up against human nature, which is altogether more recalcitrant. Professor Stengel had the root of the matter when he wrote: 'At some stage of evolution man must have discovered that he can kill not only animals and fellow-men but also himself. It can be assumed that life has never since been the same to him.'[9] It seems to me that even the most elegant and convincing sociological theories are somehow short-circuited by this simple observation that suicide is a human characteristic, like sex, which not even the most perfect society will erase.

For example, in his pioneer study of *Suicide in London* (1955) Peter Sainsbury demonstrated convincingly that social isolation is a more powerful stimulus to self-destruction than what he called 'indigenous poverty'. He showed that in the deprived but relatively close-knit working-class areas of London's East End the rate was startlingly lower than in wealthier Bloomsbury, with its warrens of lonely bedsitters and not quite seedy transient hotels. The implication – though Sainsbury refrained from making it himself – is that if the circle of loneliness can be broken, if the isolated can be brought out of their dank rooms into the relative cheer of a community centre, the 'problem' of suicide may begin to be solved. No doubt this is partly true. No doubt the fault does partly lie with a society which takes as little notice as it decently can of the elderly, the sick, the unstable, the foreign and the drifting. Yet it is also true that the suicide creates his own society: to shut yourself off from other people in some dingy, rented box and stare, like Melville's Bartleby, day in and day out at the dead wall outside your window is in itself a rejection of the world which is said to be rejecting you. It is a way of saying, like Bartleby, 'I prefer not to' to every offer and every possibility, which is a condition no amount of social engineering will cure. The best the sociologist can hope for is that his findings and recommendations will lengthen the odds against the private final solution.

Despair, in short, seeks its own environment as surely as water finds its own level. Thus the sociological theories woven around suicide are all to some extent true – though some are truer than others and most are conflicting – but they are also partial and circular. They return constantly to an inner negation and hopelessness which social pressures may bring to the surface but which existed before those pressures and will probably continue even after they are removed. Consider, for example, the case-histories used by the Viennese psychiatrist Margarethe von Andics. She believed that 'the suicidal situation [is] ... a unique, extreme experimental condition for observing human conduct', like the extremes of temperature and pressure under which experimental physicists examine nature. So she visited the Vienna Psychiatric Clinic, interviewing survivors as soon as possible after their attempts, when their defences were down and all they lacked most obvious. She hoped that an understanding of the reasons which impelled an individual to choose death might throw light back on to the meaning of life. There are two drawbacks to this method. The first is obvious: in the confusion following a failed attempt a survivor, however skilfully questioned, will offer only excuses, handy rationalizations to cover his depression and shame. As a result, Dr von Andics learned a certain amount about the triggering mechanism of the attempt and almost nothing of the chemistry of the explosives. The other drawback is the doctor's stern allegiance to the doctrine of Alfred Adler, one of the original circle of Viennese psychoanalysts, who was excommunicated by Freud for proposing that the primary human drive was nothing more primitive than social aggression. Not surprisingly, Dr von Andics came to the conclusion that the meaning of life and the reasons for suicide were all explicable in terms of social success or failure with colleagues at work, with neighbours and with family.

In these limiting circumstances, her case-histories are consistently more eloquent than her conclusions. She proposes, for instance, that 'injured self-esteem' is one of the prime motives for suicide:

That such importance attaches to what others think of us, is due to the fact that we can only realize our value in the opinion of others, for what we call our value can, ultimately, only consist in services (emotional or practical) rendered to others ... Our value is what we are worth *to* others, and *in the eyes of* others – at whom, in the last resort, all our personal and practical achievements are aimed.[10]

The bland and reductive confidence of her theory is a world apart from her examples:

> Fanny, aged twenty-nine, worked in the building trade and was very unpopular for accepting less than standard wages. In the course of a quarrel, one of the men punched her head: 'All of a sudden I was fed up with life.' She immediately took the rope which she daily used for carrying home wood, in order to hang herself.

This, says the doctor, is an illustration of subdivision three of the principle just quoted:

> The fact that they had been undeservedly abused and unjustly charged with negative qualities, and called contemptuous names, was, in the case of eight women, the direct motive for suicide. The motive 'quarrels' as a motive for suicide, really means the mortification at being abused and humiliated.

Poor Fanny. Maybe the final insult was to write off her long history of degradation with such a pat and trivial explanation. The facts so baldly stated by Dr von Andics make her sound like a character from Zola. She is no longer young and is presumably unattractive – had she been otherwise the men on the site would surely have treated her more gently despite union principles. She is so poor that she not only works as a manual labourer, she also accepts less than the already derisory wages (derisory since the period is the Great Depression). She can't even afford fuel to heat her room at night. It is a question, in short, of a poverty so grinding that it erodes her identity: being a woman didn't save her from labouring like a man; it didn't save her from being despised by the men she laboured with and getting less pay; it didn't finally save her from being beaten up as though she really were a man. When she seemed to have touched bottom, the punch forced her down still further. After that, there was nothing left and nowhere to go except death. Whatever else, it adds up to something more than 'injured self-esteem' and 'mortification'.

Or maybe it adds up to less. The social meanings which even a psychiatrist like Dr von Andics extrapolates from the suicidal act may explain something of its local and immediate causes; but they say nothing at all of the long, slow, hidden processes that lead up to it. 'An act like this,' said Camus, 'is prepared within the silence of the heart, as is a great work of art.' Perhaps this is why the more convincing the social theories, the more independent they seem of the material on which they are based. They are superstructures, often elegant and lovingly detailed, but built on simple misery, a terminal inner loneliness which no amount of social engineering will alleviate. This is as true of poor Fanny as of Marilyn Monroe, of the seedy Stephen Ward, the pimp in the Profumo affair, as of the great and eminently successful Mark Rothko. They killed themselves because their lives, by all the standards they had built up for themselves, no longer made sense. Like divorce, suicide is a confession of failure. And like divorce, it is shrouded in excuses and rationalizations spun endlessly to disguise the simple fact that all one's energy, passion, appetite and ambition have been aborted. Those who survive suicide, like those who make a new marriage, survive into a changed life, with different standards and motives and satisfactions.

It goes without saying that external misery has relatively little to do with suicide. The figures are higher in the wealthy industrialized countries than in the underdeveloped, higher among the comfortable professional middle classes than among the poor; they were extraordinarily low in the Nazi concentration camps. Indeed, deprivation can be a stimulus. Witness the classic case of George Orwell who, after he left the Burma Police, deliberately turned his back on all help and opportunities and, by choosing to be 'down and out in Paris and London', turned himself into a serious artist. More recently, the young Russian author Andrei Amalrik unwillingly had a similar fate thrust on him: he was exiled to a remote collective farm in Siberia where, despite his weak heart, he survived the grinding physical labour and, with his even younger wife, made his home in a ruined hovel, subsisting on a diet of potatoes and milk, lighting the stove only three times a day to cook, in a Siberian winter so cold that calves froze in their mothers' wombs. Far from being subdued, he emerged from all this more spoiling for a fight than he had been when he was sentenced, and has produced, so far, two excellent books about the experience. They have, incidentally, earned him a further term of hard labour in a prison camp. In short, given a certain temperament, adversity sharpens the spirit and reinforces the urge to survive, as though out of a kind of bloody-mindedness.*

*The most extreme example of this is described by a psychiatrist, who observed that many people with neurotic or psychotic complaints fared remarkably well in the concentration camps: 'As regards patients suffering from anxiety, one might think that anxiety has become canalized through the actual causes of terror, which of course were abundant. Realistic anxiety in these cases took the place of neurotic anxiety. The improvement of patients with depressive symptoms might be explained by the fact that their need for punishment had been gratified through the frightful circumstances, just as a depressive state may often improve when an organic disease develops.' He also has an explanation for the low suicide-rate in the Nazi camps: 'I observed only four suicide attempts, three of the victims of which were saved only with great effort. This seems a low number in a group of approximately 3,000 persons living under such terrifying circumstances. However, in my opinion this can be explained by the fact that if, under these conditions, somebody had no desire to continue life, no active deed of self-murder was necessary; the only thing one had to do was ... to give up the grim struggle for life; i.e. the struggle to do everything possible to obtain food and keep up one's spirits. If one did give this up, then death came by itself.'[11]

In comparison, suicide often seems to the outsider a supremely motiveless perversity, performed, as Montesquieu complained, 'most unaccountably ... in the very bosom of happiness', and for reasons which seem trivial or even imperceptible. Thus Pavese killed himself at the height both of his creative powers and his public success, using as his excuse an unhappy affair with a dim little American actress whom he had known only briefly. On hearing of his death, her only comment was, 'I didn't know he was so famous.' There is even a case of an eighteenth-century gentleman who hanged himself out of sheer boredom and good taste, in order to save himself the trouble of pulling his clothes off and on. In other words, a suicide's excuses are mostly by the way. At best they assuage the guilt of the survivors, soothe the tidy-minded and encourage the sociologists in their endless search for convincing categories and theories. They are like a trivial border incident which triggers off a major war. The real motives which impel a man to take his own life are elsewhere; they belong to the internal world, devious, contradictory, labyrinthine, and mostly out of sight.

Yet oddly enough, a psycho-analytic theory of suicide is hard to find. Indeed, the analysts are so reticent about the subject that one of them has remarked: 'The important scientific problem is this: is the taboo on suicide so intense that even psychoanalysts are reluctant to expose their case materials and personal experiences in this area?'[12] One reason for this unusual diffidence is obvious: the patient who succeeds in killing himself represents for his analyst an unequivocal failure, since the final purpose of the treatment is to make life livable despite the patient himself, despite life itself.* There is also a simple, practical difficulty:

*The one notable exception is Ludwig Binswanger's long, detailed and, for the most part, extremely obscure analysis of 'The Case of Ellen West', a patient who, just before taking her own life, seemed the analyst can deal only with suicidal threats and attempts; the successful suicide is, in every sense, beyond him. As a result, suicide has been dealt with largely on the side, in its relationship to topics which provide the analysts with more precise and verifiable clinical material. Such theories as there are have, despite the large changes in psycho-analytic thinking in the last fifty years, stayed close to Freud's tentative, relatively early grappling with the subject.

In April 1910, Freud's original Vienna Psycho-analytic Society held a symposium on suicide.[14] Most of the theorizing was done by Stekel and Adler, who were soon to part company with Freud and go their own revisionist ways. Each used the subject to illustrate his own preoccupations: Adler talked at length about inferiority, revenge and antisocial aggression; Stekel related the act to masturbation and

calm and happy, perhaps for the first time ever. Binswanger's explanation of this 'festive mood' is that '. . . the existence in the case of Ellen West had become ripe for its death, in other words, that the death, this death, was the necessary fulfillment of the life-meaning of this existence . . . As a young woman Ellen West had already become old . . . Existential aging had hurried ahead of biological aging, just as existential death, the "being-a-corpse among people", had hurried ahead of the biological end of life. The suicide is the necessary-voluntary consequence of this existential state of things. And just as we can only speak of the gladness of old age as the "most intimate and sweetest anticipatory relish of death" when the existence is ripening towards its death, so too in the face of self-induced death only gladness and a festive mood can reign when death falls like a ripe fruit into the lap of the existence.'[13] As I understand him, Binswanger seems to be implying that Ellen West's suicide was not merely inevitable, it was also the most completely meaningful act she ever committed, and one to which the whole of her previous life had ineluctably led her. He also seems to be implying that his existential analysis had helped her to understand this; thus her suicide almost becomes a vindication of his treatment. But I may well be misreading him.

the guilts attendant upon that. He also came out with the famous principle on which so much subsequent theory has been based: 'No one kills himself who has never wanted to kill another, or at least wished the death of another.' Historically, all this represented a great change from the social determinism which had prevailed since Durkheim published his masterpiece thirteen years before. But it offered as an explanation only a rather simple psychic mechanism which Freud himself was not willing to accept. So he held his peace until the end of the discussion, when he suggested that suicide would not be understood until more was known about the intricate process of mourning and melancholia.

Yet, as Dr Litman shows, Freud knew more about the subject than he was saying. It had occurred, in one manifestation or another, in all his early case-histories, except that of the five-year-old Little Hans. His difficulty was theoretical: how to reconcile the impulse to self-destruction with the pleasure principle? If the basic instinctual drives were libido and self-preservation, then suicide was incomprehensible as well as unnatural:

So immense is the ego's self-love, which we have come to recognize as the primal state from which instinctual life proceeds, and so vast is the amount of narcissistic libido which we see liberated in the fear that emerges at a threat to life, that we cannot conceive how that ego can consent to its own destruction. We have long known, it is true, that no neurotic harbours thoughts of suicide which he has not turned back upon himself from murderous impulses against others, but we have never been able to explain what interplay of forces can carry such a purpose through to execution. The analysis of melancholia now shows that the ego can kill itself only if, owing to the return of the object-cathexis, it can treat itself as an object – if it is able to direct against itself the hostility which relates to an object and which represents the ego's original reaction to objects in the external world. Thus in regression from narcissistic object-choice the object has, it is true, been got rid of, but it has nevertheless proved more powerful than the ego itself. In the two most opposed situations of being most intensely in love and of suicide the ego is overwhelmed by the object, though in totally different ways.[15]

That is from Freud's seminal essay 'Mourning and Melancholia', written five years after the symposium on suicide, though not published until 1917. The passage is often quoted as though to give the master's blessing on the idea that suicide is simply displaced hostility. But as Dr Litman suggests, it was in fact the first sketch of the altogether more complex picture of the internal world which Freud was gradually to draw.

The essence of Freud's genius was to be able to see with uncanny clearness the theoretical implications of each piece of evidence, and to follow them without regard for the sanctity of the positions he had already established. In this essay, this continually probing, continually sceptical process expressed itself on two themes: one had to do with the structure of the psyche; the other was concerned with the problem of sadism and masochism, and led towards the concept of what Freud later called the death instinct.

First, then, he showed that in mourning and its pathological equivalent, melancholia, the ego tries to restore to life whatever has been lost by identifying with it, and then incorporating, or introjecting, the lost object in itself. Thus the mourner sets up the lost object in his own ego, where it lives on as part of himself. Freud's use of this concept may have been new, like his technical way of putting it, but the idea itself is at least as old as John Donne who, in his poems of parting and mourning, returns continually, as though to some comforting old truism, to the theme that each lover carries within him the soul and image of his mistress:

> Feed on this flattery,
> That absent Lovers one in th'other be.

In normal mourning the painful process of coming slowly to terms with the fact that the loved object really exists no longer in the outside world is gradually compensated for by its establishment within the ego as something loved, loving and strengthening. Thus Hardy's later poems are peopled by the ghosts of women he had once loved disastrously, who now return, tender and forgiving.

In melancholia, on the other hand, guilt and hostility are too much for the sufferer. It is as though the melancholic believed that whatever had been lost, by death or separation or rejection, had somehow been murdered by him. It therefore returns as an internal persecutor, punishing, seeking revenge and expiation. Sylvia Plath put this clearly and without shuffling in the poem on her dead father, 'Daddy':

> If I've killed one man, I've killed two –
> The vampire who said he was you
> And drank my blood for a year,
> Seven years, if you want to know.
> Daddy, you can lie back now.
> There's a stake in your fat black heart . . .

She is both the guilty woman who has committed murder and the innocent victim fed upon by vampires. This is the vicious circle of melancholia, in which a man may take his own life partly to atone for his fantasied guilt for the death of someone he loves, and partly because he feels the dead person lives on inside him, crying out, like Hamlet's father, for revenge.

Later, in his work *The Ego and the Id*, Freud developed his concept of the super-ego, a censuring, critical force working on a far deeper, more unconscious level than that ordinary conscience that makes cowards of us all. He

believed that the super-ego is formed by the child's identifi-
cations with parent figures – or rather, with his fantasies of
them – which are then introjected so that they become part
of the child's self. The voice of conscience, he was suggesting, is really the stern but distorted voice of the father and
the mother re-echoing through the child's fantasies. Analysts since Freud, particularly Melanie Klein, have taken this
theory a good deal further. Mrs Klein believed that the unconscious super-ego develops much earlier in life than Freud
thought, not at two years or three but in those first few
months before the baby is even able to recognize that objects in the external world have a separate existence of
their own. Thus a baby's earliest, most primitive experience
of reality is of 'part-objects' which are the sources of both
pleasure and pain, satisfaction and frustration, love and
anger, good and bad. In the simplest possible terms, the
baby defends itself from the 'bad' by splitting it off and
projecting it on to external part-objects; it also defends itself by identifying with the 'good' and taking that into itself. All that concerns us here is that from the complex
defence mechanisms of projection and introjection, splitting, denial and identification there emerges a proportionately complex image of the psyche: not a neatly divided
egg of conscious and unconscious, nor even a three-layer
cake of super-ego ego and id; instead, from the earliest
days, there is an area seamed and fissured like an earth-
quake zone. So far as the mechanics of suicide are concerned, this means that the simple push-pull model of aggression, turned away from an external figure and directed
towards the self, is never wholly adequate.

The Freudian analyst, Karl Menninger, has said that there
are three components of suicide : the wish to kill, the wish
to be killed, the wish to die. Kleinian theory would suggest
that each of these processes is highly complex, ambiguous

and rarely separate from the others. For instance, a man may wish to kill only some aspect of himself under the illusion that its death will free some other part to live. In part he wishes to kill, in part to be killed. But in part death itself is by the way; what is at issue is not self-murder but an extreme act of placation which will restore some injured part of himself to health and enable it to flourish: 'If thy eye offend thee, pluck it out.' But for the suicide, overwhelmed by his obscure and obscuring sense of inner chaos and worthlessness, the 'eye', the part, is his life itself as he is leading it. He casts away his life in order properly to live.

This psychic double-take occurs even in what seem to be the crudest cases of aggression. The angry child who says to his parents, 'I'll die and then you'll be sorry', is not merely seeking revenge. He is also projecting the guilt and anger that possesses him on to those who control his life. In other words, he is defending himself from his own hostility by the mechanism of projective identification; he becomes the victim, they the persecutors. Similarly, but on a more sophisticated level, a man may take his own life because he feels the destructive elements inside him are no longer to be borne; so he sheds them at the expense of the guilt and confusion of his survivors. But what is left, he hopes, is a purified, idealized image of himself which lives on like the memory of all those noble Romans who fell on their own swords with equanimity for the sake of their principles, their reputations and their proper name in history. Without those high Roman ideals, suicide is simply the most extreme and brutal way of making sure that you will not readily be forgotten. It is a question of a kind of posthumous rebirth in the memory of others, rather like that imagined by the primitive warrior-tribesmen who thought Paradise was reserved only for those who died violently; so they destroyed themselves in order to forestall a degrading natural death by sickness or old age which would otherwise have shut them out for eternity from the best of all possible afterworlds.

But what of the survivors? On the evidence of fifty attempted suicides, two New York psychiatrists made an interesting discovery: in ninety-five per cent of all their cases there had been 'the death or loss under dramatic and often tragic circumstances of individuals closely related to the patient, generally parents, siblings, and mates. In 75 per cent of our cases, the deaths had taken place before the patient had completed adolescence.'[16] They call this pattern 'the death trend'. Unfortunately, they draw from it only the narrowest conclusions:

> If one assumes that suicidal fantasies are possible forms of reacting to intense inner conflict and in some way represent problem-solving behaviour, we may conclude from our study that the occurrence of the 'death trend' in the patient's background would predispose him to act out self-destructive preoccupations. This may shed some light on why one individual with suicidal fantasies will act upon them with a suicidal attempt, while another, with similar fantasies, and equal emotional tensions, will not.

This seems to mean no more than that one suicide encourages another, rather as the first athlete who broke the barrier of the four-minute mile made it easier for those who came after him. But this has always been the recognized syndrome in those strange, periodic epidemics of suicide which break out from time to time: for example, the maidens of Miletos who, according to Plutarch, rushed to hang themselves until one of the city elders suggested shaming their bodies by carrying them through the market-place – whereupon vanity, if not sanity, prevailed; or the fifteen wounded soldiers in Les Invalides Hospital in Paris who hanged themselves from the same hook in 1772 – the epidemic stopped when the hook was removed; or the thousands of Russian peasants who burned themselves to death in the seventeenth century in the belief that the Antichrist was coming; or the hundreds of Japanese who threw themselves into the crater of Mihara-Yama from 1933 until access to the mountain was closed in 1935; or all those Chicagoans who jumped off 'Suicides' Bridge' until the authorities, in despair, finally tore the thing down. In each case, one dramatic example was enough to spark off a crazy chain reaction.

But the idea of 'the death trend' seems also to imply something subtler and less quirky. The process of mourning, Freud thought, was completed when whatever had been lost, for whatever reason, was somehow restored to life within the ego of the mourner. But when the loss occurs at a particularly vulnerable age, the slow process of introjection becomes not only more difficult but also more hazardous. Every child who loses a parent, or someone loved equally passionately and helplessly, must cope as best he can with a confusion of guilt and anger and his outraged sense of abandonment; since in his innocence he does not understand this, his natural grief is made doubly painful. In order to relieve himself of this apparently gratuitous and inappropriate hostility, he splits it off from himself and projects it on to the lost figure. As a result, it is possible that when the fantasied identification finally takes place it is invested with all sorts of unmanageable horror. Thereafter, hidden away in some locked cupboard of the mind, he carries the murderous dead thing within him, an unappeased *Doppelgänger*, not to be placated, crying out to be heard, and ready to emerge at every crisis.

Perhaps, then, 'the death trend' appears later in life as that curious impregnability of so many suicides, their imperviousness to solace. Like sleep-walkers or those who were once thought to be possessed by devils, their life is elsewhere, their movements are controlled from some dark and unrecognized centre. It is as though their one real purpose were to find a proper excuse to take their own lives. So, however convincing the immediate causes, imaginary rewards and blind provocations of their final suicide, the act, successful or not, is fundamentally an attempt at exorcism.

There seems to have been, incidentally, a number of writers in whom 'the death trend' was at work. The father of Thomas Chatterton, the first and most famous English literary suicide, died before his son was born. In our own time, Hemingway, Mayakovsky, Pavese and Plath all lost their fathers when they were children. Hemingway's father, in fact, shot himself, as his son did later. So did the father of John Berryman, whose major theme in his poetic maturity was mourning, and who killed himself in 1972.

Psycho-analytic theory, then, offers no simple explanation of the mechanics of suicide. On the contrary, the closer the theory gets to the facts of any case, the more complex it becomes and the less the act is explained. The best it can do is illuminate the profound ambiguity of motives even when they seem most clear-cut. For example, when Sylvia Plath writes:

> So daddy, I'm finally through.
> The black telephone's off at the root,
> The voices just can't worm through

I think she is talking about something more than that total loneliness which is the precondition of all suicidal depression. The voices, I mean, are not just those of outsiders hooked up elsewhere on the London telephone exchange; they may also be the internal voices of those parts of herself which loved and sustained her. But they have been split off and now have become distant, no longer audible.

This concept of splitting helps, perhaps, to explain the weird tenacity with which people survive the most devastating attempts on their own lives. One girl, for example, so wanted to die that she swallowed fifty barbiturates. When she was finally found, in a deep coma, and rushed to the hospital, she failed to respond to any treatment. In the end, the doctors gave her up for dead. Yet her heart kept on beating. At some point in her coma she had a strange spatial vision: she was looking down at her husband, as though from another plane. He seemed quite near yet the gulf between them was impassable, as if they were inhabiting different dimensions. Watching him, she felt a sudden, absolute need – as sharp and present as a physical convulsion – to reach down to him and explain why she had done this thing. But she couldn't. However loudly she called, he could not or would not hear her. So heavily, unwillingly, she decided she must go back down to him. That was all she remembered of the whole episode. Her coma lasted four days but she recovered. Consciously, she was disappointed to have survived, since neither her life nor her attitude to it seemed much altered. Yet somewhere under the despair, some split-off part of her was passionately and tenaciously alive, refusing to surrender.

The constant impurity of motive, this conflict between opposing forces in the psyche, became Freud's theme in the latter half of his career. I mentioned earlier that he gradually developed two themes from his essay 'Mourning and Melancholia'. The first concerned a more complex view of the psyche. The second was what came to be called 'the death instinct'. Like many of Freud's theories, the first faint hint of it was in a shrewd, rather worldly insight into human behaviour:

It must strike us that after all the melancholic does not be-have in quite the same way as a person who is crushed by remorse and self-reproach in a normal fashion. Feelings of shame in front of other people, which would more than any-thing characterize this latter condition, are lacking in the melancholic, or at least they are not prominent in him. One might emphasize the presence in him of an almost opposite trait of insistent communicativeness which finds satisfaction in self-exposure.[17]

The pain of melancholia, in short, can itself be a source of pleasure. With that insight he is moving towards what he later called 'the economic problem of masochism', a trait which he decided was not secondary to sadism, as he had earlier thought, but was instead a primary impulse. But there was also other, more compelling evidence to hand. In the simplest terms, at the basis of his great early book *The Interpretation of Dreams* is the belief that all dreams are wish-fulfilling; in their various, devious ways they gratify instinctual erotic drives. Whence his theory of the libido, the ubiquitous principle of pleasure and self-preservation which runs below the surface of even the most improbably contorted fantasies. But his subsequent study of what are called 'repetition compulsions', which he noticed in some forms of children's play and, more powerfully, in the nightmares of shell-shocked soldiers, went directly against all this. In both instances, the patient's dreams and fantasies seemed to be compelling him to suffer again, in all its an-guish and without any of the usual dream distortion and displacement, the situation where his trouble had begun, like the sleep-walking Lady Macbeth returning obsession-ally to the scene of her crime. In certain types of neurosis, in short, a force was at work which was the complete opposite of any pleasure principle. No wishes were fulfilled, no gratifications, however perverse, were achieved. Instead, the purpose of the repetition compulsion was to attempt to contain this overwhelming *un*pleasure principle, this death instinct. By obsessively repeating the trauma again and again the sufferer was, Freud thought, trying to gain control over it. In much the same way, when a drowning man sees his whole life flash before him it may be, someone has suggested, that his unconscious is somehow 'racking its brains' for a solution to this terrible crisis.

From these various strands Freud wove his theory of the death instinct, a non-erotic 'primary aggression', present from the very beginning of life and working as continually to unbind connections, to destroy, to return what is living to a null but peaceful inorganic state as Eros, the pleasure principle, was continually seeking to unite, to renew, to preserve, to disturb. The death instinct is a moving bass against which all the restless intricacies of desire are patterned:

> Beyond all this the wish to be alone:
> However the sky grows dark with invitation-cards
> However we follow the printed directions of sex
> However the family is photographed under the flagstaff –
> Beyond all this, the wish to be alone.
>
> Beneath it all, desire of oblivion runs:
> Despite the artful tensions of the calendar,
> The life insurance, the tabled fertility rites,
> The costly aversion of the eyes from death –
> Beneath it all, desire of oblivion runs.

That is by Philip Larkin, a poet whose constant theme is that of *not* succumbing to the pleasure principle, of avoiding the confusions and demands and uproar of life in order to maintain a certain austere inviolability, however starved and haunted, and at whatever cost.

So far as suicide is concerned, Freud thought that the

death instinct took over in melancholia as a kind of disease of the super-ego. The more virulent the disease, the more suicidal the patient becomes:

[In melancholia] we find that the excessively strong super-ego which has obtained a hold upon consciousness rages against the ego with merciless violence, as if it had taken possession of the whole of the sadism available in the person concerned. Following our view of sadism, we should say that the destructive component had entrenched itself in the super-ego and turned against the ego. What is now holding sway in the super-ego is, as it were, a pure culture of the death instinct, and in fact it often enough succeeds in driving the ego into death . . . [18]

Moreover, the more fragile the ego, for whatever complicated historical reasons, the more vulnerable it is to the raging of the super-ego: 'The fear of death in melancholia only admits of one explanation: that the ego gives itself up because it feels itself hated and persecuted by the super-ego, instead of loved. To the ego, therefore, living means the same as being loved – being loved by the super-ego. . .' [19]

The Kleinians who, unlike many schools of analytic thought, accept the death instinct as a basic clinical concept, interpret it with less structural neatness. For them, the infant derives its primitive notion of death from those periods when its defences against the 'bad' fail and it feels itself overwhelmed by its own destructive anger and pain. Thus its inner world is felt to be fragmented, murderous and desolate. In contrast, its notion of life as something positive, pleasurable and desirable comes when this intolerable chaos gives way to an inner sense of integration, of containing a whole world, sustaining and sustained. The image of one is the baby screaming with hunger and frustration, and of the other the baby peacefully feeding. In the adult, traces of these primitive experiences remain, buried like fragments of a pre-historic settlement far below a modern city, but emerging when the elaborate superstructure is shattered by some psychic explosion. Thus one aim of analytic treatment, as I understand it, is to help the patient to come to terms with the destructiveness – the death instinct – working constantly within him.

The technicalities of Freud's theory, and the intricate arguments between the Freudians and the Kleinians, are not my business here, nor am I qualified to discuss them. What matters is the implications for the tone of Freud's whole conception of the human personality. He outlined his theory of the death instinct in *Beyond the Pleasure Principle*, which he began in 1919 and finished in 1920. The dates are important. Behind all the clinical examples and the now disproved biological theories was evidence of a larger and more undeniable kind: the vast and senseless destruction of the First World War to which Freud, who later called himself a pacifist, reacted with horror and despair. So perhaps the death instinct was not just a question of 'primary aggression'; it entailed also the *primary pessimism* of a supremely civilized man who had watched appalled while the whole civilization he so passionately believed in began to fall to pieces.

Much later, in 1937, when cancer was already raging in him like the death instinct itself, he wrote a paper, 'Analysis Terminable and Interminable', in which he called in question the effectiveness of the therapeutic method he had devoted his life to developing. He in part blamed the death instinct for the tenaciousness with which the patient clings to his sickness, the reluctance with which he accepts the possibilities of cure and health. Just as this innate destructive force seemed to undermine the theoretical structure on which all his earlier work was based, so now he saw it casting doubt over his whole life's work. Perhaps this is why the death instinct is still not accepted by the 'classical'

Freudians, whereas it is a theoretical corner-stone for the Kleinians, with their more complex view of the psyche and its mechanisms, with their constant emphasis on the workings of the death instinct through envy and destructiveness and, incidentally, their acceptance of the possibility of an analysis which is, if not literally interminable, at least extraordinarily long. For Freud's restless, sceptical genius, a discipline which had begun in the settled society of Vienna at the turn of the century with the treatment of weathly, almost amiable hysterics, no longer seemed adequate in 1937 to a culture which had already been split apart by one world war and was now preparing for another, enduring meanwhile a massive economic depression and the rise of Nazism. In the circumstances, any notion of the perfectibility of man – by psycho-analysis or any other panacea – seemed wholly inappropriate. A grimmer, more tragic response was needed.

Since then, the theory of a death instinct working constantly away to disrupt and destroy has gathered considerable power as a kind of historical metaphor. Sixty odd years of genocide and intermittent war between superpowers which, like Freud's diseased super-ego, have become progressively harsher, more repressive and totalitarian, have made the modified ego-gratifications of civilization seem peculiarly fragile. The response of the arts has been to reduce the pleasure principle to its most archaic forms – manic, naked, beyond culture. The new strategy of aesthetic sophistication is primitivism: tribal rhythms on every radio, fertility rites on the stage, real or televized Gold Coast customs in the living-room, concrete poets grunting and oinking beyond language and beyond expression, *avant-garde* musicians exploring the possibilities of random noise, painters immortalizing industrial waste, radical politicians modelling their behaviour on the clowns of a Roman saturnalia, and a youth culture devoted to the gradual, chronic suicide of drug addiction. As the pleasure principle becomes less pleasurable and more manic, so the death instinct seems more powerful and ubiquitous: every perspective closes with the possibility of international suicide by nuclear warfare. It is as though the discontents of civilization itself had now reached that point of extreme suicidal melancholia which Freud so eloquently described: 'What is now holding sway in the super-ego is, as it were, a pure culture of the death instinct and in fact it often enough succeeds in driving the ego into death, if the latter does not fend off its tyrant in time by the change round into mania.' Shakespeare, too, described the same process, though in a less technical way:

> As surfeit is the father of much fast,
> So every scope by the immoderate use
> Turns to restraint. Our natures do pursue,
> Like rats that ravin down their proper bane,
> A thirsty evil; and when we drink we die.

In both languages, the outlook is bleak. 'Of the world as it exists,' wrote Theodor Adorno, 'one cannot be enough afraid.'

Listen to the newborn infant's cry in the hour of birth
– see the death struggles in the final hour – and then
declare whether what begins and ends in this way can
be intended to be enjoyment.

True enough, we human beings do everything as
fast as possible to get away from these two points,
hurry as fast as possible to forget the birth-cry and
change it to delight in having given a being life. And
when someone dies we immediately say : Softly and
gently he slipped away, death is a sleep, a quiet sleep
– something we do not say for the sake of the one
who died, for our talking cannot help him, but for our
own sake, in order not to lose any of the zest for life,
in order to change everything to serve an increase in
the zest for life during the interval between the birth-
cry and the death-wail, between the mother's shriek
and the child's repetition of it, when the child at some
time dies.

Imagine somewhere a great and splendid hall
where everything is done to produce joy and
merriment – but the entrance to this room is a nasty,
muddy, horrible stairway and it is impossible to pass
without getting disgustingly soiled, and admission is
paid by prostituting oneself, and when day dawns the
merriment is over and all ends with one's being
kicked out again – but the whole night through

everything is done to keep up and inflame the merriment and pleasure!

What is reflection? Simply to reflect on these two questions: How did I get into this and this and how do I get out of it again, how does it end? What is thoughtlessness? To muster everything in order to drown all this about entrance and exit in forgetfulness, to muster everything to re-explain and explain away entrance and exit, simply lost in the interval between the birth-cry and the repetition of this cry when the one who is born expires in the death struggle.

— SOREN KIERKEGAARD

3. Feelings

The psycho-analytic theories of suicide, prove, perhaps, only what was already obvious: that the processes which lead a man to take his own life are at least as complex and difficult as those by which he continues to live. The theories help untangle the intricacy of motive and define the deep ambiguity of the wish to die but they say little about what it means to be suicidal, and how it feels.

First and most important, suicide is a closed world with its own irresistible logic. This is not to say that people commit suicide, as the Stoics did, coolly, deliberately, as a rational choice between rational alternatives. The Romans may have disciplined themselves into accepting this frigid logic but those who have done so in modern history are, in the last analysis, monsters. And like all monsters, they are hard to find. In 1735 John Robeck, a Swedish philosopher, completed a long Stoic defence of suicide as a just, right and desirable act; he then carefully put his principles into practice by giving away his property and drowning himself in the Weser. His death was the sensation of the day. It provoked Voltaire to comment, through one of the characters in *Candide*: 'I have seen a prodigious number of people who hold their existence in execration; but I have only seen a dozen who voluntarily put an end to their misery, three negroes, four Englishmen, four Genevois, and a German professor called Robeck.' Even for Voltaire, the supreme rationalist, a purely rational suicide was something prodigious and slightly grotesque, like a comet or a two-headed sheep.

The logic of suicide is, then, not rational in the old Stoic sense. It scarcely could be since there is almost no one now, even among the philosophers, who believes that reason is clean and straightforward, or that motives can ever be less than equivocal. 'The desires of the heart,' said Auden, 'are as crooked as corkscrews.' To the extent to which suicide *is* logical, it is also unreal: too simple, too convincing, too total, like one of those paranoid systems, such as Ezra Pound's Social Credit, by which madmen explain the whole universe. The logic of suicide is different. It is like the unanswerable logic of a nightmare, or like the science-fiction fantasy of being projected suddenly into another dimension: everything makes sense and follows its own strict rules; yet, at the same time, everything is also different, perverted, upside-down. Once a man decides to take his own life he enters a shut-off, impregnable but wholly convincing world where every detail fits and each incident reinforces his decision. An argument with a stranger in a bar, an expected letter which doesn't arrive, the wrong voice on the telephone, the wrong knock at the door, even a change in the weather – all seem charged with special meaning; they all contribute. The world of the suicide is superstitious, full of omens. Freud saw suicide as a great passion, like being in love: 'In the two opposed situations of being most intensely in love and of suicide the ego is overwhelmed by the object, though in totally different ways.' As in love, things which seem trivial to the outsider, tiresome or amusing, assume enormous importance to those in the grip of the monster, while the sanest arguments against it seem to him simply absurd.

The imperviousness to everything outside the closed world of self-destruction can produce an obsession so weird and total, so psychotic, that death itself becomes a side-issue. In nineteenth-century Vienna an old man of seventy drove seven three-inch nails into the top of his head with a heavy blacksmith's hammer. For some reason he did not die immediately, so he changed his mind and walked to the hospital, streaming blood.[20] In March 1971 a Belfast business man killed himself by boring nine holes in his head with a power drill. There is also the case of a Polish girl, unhappily in love, who in five months swallowed four spoons, three knives, nineteen coins, twenty nails, seven window-bolts, a brass cross, one hundred and one pins, a stone, three pieces of glass and two beads from her rosary.[21] In all these instances the suicidal gesture seems to have mattered more than its outcome. People try to die in such operatic ways only when they are obsessed more by the means than by the end, just as a sexual fetishist gets more satisfaction from his rituals than from the orgasm to which they lead. The old man driving nails into his skull, the company director with his power drill and the love-lorn girl swallowing all that hardware seem to be acting wildly out of despair. Yet in order to behave in precisely that way they must have brooded endlessly over the details, select-in.;, modifying, perfecting them like artists, until they produced that one, unrepeatable happening which expressed their madness in all its uniqueness. In the circumstances, death may come but it is superfluous.*

* A perfect example of a suicide which summed up a man's whole life and yearnings occurred in March 1970. A body was found jammed in a crevice one hundred feet down the sheer cliffs near Land's End. It was dressed in full 'city gent's' uniform: pin-striped trousers, black jacket, polished shoes and bowler hat. Over the dead arm was a neatly rolled umbrella. The man, who carried no identi-fication, was looking westwards, out to sea. He had died from an overdose of sleeping pills. The police eventually discovered that he was a much Anglicized and Anglophile American who had lived and

Without this wild drama of psychosis, there is a kind of suicide, more commonplace but also more deadly, which is simply an extreme form of self-injury. The psycho-analysts have suggested that a man may destroy himself not because he wants to die but because there is a single aspect of himself which he cannot tolerate. A suicide of this order is a perfectionist. (The flaws in his nature exacerbate him like some secret itch he cannot get at) So he acts suddenly, rashly, out of exasperation. Thus Kirilov, in *The Possessed*, kills himself, he says, to show that he is God. But secretly he kills himself because he knows he is not God. Had his ambitions been less, perhaps he would have only attempted the deed or mutilated himself. He conceived of his mortality as a kind of lapse, an error which offended him beyond bearing. So in the end he pulled the trigger in order to shed this mortality like a tatty suit of clothes, but without taking into account that the clothes were, in fact, his own warm body.

Compared with the other revolutionaries in the novel, Kirilov seems sane, tender-hearted and upright. Yet maybe his concern with godhead and metaphysical liberty consigned him, too, to the suburbs of psychosis. And this sets

worked in London for a long time. His marriage had gone on the rocks and he had finally left his wife. He had chosen Land's End to die because that was the point nearest America. By jamming himself in the rock, he was able to gaze towards the States until he lost consciousness.

Another, though less odd, example is that of a young American climber, very gifted and graceful, who was badly depressed at breaking up with his girl. One Saturday morning he called on friends who live near the Shawangunks, a popular outcrop north of New York City. He seemed quite relaxed and played in the garden with the friends' small children, of whom he had always been fond. Then he drove over to the cliffs, which are vertical and between two and three hundred feet high, and jumped off. Physical perfectionist to the last, he performed as he fell an immaculate swallow-dive.

him apart from the majority of the inhabitants of the closed world of suicide. For them, the act is neither rash nor operatic nor, in any obvious way, unbalanced. Instead it is, insidiously, a vocation. Once inside the closed world, there seems never to have been a time when one was not suicidal. Just as a writer feels himself never to have been anything except a writer, even if he can remember with embarrassment his first doggerel, even if he has spent years, like Conrad, disguised as a sea-dog, so the suicide feels he has always been preparing in secret for this last act. There is no end to his sense of *déjà vu* or to his justifications. His memory is stored with long, black afternoons of childhood, with the taste of pleasures that gave no pleasure, with sour losses and failures, all repeated endlessly like a scratched gramophone record.

An English novelist, who had made two serious suicide attempts, said this to me:

'I don't know how much potential suicides *think* about it. I must say, I've never really thought about it much. Yet it's always there. For me, suicide's a constant temptation. It never slackens. Things are all right at the moment. But I feel like a cured alcoholic: I daren't take a drink because I know that if I do I'll go on it again. Because whatever it is that's there doesn't alter. It's a pattern of my entire life. I would like to think that it was only brought on by certain stresses and strains. But in fact, if I'm honest and look back, I realize it's been a pattern ever since I can remember.

My parents were very fond of death. It was their favourite thing. As a child, it seemed to me that my father was constantly rushing off to do himself in. Everything he said, all his analogies, were to do with death. I remember him once telling me that marriage was the last nail in the coffin of life. I was about eight at the time. Both my parents, for different reasons, regarded death as a perfect release from their troubles. They were very unhappy together, and I think this sunk in very much. Like my father, I have always demanded too much of life and people and relationships – far more than exists, really. And when I find that it doesn't exist, it seems like a rejection. It probably isn't a rejection at all; it simply isn't there. I mean the empty air doesn't reject you, it just says, "I'm empty." Yet rejection and disappointment are two things I've always found impossible to take.

In the afternoons my mother and father both retired to sleep. That is, they retired to death. They really died for the afternoons. My father was a parson. He had nothing to do, he had no work. I begin now to understand how it was for him. When I'm not working, I'm capable of sleeping through most of the morning. Then I start taking sleeping pills during the day to keep myself in a state of dopiness, so that I can sleep at any time. To take sleeping pills during the day to sleep isn't so far from taking sleeping pills in order to die. It's just a bit more practical and a bit more craven. You only take two instead of two hundred. But during those afternoons I used to be alive and lively. It was a great big house but I never dared make a sound. I didn't dare pull a plug in case I woke one of them up. I felt terribly rejected. Their door was shut, they were absolutely unapproachable. Whatever terrible crisis had happened to me, I felt I couldn't go and say, "Hey, wake up, listen to me." And those afternoons went on a long time. Because of the war I went back to live with them, and it was still exactly the same. If I ever bumped myself off, it would be in the afternoon. Indeed, the first time I tried was in the afternoon. The second time was after an awful afternoon. Moreover, it was after an afternoon in the country, which I hate for the same reasons as I hate afternoons. The reason is simple: when I'm alone, I stop believing I exist.'

Although the speaker is well into a successful middle age, the injured and rejected child she had once been still lives powerfully on. Perhaps it is this element which makes the closed world of suicide so inescapable: the wounds of the past, like those of the Fisher King, will not heal over – the ego, the analysts would say, is too fragile – instead, they continually push themselves to the surface to obliterate the modified pleasures and acceptances of the present. The life of the suicide is, to an extraordinary degree, unforgiving. Nothing he achieves by his own efforts, or luck bestows, reconciles him to his injurious past.

Thus on 16 August 1950, ten days before he finally took sleeping pills, Pavese wrote in his notebook: 'Today I see clearly that from 1928 until now I have always lived under this shadow.' But in 1928 Pavese was already twenty. From what we know of his desolate childhood – his father dead when he was six, his mother of spun steel, harsh and austere – the shadow was probably on him much earlier; at twenty he simply recognized it for what it was. At thirty he had written flatly and without self-pity, as though it were some practical detail he had just noticed: 'Every luxury must be paid for, and everything is a luxury, starting with being in the world.'

A suicide of this kind is born, not made. As I said earlier, he receives his reasons – from whatever nexus of guilt, loss and despair – when he is too young to cope with them or understand. All he can do is accept them innocently and try to defend himself as best as he is able. By the time he recognizes them more objectively they have become part of his sensibility, his way of seeing and his way of life. Unlike the psychotic self-injurer, whose suicide is a sudden fatal twist in the road, his whole life is a gradual downward curve, steepening at the end, on which he moves knowingly, unable and unwilling to stop himself. No amount of success will change him. Before his death Pavese was writing better than ever before – more richly, more powerfully, more easily. In the year before he died he turned out two of his best novels, each in less than two months of writing. One month before the end he received the Strega Prize, the supreme accolade for an Italian writer. 'I have never been so much alive as now,' he wrote, 'never so young.' A few days later he was dead. Perhaps the sweetness itself of his creative powers made his innate depression all the harder to bear. It is as though those strengths and rewards belonged to some inner part of him from which he felt himself irredeemably alienated.

It is also characteristic of this type of sucide that his beliefs do not help him. Although Pavese called himself a Communist, his politics permeate neither his imaginative work nor his private notebooks. I suspect they were merely a gesture of solidarity with the people he liked, against those he disliked. He was a Communist not because of any particular conviction but because the Fascists had imprisoned him. In practice, he was like nearly everybody else in this present time: sceptical, pragmatic, adrift, sustained neither by the religion of the Church nor by that of the Party. In these circumstances, 'this business of living' – the title of his notebooks – becomes peculiarly chancy. What Durkheim called 'anomie' may lead to a social conception of man infinitely more impoverished than any religious formulation of his role as a servant of God. Yet since the decline of religious authority,* the only alternative to the ersatz and unsatisfactory religions of science and politics has been an uneasy and perilous freedom. This is summed up in an eerie note found in an empty house in Hampstead: 'Why suicide? Why not?'

Why not? The pleasures of living – the hedonistic plea-

---

*'What undermined the Christian faith was not the atheism of the eighteenth century or the materialism of the nineteenth – their arguments are frequently vulgar and, for the most part, easily refutable by traditional theology – but rather the doubting concern with salvation of genuinely religious men [like Pascal and Kierkegaard], in whose eyes the traditional Christian content and promise had become "absurd".'[23]

sures of the five senses, the more complex and demanding pleasures of concentration and doing, even the unanswerable commitments of love – seem often no greater and mostly less frequent than the frustrations – the continual sense of unfinished and unfinishable business, jangled, anxious, ragged, overborne. If secularized man were kept going only by the pleasure principle, the human race would already be extinct. Yet maybe his secular quality is his strength. He chooses life because he has no alternative, because he knows that after death there is nothing at all. When Camus wrote *The Myth of Sisyphus* – in 1940, after the fall of France, a serious personal illness and some kind of depressive crisis – he began with suicide and ended with an affirmation of individual life, in itself and for itself, desirable because it is 'absurd', without final meaning or metaphysical justification. 'Life is a gift that nobody should renounce,' the great Russian poet Osip Mandelstam said to his wife when, in exile after his imprisonment, she proposed that they commit suicide together if Stalin's secret police took them again.* Hamlet said that the only obstacle

---

* Mandelstam was, in fact, rearrested and died in a forced-labour camp somewhere in Siberia. Yet right up to the end he refused his wife's alternative: 'Whenever I talked of suicide, M. used to say: "Why hurry? The end is the same everywhere, and here they even hasten it for you." Death was so much more real, and so much simpler than life, that we all involuntarily tried to prolong our earthly existence, even if only for a few brief moments – just in case the next day brought some relief! In war, in the camps and during periods of terror, people think much less about death (let alone about suicide) than when they are living normal lives. Whenever at some point on earth mortal terror and the pressure of utterly insoluble problems are present in a particularly intense form, general questions about the nature of being recede into the background. How could we stand in awe before the forces of nature and the eternal laws of existence if terror of a mundane kind was felt so tangibly in everday life? In a strange way, despite the horror of it,

to self-slaughter was fear of the after-life, which was an unconvinced but Christian answer to all those noble suicides which the heroes of Shakespeare's Roman plays performed so unhesitatingly. Without the buttress of Christianity, without the cold dignity of a Stoicism which had evolved in response to a world in which human life was a trivial commodity, cheap enough to be expended at every circus to amuse the crowd, the rational obstacles begin to seem strangely flimsy. When neither high purpose nor the categorical imperatives of religion will do, the only arguments left are circular. In other words, the final argument against suicide is life itself. You pause and attend: the heart beats in your chest, outside the trees are thick with new leaves, a swallow dips over them, the light moves, people are going about their business. Perhaps this is what Freud meant by 'the narcissistic satisfactions [the ego] derives from being alive'. Most of the time, they seem enough. They are, anyway, all we ever have or can ever expect.

Yet they can also be very fragile. A shift of focus in one's life, a sudden loss or separation, a single irreversible act can suffice to make the whole process intolerable. Perhaps this is what is implied by the phrase 'suicide when the balance of mind was disturbed'. It is, of course, a legal formula evolved to protect the dead man from the law and to spare the feelings and insurance benefits of his family. But it also has a certain existential truth: without the checks of belief, the balance between life and death can be perilously delicate.

---

this also gave a certain richness to our lives. Who knows what happiness is? Perhaps it is better to talk in more concrete terms of the fullness or intensity of existence, and in this sense there may have been something more deeply satisfying in our desperate clinging to life than in what people generally strive for.'[23]

Consider a climber poised on minute holds on a steep cliff. The smallness of the holds, the steepness of the angle, all add to his pleasure, provided he is in complete control. He is a man playing chess with his body; he can read the sequence of moves far enough in advance, so that his physical economy – the ratio between the effort he uses and his reserves of strength – is never totally disrupted. The more improbable the situation, the greater the demands made on him, the more sweetly the blood flows later in release from all that tension. The possibility of danger serves merely to sharpen his awareness and control. And perhaps this is the rationale of all risky sports: you deliberately raise the ante of effort and concentration in order, as it were, to clear your mind of trivialities. It is a small-scale model for living but with a difference: unlike your routine life, where mistakes can usually be recouped and some kind of compromise patched up, your actions, for however brief a period, are deadly serious.

I think there may be some people who kill themselves like this: in order to achieve a calm and control they never find in life. Antonin Artaud, who spent most of his life in lunatic asylums, once wrote:

If I commit suicide, it will not be to destroy myself but to put myself back together again. Suicide will be for me only one means of violently reconquering myself, of brutally invading my being, of anticipating the unpredictable approaches of God. By suicide, I reintroduce my design in nature, I shall for the first time give things the shape of my will. I free myself from the conditioned reflexes of my organs, which are so badly adjusted to my innner self, and life is for me no longer an absurd accident whereby I think what I am told to think. But now I choose my thought and the direction of my faculties, my tendencies, my reality. I place myself between the beautiful and the hideous, the good and evil. I put myself in suspension, without innate propensities, neutral, in the state of equilibrium between good and evil solicitations.[24]

There is, I believe, a whole class of suicides, though infinitely less gifted than Artaud and less extreme in their perceptions, who take their own lives not in order to die but to escape confusion, to clear their heads. They deliberately use suicide to create an unencumbered reality for themselves or to break through the patterns of obsession and necessity which they have unwittingly imposed on their lives.* There are also others, similar but less despairing, for whom the mere idea of suicide is enough; they can continue to function efficiently and even happily provided they know they have their own, specially chosen means of escape always ready : a hidden cache of sleeping pills, a gun at the back of a drawer, like the wife in Lowell's poem who sleeps every night with her car key and ten dollars strapped to her thigh.

But there is also another, perhaps more numerous, class of suicides to whom the *idea* of taking their own lives is

---

*Perhaps the most famous example is that of the distinguished scholar who had worked for years on the definitive edition of one of the gloomier American novelists. Maybe the long, deadening grind and obsessional detail got to him in the end. Add to that the even deeper gloom of McCarthyism and vague hints of a private scandal. It doesn't matter. One afternoon he finally put all his papers in order, paid every bill to the last cent, wrote farewell letters to all his friends, saying he was sorry, put out food and milk for his cat, packed an overnight case and carefully locked his apartment. Down in the street, he mailed the letters – they would arrive too late – and then took a taxi downtown. He checked into a scruffy hotel and took a room on an upper floor. Every meticulous detail had been attended to; he had added the final footnote to his own life. Then his whole obsessionally controlled, minutely organized universe exploded like a grenade. He hurled himself across the room and crashed through the window he hadn't even bothered to open. He burst, lacerated, into free space and smashed on to the shocked sidewalk.

utterly repugnant. These are the people who will do everything to destroy themselves, except admit that that is what they are after; they will, that is, do everything except take the final responsibility for their actions. Hence all those cases of what Karl Menninger calls 'chronic suicide', the alcoholics and drug addicts who kill themselves slowly and piecemeal, all the while protesting that they are merely taking the necessary steps to make an intolerable life tolerable. Hence, too, those thousands of inexplicable fatal accidents – the good drivers who die in car crashes, the careful pedestrians who get themselves run over – which never make the suicide statistics. The image recurs of the same climber in the same unforgiving situation. In the grip of some depresssion he may not even recognize, he could die almost without knowing it. Impatiently, he fails to take the necessary safety measures, he climbs a little too fast and without working out his moves far enough in advance. And suddenly, the risks have become disproportionate. For a fatal accident, there is no longer the need of any conscious thought or impulse of despair, still less a deliberate action. He has only to surrender for a moment to the darkness beneath the threshold. The smallest mistake – an impetuous move not quite in balance, an error of judgement which leaves him extended beyond his strength with no way back and no prospect of relief – and the man will be dead without realizing that he wanted to die. 'The victim lets himself act,' said Valéry, 'and his death escapes from him like a rash remark. . . He kills himself because it is too easy to kill himself.'[25] Whence, I suppose, all those so-called 'impetuous suicides' who, if they survive, claim never to have considered the act until moments before their attempt. Once recovered, they seem above all embarrassed, ashamed of what they have done, and unwilling to admit that they were ever genuinely suicidal. They can return to life, that is, only by denying the strength of their despair, transforming their unconscious but deliberate choice into an impulsive, meaningless mistake. They wanted to die without seeming to mean it.

Every so often the opposite of all this occurs: there is a cult of suicide which has very little to do with real death. Thus early nineteenth-century Romanticism – as a pop phenomenon rather than as a serious creative movement – was dominated by the twin stars of Chatterton and Young Werther. The ideal was 'to cease upon the midnight with no pain' whilst still young and beautiful and full of promise. Suicide added a dimension of drama and doom, a fine black orchid to the already tropical jungle of the period's emotional life. One hundred years later a similar cult grew up around the *Inconnue de la Seine*. During the 1920s and early 1930s, all over the Continent, nearly every student of sensibility had a plaster-cast of her death-mask: a young, full, sweetly smiling face which seems less dead than peacefully sleeping. I am told that a whole generation of German girls modelled their looks on her.* She appears in appropriately aroused stories by Richard Le Gallienne, Jules Supervielle and Claire Goll and, oddly enough since the author is a Communist, is the moving spirit behind the heroine of *Aurélian*, a long novel which Louis Aragon thought his masterpiece. But her fame was spread most effectively by a sickly, though much translated best-seller, *The Unknown*, by Reinhold Conrad Muschler. He makes her an innocent young country girl who comes to Paris, falls in love with a handsome British diplomat – titled, of

*I owe this information to Hans Hesse of the University of Sussex. He suggests that the *Inconnue* became the erotic ideal of the period, as Bardot was for the 1950s. He thinks that German actresses like Elisabeth Bergner modelled themselves on her. She was finally displaced as a paradigm by Greta Garbo.

course – has a brief but idyllic romance and then, when milord regretfully leaves to marry his suitably aristocratic English fiancée, drowns herself in the Seine. As Muschler's sales show, this was the style of explanation the public wanted for that enigmatic, dead face.

Yet, in fact, the girl was genuinely *inconnue*. All that is known of her is that she was fished out of the Seine and exposed on a block of ice in the Paris Morgue, along with a couple of hundred other corpses waiting identification. She was never claimed but someone was sufficiently impressed by her peaceful smile to take a death-mask. On the evidence of her hair-style, Sacheverell Sitwell believes this happened not later than the early 1880s.

It is also possible that it never happened at all. In another version of the story a researcher, unable to obtain information at the Paris Morgue, followed her trail to the German source of the plaster-casts. At the factory he met the *Inconnue* herself, alive and well and living in Hamburg, the daughter of the now prosperous manufacturer of her image.

There is, however, no doubt at all about her cult. It seemed to attract young people between the two world wars in much the same way as drugs call them now: to opt out before they start, to give up a struggle that frightens them in a world they find distasteful, and to slide away into a deep inner dream. Death by drowning and blowing your mind with dope, amount, in fantasy, to the same thing: the sweetness, shadow and easy release of a successful regression. So the cult of the *Inconnue* flourished in the absence of all facts, perhaps it even flourished because there were no facts. Like a Rorschach blot, her dead face was the receptacle for any feelings the onlookers wanted to project into it. And like the Sphinx and the Mona Lisa, the power of *the Inconnue* was in her smile – subtle, oblivious, promising peace. Not only was she out of it all, beyond troubles, beyond responsibilities, she had also remained beautiful; she had retained the quality the young most fear to lose – their youth. Although Sitwell credits to her influence an epidemic of suicide among the young people of Evreux, I suspect she may have saved more lives than she destroyed: to know that it can be done, that the option really exists and is even becoming, is usually enough to relieve a mildly suicidal anxiety. In the end, the function of the Romantic suicide cult is to be a focus for wandering melancholy; almost nobody actually dies.

The expression on the face of the *Inconnue* implies that her death was both easy and painless. These, I think, are the twin qualities, almost ideals, which distinguish modern suicide from that of the past. Robert Lowell once remarked that if there were some little switch in the arm which one could press in order to die immediately and without pain, then everyone would sooner or later commit suicide. It seems that we are rapidly moving towards that questionable ideal. The reason is not hard to find. Statistics, for what they are worth, show that in Great Britain, France, Germany and Japan there has been an enormous increase in death by drugs. In a brilliant essay, 'Self-Poisoning', Dr Neil Kessel has written:

In every century before our own, poisons and drugs were dissimilar. Poisons were substances which should not be taken at all, the province not of physicians but of wizards. Their properties verged upon the magical. They were, indeed, 'unctions bought of mountebanks'. By the second half of the nineteenth century, science had displaced sorcery and poisons were purchased from the chemist, not the alchemist. But they still differed from drugs. Drugs, with few exceptions, though recognized to produce undesirable actions if taken in excess, were not considered lethal agents and were not used to kill. The growth of self-poisoning has come about in the train of a rapid rise in the number of highly dangerous preparations employed therapeutically, together with a great contemporaneous increase in prescribing.

The effect of this medical revolution has been to make poisons both readily available and relatively safe. The way has thus been opened for self-poisoning to flourish ... Facilities for self-poisoning have been placed within the reach of everyone.[26]

Along with the increase in suicide by drugs has gone a proportionate decrease in the older, more violent methods: hanging, drowning, shooting, cutting, jumping. What is involved, I think, is a massive and, in effect, a qualitative change in suicide. Ever since hemlock, for whatever obscure reason, went out of general use, the act has always entailed great physical violence. The Romans fell on their swords or, at best, cut their wrists in hot baths; even the fastidious Cleopatra allowed herself to be bitten by a snake. In the eighteenth century the kind of violence you used depended on the class you came from: gentlemen usually took their lives with pistols, the lower classes hanged themselves. Later it became fashionable to drown yourself or endure the convulsions and agonies of cheap poisons like arsenic and strychnine. Perhaps the ancient, superstitious horror of suicide persisted so long because the violence made it impossible to disguise the nature of the act. Peace and oblivion were not in question; suicide was as unequivocally a violation of life as murder.

Modern drugs and domestic gas have changed all that. They have not only made suicide more or less painless, they have also made it seem magical. A man who takes a knife and slices deliberately across his throat is murdering himself. But when someone lies down in front of an unlit gas-fire or swallows sleeping pills, he seems not so much to be dying as merely seeking oblivion for a while. Dostoievsky's Kirilov said that there are only two reasons why we do not all kill ourselves: pain and the fear of the next world. We seem, more or less, to have got rid of both. In suicide, as in most other areas of activity, there has been a technological breakthrough which has made a cheap and relatively painless death democratically available to everyone. Perhaps this is why the subject now seems so central and so demanding, why even governments spend a little money on finding its causes and possible means of prevention. We already have a suicidology; all we mercifully lack, for the moment, is a thorough-going philosophical rationale of the act itself. No doubt it will come. But perhaps that is only as it should be in a period in which global suicide by nuclear warfare is a permanent possibility.

It will generally be found that as soon as the terrors of life reach the point where they outweigh the terrors of death, a man will put an end to his life. But the terrors of death offer considerable resistance; they stand like a sentinel at the gate leading out of this world. Perhaps there is no man alive who would not have already put an end to his life, if this end had been of a purely negative character, a sudden stoppage of existence. There is something positive about it; it is the destruction of the body; and a man shrinks from that, because his body is the manifestation of the will to live.

However, ... great mental suffering makes us insensible to bodily pain; we despise it; nay, if it should outweigh the other, it distracts our thoughts and we welcome it as a pause in mental suffering. It is this feeling that makes suicide easy . . .

When, in some dreadful and ghastly dream, we reach the moment of greatest horror, it awakes us; thereby banishing all the hideous shapes that were born of the night. And life is a dream: when the moment of greatest horror compels us to break it off, the same thing happens.

Suicide may also be regarded as an experiment – a question which man puts to Nature, trying to force her to answer. The question is this: What change will death produce in a man's existence and in his insight into the nature of things? It is a clumsy experiment to make, for it involves the destruction of the very consciousness which puts the question and awaits the answer.

— ARTHUR SCHOPENHAUER

Part 4
Suicide and Literature

To express an inward tragedy in an art form, and so
purge himself of it, is something that can only be
achieved by an artist who, even while living through
his tragedy, was already putting forth sensitive feelers
and weaving his delicate threads of construction;
who, in short, was already incubating his creative
ideas. There can be no such thing as living through
the storm in a state of frenzy and then liberating pent-
up emotions in a work of art as an alternative to
suicide. How true that is can be seen from the fact
that artists who really have killed themselves because
of some tragedy that happened to them are usually
trivial songsters, lovers of sensation, who never, in
their lyrical effusions, even hint at the deep cancer
that is gnawing them. From which one learns that the
only way to escape from the abyss is to look at it,
measure it, sound its depths and go down into it.

— CESARE PAVESE

Suicides were the aristocrats of death – God's
graduate students, acting out their theses to prove
how limited were the alternatives He had allowed
Himself and His creatures. Their act was, at its best,
superb literary criticism.

— DANIEL STERN

My subject is suicide *and* literature, not suicide *in* literature. I am not, I mean, concerned with all those tragic deaths at their own hands by which authors, since the beginning of literature, have disposed of the characters they have created. No doubt much could be learned from such a study, indirectly about the authors themselves, more directly about the social habits and expectations of their period. My subject is less precise and easy to pin down: it has to do not with specific literary suicides but with the power the act has exerted over the creative imagination. I make no apology for the fact that this is a specialized way of looking at literature since, if my arguments are right, it becomes dramatically less specialized as we come near to our own time. But inevitably, this special perspective has led me from a historical reading of literature to something altogether more theoretical and tendentious.

1. Dante and the Middle Ages

In the Middle Ages suicide was beyond literature. It was a mortal sin, a horror, the object of such total moral revulsion that the outrages against the corpse of the suicide were carried out not only with all due ecclesiastical and legal solemnity but also gratefully. Any brutality was justified *pour décourager les autres*. It may be that suicide was anathema to the medieval Church for much the same ambiguous reasons as Trotsky was the spectre haunting Stalinist Russia: because he was too potent, too stirring a figure, and too present in the structure which now rejected him. Just as Trotsky had created the Red Army, so the Church was buttressed by the glorious army of martyrs. Inevitably, an act which had once been fiercely desired in time became equally fiercely hated.

Certainly, Dante never questioned the orthodox judgement of the crime. Instead, he sustained it by devoting one of the grimmest cantos of the *Inferno* to the suicides. In the seventh circle, below the burning heretics and the murderers stewing in their river of hot blood, is a dark, pathless wood where the souls of suicides grow for eternity in the shape of warped poisonous thorns. The harpies, with their great wings and feathered bellies, human faces and clawed feet, nest in these stunted trees and pick at their leaves. The whole wood is full of the sound of lament. When Dante, frightened and uncomprehending, breaks off a twig, the trunk turns dark with blood and cries out, 'Why doest thou tear me?' It is a moment and image of great power and menace:

> Come d'un stizzo verde ch'arso sia
>   dall'un de' capi, che dall'altro geme
>   e cigola per vento che va via,
> sì della scheggia rotta usciva inseme
>   parole e sangue; ond'io lasciai la cima
>   cadere, e stetti come l'uom che teme.*

The tree harbours the soul of Piero delle Vigne, Chancellor and chief advisor to the Emperor Frederick II. Accused of treason, publicly disgraced, blinded and imprisoned, Piero had dashed out his brains against the walls of his cell sixteen years before Dante was born. He explains to the poet that when the soul violently tears itself from its own body, it is thrown by ~~Minos~~ haphazardly into the terrible wood, where it springs up like a grain of wheat and eventually grows into a thorn tree. Then the harpies make their nests in its branches and tear at the leaves, endlessly repeating the violence the soul had inflicted on itself. At the Day of Judgement, when bodies and souls are reunited, the bodies of suicides will hang from the branches of these trees, since divine justice will not bestow again on their owners the bodies they have wilfully thrown away.

The commentators have pointed out that Dante seems unusually involved in Canto III. It is not simply a matter of the gloomy power of the poetry in creating a fitting landscape for despair. There is also the question of the narrator-poet himself insisting, as he does not elsewhere, on his own reactions: fear, pity, horror. With most of the other sinners in hell he remains more or less detached,

---

*'As a green brand that is burning at one end drips from the other and hisses with the escaping wind, so from the broken splinter came forth words and blood together; at which I let fall the tip and stood as one afraid.'

sometimes grimly satisfied by their tortures. In comparison, the despair of the suicides seems to touch him closely, as though, however little he approved, he understood the quality of it from the inside.

Perhaps this is why he described the hell of suicides with the same image as that with which his great works began.

> *Nel mezzo del cammin di nostra vita*
> *mi ritrovai per una selva oscura*
> *che la diritta via era smarrita.*

> *Ah quanto a dir qual era è cosa dura*
> *esta selva selvaggia e aspra e forte*
> *che nel pensier rinova la paura!*
> *Tant' è amara che poco è piu morte ...* *

It was by no means a random image; the way to Hell-Gate lay, traditionally, through the blackest, most impenetrable primeval forest. We know, too, that Dante began *The Divine Comedy* in a black period, after he had been banished from Florence at the age of thirty-seven. But a psychoanalyst, Elliott Jaques, has also interpreted the lines as a classic description of what he calls 'the mid-life crisis',[1] that long period of hopelessness and confusion, a kind of male menopause, which often occurs at some point in the thirties or early forties and marks the transition from youth to middle age. It is a crisis about death and the death instinct and, according to Professor Jaques, it comes at that moment when, with your own children growing up and your parents dead, you find yourself suddenly at the head of the queue. You have to come to terms with the fact that

---

*'In the middle of the journey of our life I came to myself within a dark wood where the straight way was lost. Ah, how hard a thing it is to tell of that wood, savage and harsh and dense, the thought of which renews my fear! So bitter is it that death is hardly more.'

you too, are really going to die. You also begin painfully to recognize that you, too, have your share of destructiveness working away inside. It is too late for youthful optimism, too soon for acceptance.

For creative artists, this brings a new element, a new tone to their work. Some never negotiate the crisis. Professor Jaques points out that Mozart, Raphael, Chopin, Rimbaud, Purcell, Schubert and Watteau all died in their thirties. It is as though the intensity of their creative powers was such that they lived their whole lives in half the normal span. Others lapse into silence, like Sibelius or Rossini, who wrote no opera from the age of forty until his death at seventy-four. Some, like Wordsworth, drone on and on, vainly trying to recapture the inspiration of their youth. Others only begin in middle age, like Gauguin abandoning his family and his job in order to paint or Conrad changing from master-mariner to master-novelist. But for some of the greatest artists – Dante, Shakespeare, Bach, Dickens, Donatello, Beethoven – the mid-life crisis is the way through to their finest work, more profound, tragic, reflective and ultimately more serene than anything they have achieved before.

The need to face the fact that your own death is coming and the seeds of it are already at work produces, according to Professor Jaques, a long, bitter period of depression during which all your values slowly and painfully change. The optimism and idealism of youth fall away before a more sombre, less hopeful sense of the world as it is, unredeemed, uneasy, unforgiving. And in the warren of this depression all your past work seems trivial or worthless, and your internal resources hopelessly inadequate for the dour task of finding a way through in some new, untested direction. It is a despair not many steps from suicide.

The fact that Dante gives the suicides the same landscape

as that with which he began the whole poem makes me suspect that he at least understood something of their anguish, and had probably shared it in his time. But the signs are also clear that he rejected it unequivocally. Indeed, he goes out of his way to emphasize the horror of the act by making Piero an otherwise wholly virtuous figure, brought down simply by the envy of others, and through no fault of his own. John Sinclair remarks: 'The story, as it is told here, is in effect Dante's vindication of Piero's memory from the charges of treason for which he had suffered and under which, after half a century, his name lay still.'[2] So Dante is at once clearing Piero's reputation and, at the same time, damning him to an eternity of pain. It is an oddly ambivalent performance, as though the artist and the Christian were pulling in opposite directions. Although the tone and reverberations of the poetry in no way condone the sin, they render it at least understandable, and they link it implicitly with a more qualified despair which Dante himself seems to have known. Meanwhile, the orthodox believer rejects the act flatly and in horror.

Inevitably, the Christian has the last word. After Piero has said his say and the spendthrifts – whose ostentation has made them suicides of their worldly goods – have been hunted through the woods, another suicide speaks. He is an anonymous Florentine who has killed himself for no good reason that Dante cares to mention:

*Io fei giubbetto a me delle mie case.**

In other words, he has debased all propriety and all values: his name, his home, his family, his native city and his religion. For Dante, whose loyalty to Florence flourished even in Paradise, this style of wilful baseness is beyond contempt and excuse, certainly beyond redemption. He ends the

*'I made a gibbet for myself of my own house.'

canto with this line, as though to cauterize any trace of sympathy which his treatment of Piero might have suggested for nobler and apparently more justifiable suicides. In the end, a mortal sin is a mortal sin. What the Church condemns, no poetry can exonerate.

2. John Donne and
the Renaissance

In the Middle Ages, the taboo against suicide went with an intense preoccupation with death in all its most horrifying details: with worms and putrefaction, with the transitoriness of earthly glory, the remorselessness of decay and God's savage, cheese-paring judgement. The great popular image of all this – acted, painted, carved in churches and endlessly circulated in cheap and proportionately gruesome woodcuts – was the Dance of Death, in which a jaunty skeleton waltzes away forty times with the different orders of the living. Nobody escaped, whatever his rank or profession. Death was the one form of political equality the Middle Ages understood, an equality of terror:

> Nothing betrays more clearly the excessive fear of death felt in the Middle Ages than the popular belief, then widely spread, according to which Lazarus, after his resurrection, lived in a continual misery and horror at the thought that he should have again to pass through the gate of death. If the just had so much to fear, how could the sinner soothe himself?[3]

Life was grim and pinched, death unspeakable, eternity probably worse. The difference between this horrified obsession and the cool tones of the Renaissance is profound:

> Death is a remedy against all evils: It is a most assured haven, never to be feared, and often to be sought: All comes to one period, whether man make an end of himself, or whether he endure it; whether he run before his day, or whether he

expect it: whence soever it come, it is ever his owne, where ever the thread be broken, it is all there, it's the end of the web. The voluntariest death is the fairest. Life dependeth on the will of others, death on ours.[4]

That is Montaigne writing his defence of 'A Custome of the Ile of Cea', the custom in question being legal suicide for those whose life had lost purpose and meaning. He discusses it casually, as though it were the most natural act in the world, a dignified Roman usage it would be well to revive. And the authority he invokes is not that of the Church but of the classics, particularly Seneca. The implications of that change in the frame of reference – however limited it was in practice and however powerful the Church remained in fact – were enormous. Montaigne again: 'Hegesias was wont to say, that even as the condition of life, so should the qualitie of death depend on our election.' It is as though the rediscovery of the classics had returned each man's death into his own gift.

Dante was writing the *Divine Comedy* at the start of the fourteenth century. In less than two hundred years, without anyone quite mentioning it, suicide had once again become a possible subject. Sir Thomas More, like Plato, allowed it as a kind of voluntary euthanasia in his *Utopia*. Later in the sixteenth century, death before dishonour and suicide for love became the commonplace of poets and playwrights, however powerfully the preachers still thundered away about the enormity of the crime. For Tudor and Elizabethen poets, Lucretia was the model of wifely virtue.[5] Despair, however, was still a mortal sin. In *The Faerie Queene* an allegorical Despair, squatting in his cave surrounded by the corpses of suicides, tempts the Red Cross Knight in one of the best-written passages of the poem:

What if some little paine the passage have,
That makes fraile flesh to feare the bitter wave?
Is not short paine well borne, that brings long ease,
And layes the soule to sleep in quiet grave?
Sleepe after toyle, port after stormie seas,
Ease after warre, death after life does greatly please.

It has been suggested that Spenser wrote so well about despair because he himself was particularly prone to it, shut away in Ireland, miserable, broke and unrecognized. Yet the arguments he uses are perfectly traditional. (The soldier must not desert his post, says the Red Cross Knight. But the longer you live, counter-attacks Despair, the more you sin.) And when the Knight finally accepts a dagger to stab himself, Una steps forward and needs only one brisk stanza to argue him out of it. Whereupon they ride off, leaving Despair in despair.

Spenser can usually be relied on to put the conventional case elegantly but conventionally. Elsewhere the certainties seem less assured. Bacon, for instance, does not distinguish morally between death by suicide and death from natural causes; for him, as for the nineteenth-century sociologist Morselli, 'a corpse is a corpse'. All that matters is the dignity of the act, a certain stylishness in dying. It is the same with Shakespeare: as in everything else, he remains neutral, a practising dramatist. Of all the many suicides in his plays – fourteen in eight works, says Fedden – only Ophelia, the least intentional, is subject to ecclesiastical disapproval. But the priest who denies her the full funeral rites is thrust aside by Laertes, passionately and with great conviction:

I tell thee, churlish priest,
A minist'ring angel shall my sister be,
When thou liest howling.

Another priest, Friar Lawrence, narrates the double suicide of Romeo and Juliet without a hint of condemnation, and even a good Venetian Catholic like Cassio takes Othello's suicide as a sign of his nobility: 'This I did fear, but thought he had no weapon; For he was great of heart.' This is the exact reversal of Dante's treatment of Piero delle Vigne: the sin of Othello's suicide weighs not at all; what matters is its tragic inevitability and the degree to which it heightens his heroic stature. Instead of damning him, his suicide confirms his noblity.

Not much can be deduced from this. Shakespeare's attitude to moral problems was basically the same as his attitude to his sources: pragmatic. The play's the thing. His own religious prejudices – whatever they might have been – were never allowed to subvert his instinct for practical dramatic effectiveness. Moreover, High Renaissance tastes in tragedy do not imply any new toleration for real suicide. The suffering of a tragic hero, distanced and ennobled by poetic drama, is literally a world apart from suicide offstage, which is rarely tragic, never grandiose and most often sordid, depressing, muddled. There would have been no good reason why the body of a real-life Othello should not have been dragged through the streets behind a horse and buried at a crossroads with a stake through its heart. Even in the saintly Sir Thomas More's ideal republic, an unauthorized suicide would have been 'caste unburied into some stinkinge marrish'.

What, then, distinguished the Renaissance attitude to suicide from that of the Middle Ages was not a sudden access of enlightenment in practice but a new insistence on individualism which made ultimate moral problems of life, death and responsibility seem more fluid and complex than before, and very much more open to question. If nothing else, it was a moment of considerable sophistication; the moral world had tilted on its axis and the whole climate had changed.

The finest and clearest example of this is John Donne who, among his many other talents and distinctions, wrote the first English defence of suicide, *Biathanatos. A Declaration of that Paradoxe, or Thesis, That Self-homicide is not so naturally Sinne, that it may never be otherwise.** It used to be a fashion among academics to explain that Donne didn't really *mean* what he said. The book was just another example of his showing off his wit and learning, his ability, as a famous writer of paradoxes and outrageous poems, to defend any topic, no matter how apparently indefensible. Admittedly, the book is one of his less appealing performances: intricate, detailed, at times pedantic and often suffocatingly learned. It is, in short, as tightly defended as it is argued. It also matches badly with the image of the chastened and sombre Christian divine whom Donne was eventually to become.† But he himself made no bones about

---

* It is interesting that Donne was related, on his mother's side, to Sir Thomas More.

† Later Donne himself found the book an embarrassment. In 1619 he sent a copy of it to Sir Robert Ker, Earl of Ancrum, with a letter which sharply distinguishes between the unregenerate wit who wrote it and the elder churchman he had since become: 'It was written by me many years since; and because it is upon a misinterpretable subject, I have always gone so near suppressing it, as that it is onely not burnt: no hand hath passed upon it to copy it, nor many eyes to read it: onely to some particular friends in both Universities, then when I writ it, I did communicate it: And I remember, I had this answer, That certainly, there was a false thread in it, but not easily found: Keep it, I pray, with the same jealousie; lest any that your discretion admits to the sight of it, know the date of it; and that it is a book written by *Jack Donne* and not by *D. Donne*: Reserve it for me, if I live, and if I die, I only forbid it the Presse, and the Fire: publish it not, but yet burn it not; and between those, do what you will with it.'[6] Four years after taking Holy Orders, Donne's feelings about the book were still mixed: part

how close the subject was to him. That, he explains in the Preface, is why he has written the book:

Beza, a man ... eminent and illustrious, in the full glory and Noone of learning ... confesseth of himself, that only for the anguish of a Scurffe, which over-ranne his head, he had once drown'd himselfe from the Millers bridge in *Paris*, if his Uncle by chance had not then come that way; I have often such a sickely inclination. And, whether it be, because I had my first breeding and conversation with men of a suppressed and afflicted Religion, accustomed to the despite of death, and hungry of an imagin'd Martyrdome; Or that the common Enemie find that doore worst locked against him in mee; Or that there bee a perplexitie and flexibilitie in the doctrine it selfe; Or because my Conscience ever assures me, that no rebellious grudging at Gods gifts, nor other sinfull concurrence accompanies these thoughts in me, or that a brave scorn, or that a faint cowardlinesse beget it, whensoever any affliction assailes me, mee thinks I have the keyes of my prison in mine owne hand, and no remedy presents it selfe so soone to my heart, as mine own sword. Often Meditation of this hath wonne me to a charitable interpretation of their action, who dy so: and provoked me a little to watch and exagitate their reasons, which pronounce so peremptory judgements upon them.

There is nothing shuffling about this. He had written about suicide because he himself was constantly tempted to it. Later in the book Donne took pains to demonstrate his ingenuity and his mastery of the involutions of civil and canon law; he writes like a man who has read, literally, everything, and wants it known. But the Preface is scrupu-

pride in the subtlety and learning involved, part embarrassment in tackling, however privately, such a hot subject, and part a sort of tenderness for the defunct but still controversial figure of Jack Donne, now soberly resurrected as Dr Donne, the divine. His contemporaries respected his feelings; the book was not published until 1646, fifteen years after his death and nearly forty after it was written.

lously personal in a way early seventeenth-century prose rarely was. With that curious intellectual intuition which sustains everything he did, he even links his feeling for suicide, in the best psycho-analytic style, with his childhood among the oppressed Jesuits.

It is precisely this inwardness which distinguishes Donne's attitude to suicide from the easier Stoicism of his contemporaries. The essence of Stoic suicide is its deliberation: it was an act of self-conscious nobility proceeding from a philosophy of life which judged what was bearable and what was not. So there was always a hint of self-dramatization about it – which is why, among other reasons, Shakespeare found it so useful. For Donne, however, suicide seems not to have been a question of choice or action but of mood, something indistinct but pervasive, like rain. After a certain point, a kind of suicidal damp permeated his life.

So when Donne wrote *Biathanatos* he was doing more than exposing the inconsistencies of the Church's ruling against suicide, and far more than wilfully and ostentatiously defending a heretical paradox. It has been suggested that his vastly learned survey of suicide in non-Christian societies and in the animal world, and his triumphant conclusion that 'in all ages, in all places, upon all occasions, men of all conditions have affected it, and inclined to it' adds up to a primitive essay in psychology, a first rough draft for Freud's theory of the death instinct.[8] According to this view, when Donne took holy orders this obsession with death did not disappear, it was simply 'transferred from the realm of psychology to that of theology'. Hence his continual harping on death in his sermons and divine poems and the macabre drama of his last weeks, so impressive to his contemporaries, when he rose from his death-bed to preach his last and greatest sermon, 'Deaths Duell':

When to the amazement of some beholders he appeared in the Pulpit, many of them thought he presented himself not to preach mortification by a living voice: but, mortality by a decayed body and a dying face ... Many that then saw his tears, and heard his faint and hollow voice, professing they thought the Text prophetically chosen, and that Dr Donne *had preach't his own Funeral Sermon.*[9]

It seems that Donne thought so, too. He had his portrait painted in his winding-sheet, eyes closed, hands crossed. This picture of himself as a corpse was then hung by his bed where he could contemplate it for the fifteen days of life which were left to him. His last act was to settle himself into the position in which he would be buried, almost as though he wanted to know in advance what it felt like to be dead: 'As his soul ascended, and his last breath departed from him, he closed his own eyes; and then disposed his hands and body into such a posture as required not the least alteration by those that came to shroud him.'[10]

Professor Roberts feels that all this was excessive, far beyond the customs of the time, and a token of Donne's continuing obsession with death. Perhaps. But it was also a conservative gesture, in key with medieval attitudes to death and the accompanying exacerbated meditation upon the Four Last Things – Death, Judgement, Heaven and Hell. It is as though Donne, in his last days, had sanctified his obsession by channelling it into traditional forms. Perhaps this is why a pious and conventional figure like Walton found it all so easy to admire. The depressed, racked, rather twentieth-century figure Donne had cut before he entered the Church had slowly been transformed into a traditionally pious churchman thirsting for the next life.

In *Biathanatos* there is the same clash between the traditional and the new. He takes a peculiarly modern line in justifying suicide and admitting his own temptation to it.

Yet at the same time he is also summing up and disposing of all the tortured medieval arguments against the act. So the work becomes a struggle between two opposing cultural strains: the immense learning and formal logic imply a large commitment to the world of Scholasticism; yet the argument rejects this world on its own terms and by its own formulae. In short, he writes a quasi-medieval work in order to disprove the medieval belief that suicide is not a possible subject.

If it were not for the Preface, *Biathanatos*, formal, barbed and rebarbative, would seem remote enough from Donne's intimate concerns. Yet the same year in which he wrote it, 1608, he also wrote a letter to his close friend Sir Henry Goodyer which sets the book firmly in its context of depression:

Two of the most precious things which God hath afforded us here, for the agony and exercise of our sense and spirit, which are a thirst and inhiation after the next life, and   frequency of prayer and meditation in this, are often envenomed, and putrefied, and stray into a corrupt disease ... With the first of these I have often suspected my self to be overtaken; which is, with a desire of the next life: which though I know it is not meerly out of wearinesse of this, because I had the same desires when I went with the tyde, and enjoyed fairer hopes than now: yet I doubt worldly encombrances have encreased it. I would not that death should take me asleep. I would not have him meerly seise me, and onely declare me to be dead, but win me, and overcome me. When I must shipwrack, I would do it in a Sea, where mine impotencie might have some excuse; not in a sullen weedy lake, where I could not have so much as exercise for my swimming. Therefore I would fain do something; but that I cannot tell what, is no wonder. For to chuse, is to do: but to be no part of any body, is to be nothing. At most, the greatest persons, are but great wens, and excrescences; men of wit and delightfull conversation, but as moales for ornament, except they be so incorporated into the body of the world, that they contribute something to the sustentation of the whole. This I made account that I begun early, when I understood the study of our laws: but was diverted by the worst voluptuousness, which is an Hydroptique immoderate desire of humane learning and languages: beautiful ornaments to great fortunes; but mine needed an occupation, and a course which I thought I entred well into, when I submitted my self to such a service, as I thought might imploy those poor advantages, which I had. And there I stumbled too, yet I would try again: for to this hour I am nothing, or so little, that I am scarce subject and argument good enough for one of mine own letters: yet I fear, that doth not ever proceed from a good root, that I am so well content to be lesse, that is dead.[11]

The opening years of the seventeenth century were the low-point of Donne's life. His rash secret marriage to Ann More at Christmas 1601 stopped short a career which had previously been gathering brilliant momentum. His young wife's enraged father, his grandiose expectations for his daughter ruined, had him thrown briefly into prison and dismissed from his post as private secretary to the Lord Keeper of the Privy Seal. He also stopped his daughter's dowry. 'John Donne, Ann Donne, Undone,' the poet is said to have written at the bottom of a letter to his wife from prison, and, Walton added, 'God knows it proved too true.' For ten years they lived ill and poor and childridden, dependent on the hospitality of friends. His own inheritance had mostly been run through before his marriage and, despite his extraordinary gifts, his prospects were nil. *Biathanatos* and the letter to Goodyer belong to the midnight of this long period of darkness. As usual, he had been ill; as usual, his attempts to find employment had failed; he was still living in unwilling retirement at Mitcham, 'a sullen weedy lake' far from the storm and traffic and open sea of the London court, where he felt he belonged. It adds up to another instance of a particularly agonized mid-life crisis. Donne was now in his middle thirties. One career and one style of writing were over; the court, despite his efforts, was as irretrievably behind him as his early, outrageous love poetry. Another life and another style had not yet been born; it would still be years before he would be received into the Church and become the most famous and seductive preacher of his day. The passion and ambition of his brilliant youth, that 'Hydroptique immoderate desire of humane learning and languages', had given way to their suicidal opposite: 'a thirst and inhiation after the next life'. First Eros, then Thanatos; beyond the pleasure principle, the death instinct. Apparently, he sensed that they were two faces of the same power, since he used the same dropsical metaphor to describe both.

From many of his letters, particularly to his close friend Goodyer, Donne emerges as a chronic grumbler, constantly harping on his illnesses and depressions, worried about money and preferment and other men's success. But this letter is different in quality and kind; it reads as though he had reached that fine edge of crisis when he must understand or go under. In the Preface to *Biathanatos* he confessed to a perennial temptation to suicide; in the letter he qualifies that: however sharply his present troubles have increased it, it was present even when he 'went with the tyde, and enjoyed fairer hopes than now'. But previously he had defended himself against depression by activity. Hence his stunning career, first as a boy genius – he was called another Pico della Mirandola – then as a wit and lover, a brilliant poet and ambitious, successful civil servant. Now the possibility for action was gone and there was nothing between him and his despair. For Donne, as for a modern existentialist, his identity was a question of action and choice: 'to chuse, is to do: but to be no part of any body, is to be nothing.' Alienated from 'the body of the world', he becomes in himself superfluous, as his learning is superfluous without money and his talents without employment. Later and more calmly, as though from the other side of the abyss, he repeated this in the famous passage, 'No man is an island . . .'

To put it another way, the essence of his poetry lay in what he himself called its 'masculine, perswasive force', a restless, logical drive which made him argue each perception to its conclusion, impatiently and with contempt for the delays and timorousness of others. So each poem, however passionate, however tender, is also an argument complete in itself, a distinct distance travelled and a goal reached. Part of the energy of his early work comes from his own obvious enjoyment of his talents, of his sophistry as well as his sensuality, of his learning and his contempt. The essence of his despair is the opposite of all this: an overpowering sense of 'impotencie' which came from his isolation from the stirring world of possibility, choice and action. When these outlets were denied him, his energy turned inwards, turned sour and seemed to annihilate him. In these circumstances, suicide began to seem the one definite act by which he might reaffirm his identity. I wonder if *Biathanatos* didn't begin as a prelude to self-destruction and finish as a substitute for it. That is, he set out to find precedents and reasons for killing himself whilst still remaining Christian – or, at least, without damning himself eternally. But the process of writing the book and marshalling his intricate learning and dialectical skill may have relieved the tension and helped to re-establish his sense of his self.

In the end, of course, Donne's importance does not depend on his abilities as a belated Schoolman or as a letter-writer but on his poetry. So none of this would be more than an interesting sidelight on a major figure if the themes did not coalesce in one of his greatest and most baffling lyrics, 'A nocturnall upon S. *Lucies* day, Being the shortest day';*

> Tis the yeares midnight, and it is the dayes,
> *Lucies*, who scarce seaven houres herself unmaskes,
>   The Sunne is spent, and now his flasks
>   Send forth light squibs, no constant rayes;
>   The worlds whole sap is sunke;
> The generall balme th'hydroptique earth hath drunk,
> Whither, as to the beds-feet, life is shrunke,
> Dead and enterr'd; yet all these seeme to laugh,
> Compar'd with mee, who am their Epitaph.
>
> Study me then, you who shall lovers bee
> At the next world, that is, at the next Spring:
>   For I am every dead thing,
>   In whom love wrought new Alchimie.
>   For his art did expresse
> A quintessence even from nothingnesse,
> From dull privations, and leane emptinesse:
> He ruin'd mee, and I am re-begot
> Of absence, darknesse, death; things which are not.
>
> All others, from all things, draw all that's good,
> Life, soule, forme, spirit, whence they beeing have;
>   I, by loves limbecke, am the grave
>   Of all, that's nothing. Oft a flood
>   Have wee two wept, and so

---

*Although it is impossible to date any of the *Songs and Sonets* with complete certainty, there is every reason to assume that the poem, the letter and *Biathanatos* belong to roughly the same period. The scholars agree that the 'Nocturnall' is associated, in one way or another, with Lucy, Countess of Bedford. This means, says Professor Helen Gardner, that it 'must have been written after 1607'. *Biathanatos* was written in 1607 or 1608, the letter in 1608.

Drownd the whole world, us two; oft did we grow
To be two Chaosses, when we did show
Care to ought else; and often absences
Withdrew our soules, and made us carcasses.

But I am by her death, (which word wrongs her)
Of the first nothing, the Elixer grown;
   Were I am a man, that I were one,
    I needs must know : I should preferre,
      If I were any beast,
Some ends, some means; Yea plants, yea stones detest,
And love; All, all some properties invest;
If I an ordinary nothing were,
As shadow, a light, and body must be here.

But I am None; nor will my Sunne renew.
You lovers, for whose sake, the lesser Sunne
   At this time to the Goat is runne
   To fetch new lust, and give it you,
     Enjoy your summer all;
Since shee enjoyes her long nights festivall,
Let mee prepare towards her, and let mee call
This houre her Vigill, and her Eve, since this
Both the yeares, and the dayes deep midnight is.

The annihilating depression of the letter to Goodyer and the
desperate logic and learning of *Biathanatos* come together
in this poem. It is, in every sense, a 'Nocturnall', written in
the middle of the longest night, which is also the winter
midnight of the year, which is, in turn, the darkest midnight of Donne's life. In this blackness the stars (the sun's
'flasks') fail and the earth shrinks into itself like a dying
man huddling down to the foot of the bed. Once again, the
fatal disease is dropsy: the inanimate earth sucks life out
of everything just as Donne's own 'Hydroptique immoderate desire of humane learning and languages' had sucked
away his vital powers along with his inheritance.

Against this background of sickness, death, swaddling darkness and a silence in which even the poet's words have to be hissed ('*Lucies*, who scarce seaven houres herself unmaskes'), Donne gropes towards his theme: negation and emptiness, 'to be no part of any body, is to be nothing'. It is a question of a forced withdrawal from society as from the self, from action as from the feelings. But now he comes out with it factually, autobiographically: love – that is, his headlong marriage – 'ruin'd mee, and I am rebegot/Of absence, darknesse, death: things which are not.' The active lover, courtier, thinker and wit has been transformed into a passive victim of some monstrous alchemical experiment in which love, adding spiritual negation to the 'dull privations' he is already enduring, reduces him to 'a quintessence even from nothingnesse'. His only distinction is an emptiness beyond emptiness, a deprivation which is also a paralysis of the will and soul.

What follows is a desperate attempt to find some way out of this labyrinth. He even goes back to his earlier love poems, compressing into an anguished shorthand images and ideas he had used constantly before: the lovers' tears as universal floods, their ability to create a perfect world from chaos, their separation as a form of murder. Then from poetry he goes on to philosophy. In the fourth stanza the logic is insistent, contorted, wrung dry while he ransacks Aristotle's and the Schoolmen's doctrine of the soul to find some form of argument or some philosophical truth which will make him believe he exists.

But there is none. The frantic hunting of reason after reason is brought up short by the brief, stonewall assertion: 'But I am None.' After that, there is nothing left but to bring the poem back to where it began: an ironical, slightly contemptuous valediction to the lovers still at the mercy of their itch, and for the poet himself the long, dark, midwinter vigil and the acceptance that his despair, like midnight itself, cannot be overcome, it can only be endured. Yet the finality of that statement – 'I am None' – casts a new light back over the poem. Despite its theme, the piece has been driven continually forward by a curious restless energy. Yet that energy is entirely in the negations. Each phase of the argument ends in a further withdrawal into nothingness: 'The worlds whole sap is sunke', '[I] am their Epitaph', 'I am every dead thing', 'He ruin'd mee', 'things which are not', 'I . . . am the grave Of all', 'made us carcasses', 'I am . . . Of the first nothing, the Elixer grown', 'If I an ordinary nothing were', 'But I am None'. That 'masculine perswasive force' of argument, so pervasive and so effective elsewhere, is here transformed into a powerful negative current, driving the poet back step by step into his own desolation.

Yet in the end, even suicide was not a possibility. Donne's Christian training and devotion, like his intellectual energy, were ultimately stronger than his despair. Perhaps this is why the movement of the 'Nocturnall' is circular, the last line returning to the first: it is a poem about a state of mind so sterile as to be beyond even suicide. Donne finally negotiated his mid-life crisis by taking holy orders instead of his life.

Unlike *Biathanatos*, the poem is not *about* suicide. Instead, it is written as though from inside the act: it not only defines the suicidal state of mind and how it feels to reach absolute zero, it also describes how it feels to *think* when you are there. It is a poem before its time, John Donne's intimation of Kierkegaard.

Yet on one level, it would not have seemed particularly strange to his contemporaries. They would have read it as just another expression of the workings of the fashionable disease of the day, 'melancholy', What 'neurosis' and 'alienation' once were to us, what 'schizophrenia' is to R. D. Laing and his disciples, so 'melancholy' was to the Elizabethans: a blanket term which covered every quirky sensibility from the genius to the certifiable lunatic. There were melancholics who thought that they were wolves or chamber-pots, that they were made of glass or butter or brick, that they had frogs in their bellies. There were also melancholics who thought they were poets. 'The lunatic, the lover and the poet Are of Imagination all compact': Ferdinand in *The Duchess of Malfi* who suffers from lycanthropia, Hamlet who feigns madness and contemplates suicide, the Melancholy Jaques who moralizes and fancies himself as a poet, were all, in their different ways, melancholics. 'The principal reason for the popularity of melancholy [in Elizabethan and Stuart England] ... was the general acceptance of the idea that it was an attribute of superior minds, of genius. [This] Aristotelian concept had invested the melancholy character with something of sombre philosophic dignity, something of Byronic grandeur.'[12] Thus the Romantic image of the genius as someone gloomy, disturbed and apart descends ultimately from Elizabethan theories about the disrupting effect of too much black bile in the system. And black bile, said Robert Burton, is 'a shoeing horn' to suicide:

In such sort doth the torture and extremity of [the melancholic's] misery torment him, that he can take no pleasure in his life, but is in a manner enforced to offer violence unto himself, to be freed from his present insufferable pains ... 'Tis a common calamity, and a fatal end to this disease ... there remains no more to such persons, if that heavenly physician, by his assisting grace and mercy alone, do not prevent (for no humane persuasion or art can help) but to be their own butchers, and execute themselves.[13]

Although Burton is said to have hanged himself to fulfil his own astrological prophecies about the date of his death, suicide was more or less a side-issue for him, an unfortunate by-product of a malady which seemed to him to infect every aspect of life. His *Anatomy of Melancholy*, first published in 1621, is a vast, rambling compendium of a book, repetitive, discursive and idiosyncratic to breaking-point, crammed with quotations, anecdotes, and impossible references. He embroiders, invents authorities, refuses to keep to the point. It reads as though he were unsure whether to surrender to his childish need to draw attention to his own suffering – after all, he said, 'one needs must scratch where it itches' – or to distract the reader with his demented pedantry.

Yet his contribution to the debate on suicide is single and simple: sympathy. Although he quotes all the standard classical examples, he refuses the Stoic justification of suicide as an act of reasoned dignity and self-affirmation. Instead, he maintains a more obvious but less flattering truth: that suicide is neither rational, nor dignified, nor measured; people kill themselves because their lives have become intolerable: 'These unhappy men are born to misery, past all hope of recovery, incurably sick; the longer they live, the worse they are; and death alone must ease them.' The best they can hope for is God's mercy; judgement is His business, not ours. At the time, it was a brave point to make. But since Burton was labouring under the double burden of being both an Oxford don and a parson, he was finally unlikely to stick his neck out farther than was strictly necessary. In the end, he comes out with all the usual pious disclaimers and condemnations. But by then it is too late; they lack conviction. In his vacillating, fragmented way, he understands the confusion of despair, the impossibility of relief, the inadequacy of moral solutions. In the face of all that, he offers only a decent charity:

3. William Cowper, Thomas Chatterton and the Age of Reason

The eighth edition of *The Anatomy of Melancholy* appeared in 1676, the second edition of *Biathanatos* in 1700. But by that time the spiritual temper of the time had cooled considerably. Melancholy survived into the eighteenth century in a less extreme form and with a different name. It became 'spleen', a more rationally anatomical term, as befits the Augustans, for a more circumscribed and controlled gloom which found its outlet not in despair but in the rancour and mean-mindedness of the great age of satire. Once again, suicide became an extra-literary topic.

The debate on the rights and wrongs of the act continued as fiercely as ever but now the pious traditionalists had tougher opponents to fulminate against. Montesquieu, Voltaire and Hume, as well as lesser figures like Alberto Radicati, Count of Passerano, analysed the subject rationally, with controlled indignation, and a general humanitarian enlightenment began to spread downwards and outwards. After the Reformation the edicts against suicide had been transferred bodily from canon law to civil; now they began to seem disproportionately uncivilized and stupid. Although the statute books still decreed that the corpse of the self-murderer should be desecrated and his property forfeit to the Crown, coroners' juries increasingly bypassed them by returning a verdict of '*non compos mentis*'. The more this happened, the more wildly the orthodox opponents of suicide raged: the horror of the crime, they said, must be brought home to all; hang the bodies head down from gibbets, dissect them publicly in the market place.[15] But few listened. By 1788 Horace Walpole could refer, scornfully and in passing, to 'the absurd stake and highway of our ancestors'.

The key word is 'absurd'. For the eighteenth-century rationalists it was both absurd and presumptuous to inflate a trivial private act into a monstrous crime. 'The life of a man,' wrote David Hume, 'is of no greater importance to the universe than that of an oyster.' Hume's great attack on the moral prejudice against suicide was written at least twenty years before his death but not published officially until 1777, the year after he died. It was promptly suppressed. Yet it summed up brilliantly the exasperation of the most intelligent men of his time with the craven old superstitions:

Were the disposal of human life so much reserved as the peculiar province of the Almighty that it were an encroachment on his right, for men to dispose of their own lives; it would be equally criminal to act for the preservation of life as for its destruction. If I turn aside a stone which is falling upon my head, I disturb the course of nature, and I invade the peculiar province of the Almighty by lengthening out my life beyond the period which by the general laws of matter and motion he had assigned it.

A hair, a fly, an insect is able to destroy this mighty being whose life is of such importance. Is it an absurdity to suppose that human prudence may dispose of what depends on such insignificant causes? It would be no crime in me to divert the *Nile* or *Danube* from its course, were I able to effect such purposes. Where then is the crime in turning a few ounces of blood from their natural channel? . . .

'Tis impious, says the old Roman superstition, to divert rivers from their course, or invade the prerogatives of nature. 'Tis impious, says the French superstition, to innoculate for the small pox, or usurp the business of providence, by voluntarily producing distempers and maladies. 'Tis impious, says the modern *European* superstition, to put a period to our own life, and thereby rebel against our creator; and why not impious, say I, to build houses, cultivate the ground, or sail upon the ocean? In all these actions we employ our powers of mind and body, to produce some innovation in the course of nature; and in none of them do we any more. They are all of them therefore equally innocent, or equally criminal.[16]

The note is irritated and energetic, as of a man sweeping cobwebs from a musty room and opening the windows. For the great rationalists, a sense of absurdity – the absurdity of superstition, self-importance and unreason – was as natural and illuminating as sunlight.

Few of his contemporaries, perhaps, would openly have gone all the way with Hume, since the label of impiety was inconvenient. But covertly the moral revolution had already taken place; suicide had been removed from the world of taboo and installed in the realm of manners. The letters of Horace Walpole are full of casual references to aristocratic suicides, a fruitful subject for gossip, though none was as casual or cool as the legendary eighteenth-century Frenchman who, when a friend asked him to dine, replied: 'With the greatest pleasure. Yet, now I think of it, I am particularly engaged to shoot myself. One cannot get off *such* an engagement.' The polite response to the act was a yawn and even those about to die went through the motions of indifference. In 1690 Hannah More wrote feelingly to Walpole:

A poor man near our house, driven by extremity of want and other kind of despair, hung himself; not having twopence to buy a cord, he cut his clothes into strips to make one. It was in a very lonely wood where no one ever passes; but two men who were sporting saw him and cut him down; he lay dead for a while, but was at last recovered. They brought him to our house with his black and disfigured countenance! And to complete the woeful scene, there was a young but paralytic wife, and two beautiful infants.[17]

Walpole's reply was fretful: 'It is very provoking that people must always be hanging or drowning themselves or going mad ...' That mixture of aristocratic boredom and irritation is the typical eighteenth-century note. However rationally suicide was justified, however grotesque the old laws now seemed and however tactfully they were ignored, by the prevailing standards of dandified propriety the act was thought to be tiresome, rather low.

This means that, so far as literature was concerned, suicide had ceased to be imaginatively possible. Early in the century, Addison wrote a play about Cato, the noblest Roman suicide of them all. It had such a huge success that Pope, who had written the prologue, wrote to a friend, 'Cato was not such a wonder of Rome in his days, as he is of Britain in ours.' Yet Addison's *Cato* is, to a suffocating degree, concerned with Senecan nobility and high political principle. At each performance the Whigs and Tories vied with each other as to who should clap loudest. His suicide is almost by the way, although years later, in 1737, Eustace Budgell – Addison's cousin and Grub Street writer, immortalized by Pope in *The Dunciad* – leaped into the Thames with his pockets loaded with stones, leaving behind a lame suicide note:

> What Cato did and Addison approved
> Cannot be wrong.

The couplet is unfinished; his Muse was unfaithful even in death. But perhaps that was as it should have been, since suicide was no longer a subject for inspiration. Even Edward Young, who wrote *Night Thoughts*, a panegyric on death in nine books, who kept a skull always on his mantelpiece and claimed that his dreams 'infest the grave', rejected the act with high-minded Christian contempt; he blamed it on loose living. Whatever the classical precedents for suicide, it was no longer felt to be a proper topic for poetry.

There are two notable exceptions to the rule: William Cowper, who made a pathetic but elaborate attempt to take his own life, which he later described in great detail; and Thomas Chatterton, who succeeded spectacularly and thereby became a symbol for the next generation of poets. Cowper – who was, incidentally, descended on his mother's side from John Donne – seems at first sight a classic example of a man haunted by 'the death trend', deprived, guilty, injured. He was six when his adored and adoring mother died in childbirth in 1737. Within a year he had been farmed out to a shoddy little boarding-school where, for two years, he was bullied so brutally that he had some kind of breakdown. He wrote later of his chief tormentor: 'His savage treatment of me impressed such a dread of his figure on my mind, that I well remember being afraid to lift my eyes upon him higher than his knees.'[18] Not surprisingly, his breakdown took the form of acute eye trouble; he was in danger of losing his sight. So he was sent to live in the home of an oculist for another two years, until he went on to Westminster School. But his eyes stayed bad until he was fourteen, when he was seriously ill with smallpox; after which they gave less trouble. It is as though one punishing illness had driven out another.

From Westminster he went on to a solicitor's office, and from there to the Middle Temple, where he studied law in an indolent, fashionable way; that is, he spent most of his time with the young wits-about-town talking literature, politics, literary politics and women, 'giggling,' he said, 'and making giggle'. Yet almost immediately he set up on his own in the Temple and settled into what Bagehot called 'a vague, literary, omnitolerant idleness', he had another depressive breakdown. For months on end he was unable to work and unable not to work: 'Day and night I was on the rack, lying down in horror, and rising up in despair.' He dragged on like this for a year until, one day by the seaside, the depression vanished as abruptly as it had arrived. He went back to his legal and literary dabbling in London. Two years later, in 1754, he was called to the Bar; two years after that his father died, leaving him a small but providential income which for a while spared him the necessity of taking the law seriously. He devoted himself to his scribbling friends in the Nonsense Club and the usual disappointments in love. Before his twenties were out he had become a slightly old-maidish figure: shy, fidgety, ineffectual, fussy about his health and prone to claustrophobia.

By the time he was thirty-two his inheritance was nearly spent and his prospects few. Once again, he began to brood. His one hope was a clerkship in the House of Lords, a job which was at the disposal of a relative. In his anxiety about his future, his habitual helplessness and his terror of want, Cowper jokingly wished dead the man who held the post. He promptly got his wish: the clerk died and Cowper was offered his place. He was also offered two more elevated and lucrative positions. But he was overcome with guilt, as though he believed that the clerk had, in effect, been murdered by his secret hostility. By way of atonement and placation, he refused the better jobs in favour of the relatively minor and ill-paid clerkship. But there was political opposition to his appointment and he had to face a public examination in the Lords. At the best of times he was excessively shy; now his shyness was compounded with guilt. Together they made the prospect of a hostile cross-questioning before the assembled House of Lords intolerable. But he could see no way out which did not also make a fool of his sponsor, Major Cowper. A few months before, his only hope for a comfortable future had been the death of the Clerk of the Journals. Now all he could hope for was a nervous breakdown. He wanted to escape into madness and, if that failed, to atone for his guilt by taking his own life. Much later, he himself described what happened:

My chief fear was, that my senses would not fail me time enough to excuse my appearance at the bar of the House of Lords, which was the only purpose I wanted it to answer. Accordingly the day of decision drew near, and I was still in my senses; though in my heart I had formed many wishes, and by word of mouth expressed many expectations to the contrary.

Now came the grand temptation; the point to which Satan had all the while been driving me; the dark and hellish purpose of self-murder. I grew more sullen and reserved, fled from all society, even from my most intimate friends, and shut myself up in my chambers. The ruin of my fortune, the contempt of my relations and acquaintance, the prejudice I should do my patron, were all urged on me with irresistible energy. Being reconciled to the apprehension of madness, I began to be reconciled to the apprehension of death. Though formerly, in my happiest hours, I had never been able to glance a single thought that way, without shuddering at the idea of dissolution, I now wished for it, and found myself but little shocked at the idea of procuring it myself. Perhaps, thought I, there is no God; or if there be, the scriptures may be false; if so, then God has no where forbidden suicide. I considered life as my property, and therefore at my own disposal. Men of great name, I observed, had destroyed themselves; and the world still retained the profoundest respect for their memories.

But above all, I was persuaded to believe, that if the act were ever so unlawful, and even supposing Christianity to be true, my misery in hell would be more supportable. I well recollect too, that when I was about eleven years of age, my father desired me to read a vindication of self-murder, and give him my sentiments upon the question : I did so, and argued against it. My father heard my reasons, and was silent, neither approving or disapproving; from whence I inferred, that he sided with the author against me; though all the time, I believe, the true motive for his conduct was, that he wanted, if he could, to think favourably of the state of a departed friend, who had some years before destroyed himself, and whose death had struck him with the deepest affliction. But this solution of the matter never once occurred to me, and the circumstance now weighed mightily with me.

At this time I fell into company, at a chop-house, with an elderly, well-looking gentleman, whom I had often seen there before, but had never spoken to. He began the discourse, and talked much of the miseries he had suffered. This opened my heart to him; I freely and readily took part in the conversation. At length, self-murder became the topic; and in the result, we agreed, that the only reason why some men were content to drag on their sorrows with them to the grave, and others were not, was, that the latter were endued with a certain indignant fortitude of spirit, teaching them to despise life, which the former wanted. Another person, whom I met at a tavern, told me that he had made up his mind about that matter, and had no doubt of his liberty to die as he saw convenient; though, by the way, the same person, who has suffered many and great afflictions since, is still alive. Thus were the emissaries of the throne of darkness let loose upon me. Blessed be the Lord, who has brought much good out of all this evil! This concurrence of sentiment, in men of sense, unknown to each other, I considered as a satisfactory decision of the question; and determined to proceed accordingly.

One evening in November, 1763, as soon as it was dark, affecting as cheerful and unconcerned an air as possible, I went into an apothecary's shop, and asked for an half ounce phial of laudanum. The man seemed to observe me narrowly; but if he did, I managed my voice and countenance, so as to deceive him. The day that required my attendance at the bar of the

House, being not yet come, and about a week distant, I kept my bottle close in my side-pocket, resolved to use it when I should be convinced there was no other way of escaping. This, indeed, seemed evident already; but I was willing to allow myself every possible chance of that sort, and to protract the horrid execution of my purpose, till the last moment; but Satan was impatient of delay.

The day before the period above mentioned arrived, being at Richards' coffee-house at breakfast, I read the newspaper, and in it a letter, which the further I perused it, the more closely engaged my attention. I cannot now recall the purport of it; but before I had finished it, it appeared demonstratively true to me, that it was a libel, or satire, upon me. The author appeared to be acquainted with my purpose of self-destruction, and to have written that letter on purpose to secure and hasten the execution of it. My mind, probably, at this time, began to be disordered; however it was, I was certainly given up to a strong delusion. I said within myself, 'your cruelty shall be gratified; you shall have your revenge!' and, flinging down the paper, in a fit of strong passion, I rushed hastily out of the room; directing my way towards the fields, where I intended to find some house to die in; or, if not, determined to poison myself in a ditch, when I could meet with one sufficiently retired.

Before I had walked a mile in the fields, a thought struck me that I might yet spare my life; that I had nothing to do, but to sell what I had in the funds, (which might be done in an hour), go on board a ship, and transport myself to France. There, when every other way of maintenance should fail, I promised myself a comfortable asylum in some monastery, an acquisition easily made, by changing my religion. Not a little pleased with this expedient, I returned to my chambers to pack up all that I could at so short a notice; but while I was looking over my portmanteau, my mind changed again; and self-murder was recommended to me once more in all its advantages.

Not knowing where to poison myself, for I was liable to continual interruption in my chambers from my laundress and her husband, I laid aside that intention, and resolved upon drowning. For that purpose, I immediately took a coach, and ordered the man to drive to Tower wharf; intending to throw myself into the river from the Custom House quay. It would be strange, should I omit to observe here, how I was continually hurried away from such places as were most favourable to my design, to others, where it must be almost impossible to execute it; – from the fields, where it was improbable that any thing should happen to prevent me, to the Custom House quay, where every thing of that kind was to be expected; and this by a sudden impulse, which lasted just long enough to call me back again to my chambers, and was immediately withdrawn. Nothing ever appeared more feasible than the project of going to France, till it had served its purpose, and then, in an instant, it appeared impracticable and absurd, even to a degree of ridicule . . .

I left the coach upon the Tower wharf, intending never to return to it; but upon coming to the quay, I found the water low, and a porter seated upon some goods there, as if on purpose to prevent me. This passage to the bottomless pit being mercifully shut against me, I returned back to the coach, and ordered it to return to the Temple. I drew up the shutters, once more had recourse to the laudanum, and determined to drink it off directly; but God had otherwise ordained. A conflict, that shook me to pieces, suddenly took place; not properly a trembling, but a convulsive agitation, which deprived me in a manner of the use of my limbs; and my mind was as much shaken as my body.

Distracted between the desire of death, and the dread of it, twenty times I had the phial to my mouth, and as often received an irresistible check; and even at the time it seemed to me that an invisible hand swayed the bottle downwards, as often as I set it against my lips. I well remember that I took notice of this circumstance with some surprise, though it effected no change in my purpose. Panting for breath, and in an horrible agony, I flung myself back into the corner of the coach. A few drops of laudanum which touched my lips, beside the fumes of it, began to have a stupifying effect upon me.

Regretting the loss of so fair an opportunity, yet utterly unable
to avail myself of it, I determined not to live; and already half
dead with anguish, I once more returned to the Temple. Instantly I repaired to my room, and having shut both the outer
and inner door, prepared myself for the last scene of the
tragedy. I poured the laudanum into a small basin, set it on a
chair by the bedside, half undressed myself, and laid down between the blankets, shuddering with horror at what I was
about to perpetrate. I reproached myself bitterly with folly and
rank cowardice, for having suffered the fear of death to
influence me as it had done, and was filled with disdain at my
own pitiful timidity: but still something seemed to overrule
me, and to say, '*Think what you are doing! Consider, and live.*'

At length, however, with the most confirmed resolution, I
reached forth my hand towards the basin, when the fingers of
both hands were as closely contracted, as if bound with a cord,
and became entirely useless. Still, indeed, I could have made
shift with both hands, dead and lifeless as they were, to have
raised the basin to my mouth, for my arms were not at all
affected: but this new difficulty struck me with wonder; it had
the air of a divine interposition. I lay down in bed again to
muse upon it, and while thus employed, heard the key turn in
the outer door, and my laundress's husband came in. By this
time the use of my fingers was restored to me: I started up
hastily, dressed myself, hid the basin, and affecting as composed
an air as I could, walked out into the dining-room. In a few
minutes I was left alone; and now, unless God had evidently
interposed for my preservation, I should certainly have done
execution upon myself, having a whole afternoon before me.

Both the man and his wife having gone out, outward obstruc-
tions were no sooner removed, than new ones arose within.
The man had just shut the door behind him, when the convincing Spirit came upon me, and a total alteration in my sentiments took place. The horror of the crime was immediately
exhibited to me in so strong a light, that, being seized with a
kind of furious indignation, I snatched up the basin, poured
away the laudanum into a phial of foul water, and, not content

with that, flung the phial out of the window. This impulse, having served the present purpose, was withdrawn.

I spent the rest of the day in a kind of stupid insensibility; undetermined as to the manner of dying, but still bent on self-murder, as the only possible deliverance . . .

I went to bed to take, as I thought, my last sleep in this world. The next morning was to place me at the bar of the House, and I determined not to see it. I slept as usual, and awoke about three o'clock. Immediately I arose, and by the help of a rushlight, found my penknife, took it into bed with me, and lay with it for some hours directly pointed against my heart. Twice or thrice I placed it upright under my left breast, leaning all my weight upon it; but the point was broken off square, and it would not penetrate.

In this manner the time passed till the day began to break. I heard the clock strike seven, and instantly it occurred to me, there was no time to be lost: the chambers would soon be opened, and my friend would call upon me to take me with him to Westminster. 'Now is the time,' thought I, 'this is the crisis; no more dallying with the love of life!' I arose, and, as I thought, bolted the inner door of my chambers, but was mistaken; my touch deceived me, and I left it as I found it. . . .

Not one hesitating thought now remained, but I fell greedily to the execution of my purpose. My garter was made of a broad piece of scarlet binding, with a sliding buckle, being sewn together at the ends: by the help of the buckle, I formed a noose, and fixed it about my neck, straining it so tight that I hardly left a passage for my breath, or for the blood to circulate; the tongue of the buckle held it fast. At each corner of the bed was placed a wreath of carved work, fastened by an iron pin, which passed up through the midst of it: the other part of the garter, which made a loop, I slipped over one of these, and hung by it some seconds, drawing up my feet under me, that they might not touch the floor; but the iron bent, and the carved work slipped off, and the garter with it. I then fastened it to the frame of the tester, winding it round, and tying it in a strong knot. The frame broke short, and let me down again.

The third effort was more likely to succeed. I set the door open, which reached within a foot of the ceiling; by the help of a chair I could command the top of it, and the loop being large enough to admit a large angle of the door, was easily fixed so as not to slip off again. I pushed away the chair with my feet, and hung at my whole length. While I hung there, I distinctly heard a voice say three times, *''Tis over!'* Though I am sure of the fact, and was so at the time, yet it did not at all alarm me, or affect my resolution. I hung so long that I lost all sense, all consciousness of existence.

When I came to myself again, I thought myself in hell; the sound of my own dreadful groans was all that I heard, and a feeling, like that produced by a flash of lightning, just beginning to seize upon me, passed over my whole body. In a few seconds I found myself fallen on my face to the floor. In about half a minute I recovered my feet; and reeling, staggering, stumbled into bed again . . .

Soon after I got into bed, I was surprised to hear a noise in the dining-room, where the laundress was lighting a fire; she had found the door unbolted, notwithstanding my design to fasten it, and must have passed the bed-chamber door while I was hanging on it, and yet never perceived me. She heard me fall, and presently came to ask me if I was well; adding, she feared I had been in a fit.

I sent her to a friend, to whom I related the whole affair, and dispatched him to my kinsman, at the coffee-house. As soon as the latter arrived, I pointed to the broken garter, which lay in the middle of the room; and apprized him also of the attempt I had been making. – His words were, "My dear Mr Cowper, you terrify me! To be sure you cannot hold the office at this rate, – where is the deputation?" I gave him the key of the drawer where it was deposited; and his business requiring his immediate attendance, he took it away with him; and thus ended all my connexion with the Parliament office.[19]

On one level, this reads like a straightforward case-history illustrating the early Freudian theory of suicide as displaced aggression. Cowper is so appalled by his own hostility (wishing dead someone whose job he wanted) that, rather than accept responsibility for it, he turns it against himself and chooses madness and suicide. And once the decision is made, everything contributes to it: chance acquaintances in a chop-house and a tavern praise suicide as the most reasonable solution to misery. As his paranoia increases, a letter in a newspaper seems like a spiteful personal attack, urging him on to death. Above all, a vivid childhood memory of his father emerges suddenly, as though from the underworld, confirming that suicide is the answer. Yet despite all this, and despite the overwhelming sense of guilt and damnation to which he returns again and again, despite all the symptoms of a serious mental illness, Cowper was not a real suicide. Instead, the nature of his psychosis was such that it so split him into fragments that each suicidal impulse was cut short and succeeded by another impulse to self-destruction before it had any chance to take effect. The result was not suicide but a series of desperate manoeuvres each designed more to forestall death than to bring it about. It is as though the whole episode were a horrifying holding operation by which Cowper made gestures towards death – each more extreme than the last – in the hope that madness would intervene to save him. He attempted suicide in order not to die but to drive himself mad.

Madness offered an ambiguous but obvious advantage: it was an escape from the grinding responsibilities of day-to-day living. For Cowper, that meant an escape from his uncongenial profession of law, from his rapidly diminishing private income, from loneliness and pathological shyness and, above all, from the insufferable threat of a public examination for a job he, anyway, felt too guilty to take. In short, madness seemed, in his distorted perspective, to offer

a haven in which he would be cared for like a child, contained in a way he had so poignantly lacked since his
mother died.*

Certainly, his anguish was rooted in his sense of being an
outcast. At first he translated it purely theologically into an
unmovable conviction that he was guilty past redemption
and so eternally damned by God's wrath that even Hell
wouldn't have him:

> Man disavows, and Deity disowns me.
> Hell might afford my miseries a shelter;
> Therefore hell keeps her ever-hungry mouths all
> > Bolted against me . . .

These lines come from the 'Sapphics' he wrote immediately after his suicide attempt and just before he was shut
up for the first time in a mental hospital. This was, in effect,
his first serious poem. It also has the same theme as his last
and best poem, 'The Castaway', which he wrote in his final
madness thirty-six years later in 1799, the year before he
died. In that poem he compared his own fate unfavourably
to that of a sailor washed overboard and left to drown in a
storm. The sailor, incidentally, had been swept from a ship
bound from 'Albion's coast'; nine years before he had written a poem on his mother's picture in which he compared
her, in an elaborate and extended simile, to 'a gallant bark
from Albion's coast' which had safely reached port while
he himself drifted hopelessly, 'Sails ript, seams op'ning
wide, and compass lost'. What matters is that for Cowper
the destructive element is not death – the sailor dies quickly
in a business-like couplet: 'then, by toil subdued, he drank
The stifling wave, and then he sank.' The real and poignant

---

*He was right. After he was released from his lunatic asylum,
his relatives rallied round and, between them, contributed enough
to provide him with a small income for the rest of his life. He never
again had to earn his living.

horror on which he dwells in detail is the sense of being abandoned – 'Of friends, of hope, of all bereft, His floating home for ever left' – much as Cowper himself had been prematurely thrown out of his loving home as a child and set adrift in a hostile world.

The pattern of Cowper's life was one of a permanent flight. As a child he had retreated from misery into illness. Later, he sought refuge from reality in madness and suicide. Then he sought refuge from madness in religion. And when the madness returned and religion seemed beyond him, he sought refuge from both in poetry. The poetry, in fact, came late. For eight years after his first spell in the madhouse Cowper was cared for by a devoted widow while he dogsbodied for an ex-slave-trader turned evangelical Methodist called Newton, for whom he wrote a few hymns. This ended in another bout of insanity from which he never fully recovered. After it he considered himself too damned for even the mildest evangelical activity, so he devoted himself to his garden and his pets. In his mid-forties he began to write verses about them. It was these poems – 'The Task', 'John Gilpin', the verses on animals, landscape and Alexander Selkirk – which made him the most popular author of his day. All of them belong to the cosy, placid side of his character. His subject was the lovingly observed trivia of middle-class life in the Home Counties. It was, if nothing else, a distraction from the unceasing ground bass of guilt and damnation. Although Cowper ended his life in an asylum, where he wrote his masterpiece, 'The Castaway', his poems of despair, written when his madness was upon him, are slightly to one side of his main work.

Perhaps this could not have been otherwise, since the taste of his time ran altogether against any expression of private emotion, and there was no poetic style to cope with it. Even Thomas Gray was accused of impropriety in that

ideal patron: not only was he rich, influential, well connected and fashionable, a leading spirit in the Gothic Revival, he was also a forger of sorts. His novel *The Castle of Otranto* was first put out as 'a translation by William Marshall, from an Italian MS found in the library of an ancient Catholic family in the North of England, and printed in Naples in the black letter in the year 1520'. He had also mentioned those pillars of the Rowley fabric, Redcliffe Church and 'Maister Canynge' in his *Anecdotes of Painting*. Chatterton accordingly sent a contribution to the *Anecdotes*: 'The Ryse of Peyncteynge yn Englande, wroten by T. Rowlie, 1469, for Mastre Canynge'. It was an elaborate piece of fake scholarship, stuffed with detail and research, in full Rowleian dialect. As a further sweetener, he added some verse fragments. Walpole was delighted: excited to be in on a discovery and flattered to be taken for an expert by, presumably, another expert. By return he wrote Chatterton an obsequious and effusive letter, as from one learned man to another, suggesting, among other things, that he might print some of the Rowley poems.

At this point, Chatterton made a major mistake: he assumed that Walpole admired the work for its own sake, not for the snobbish gratifications it offered him. So he sent more Rowley poems and, in his enthusiasm at being taken seriously by a literary lion, he also confessed that he was not a gentleman of leisure but a penniless sixteen-year-old apprentice in search of a patron. He could scarcely have known that Walpole's meanness was as intense as his snobbery. Horrified as much at the thought of having demands made on him as at having been taken in, he dropped Chatterton flat. His own version, years later, was that he 'wrote him a letter with as much kindness and tenderness as if I had been his guardian'. The drift of it was that Chatterton's first duty was to support his widowed mother; poetry was a recreation for gentlemen. *Erst kommt das Fressen, dann kommt die Moral.* First he should make his fortune, then there would be time enough for the arts. He added that the experts he had consulted had assured him that the manuscripts were bogus. In short, he put the upstart firmly, aristocratically in his place. But he kept the manuscripts for good measure; it took several outraged letters from Chatterton to make him return them. Walpole never forgave the boy his impertinence and for years after his death he promoted an image of him as an ambitious petty swindler.

Chatterton was equally unforgiving but wholly ineffectual in his revenge. 'I cannot reconcile your behaviour to me,' he wrote to Walpole while still trying to recover his papers, 'with the notions I once entertained of you. I think myself injured, sir: and, did you not know my circumstances, you would not dare to treat me thus.'[20] Walpole called this 'singularly impertinent', but it was also singularly accurate. The overflowing talent, the facility, appetite and obsessed ingenuity which Chatterton demonstrated in every piece of writing he turned his hand to were not enough to absolve him from the original sin of having been born into the wrong class. His pride, which had always been as large as his talent, was already exacerbated by the boring, unpaid drudgery of his apprenticeship and by his menial position in the scrivener's household, where he had to eat and live exclusively with the servants and share a bedroom with the footboy. Now it was rubbed raw by Walpole's contemptuous treatment. Life among the dim, high-handed, penny-pinching Bristol elders began to seem insupportably narrow.

But it was also inescapable. As an apprentice, he was legally bound to his master, who provided only his keep, no wages. His mother gave him what she could, which was little, and the elders took his manuscripts and occasionally tipped him in return. Though his poems began to appear in magazines, he received no fees for them and, apparently, asked for none; publication was enough. Inevitably, he began to run up debts, small enough but, in his circumstances, impossible to repay.

Walpole finally returned his manuscripts in August 1769, after four months' delay. In the same month Peter Smith, a Bristol poetaster and brother of Chatterton's close school-friend William, committed suicide in a fit of pique with his family: he was twenty-one. Then, less than three months later, Thomas Phillips, who had been Chatterton's tutor and mentor at school, died suddenly. Phillips, who was only a few years older than his protégé, was himself a poet and had encouraged the boy's first efforts. It was a bad time. Chatterton began to quarrel with his pseudo-patrons and to lambast them, Walpole and anyone else who irritated him in satirical verse in the manner of the fashionable Charles Churchill. But that was, at best, a vicarious satisfaction and meanwhile his debts mounted.

By April 1770 he had reached the end of his tether. He wrote to a new friend, a distiller called Michael Clayfield, thanking him for his kindness and saying that by the time his letter arrived he would be dead. But like Freud's early patient Dora, an eighteen-year-old hysteric who wrote a suicide note in order to get her way with her parents,[21] he left the thing lying around and his master, Lambert, found it. In dismay, he passed it on to William Barrett, one of the elders with whom Chatterton had not yet quarrelled irrevocably. Barrett weighed in with advice and the following day Chatterton, who still didn't know how Barrett had got wind of the letter, wrote explaining his motives:

It is my PRIDE, my damn'd, native, unconquerable Pride, that plunges me into Distraction. You must know that 19–20th of my Composition is Pride. I must either live a Slave, a Servant;

to have no Will of my own, no Sentiments of my own which I
may freely declare as such; – or DIE – perplexing alternative!

The pride was natural enough in a boy who was not only
unprecedentedly gifted but had also been, all his life, the
only male in a doting family. It was also part of the nature
of his talent, a quality inherent in the ease with which he
deliberately created appalling medieval obstacles for his
poetry and then effortlessly overcame them. It was part,
too, of his intense personal attraction which everyone, particularly women, found so hard to resist: an unusual man-
liness, self-possession and independence; an aura, when
roused, of being passionately present, alternating with sudden fits of utter abstraction; above all, his extraordinary
grey eyes with, said Barrett, 'fire rolling at the bottom of
them'; 'a kind of hawk's eye', said George Catcott, another of the elders, 'you could see his soul through it'.

Given a character like this, his penury and social impotence, his place among servants he despised, the snubs
and condescension he had to put up with from everyone,
all created in him a sense of intolerable outrage. As a final
petty injury Henry Burgum, the stupidest of the Bristol
elders, had refused to lend Chatterton the small sum – 'in
the whole not five Pounds' – which would have cleared his
debts. His bluff had already been called humiliatingly when
his first suicide note was found. Now his pride would allow
no alternative but to try again. On Easter Saturday, with
the office presumably to himself, he settled down to write
his Last Will and Testament, prefacing it with a note announcing: 'All this wrote bet 11 & 2 oclock Saturday in the
utmost Distress of Mind.' Yet his distress is a good deal less
obvious than his anger. The Will begins with a long section
of vitriolic couplets on the three elders. The tone of the
prose that follows is equally contemptuous of the philis-

tinism of Bristol and its merchants. But he was careful not to mention his master, Lambert, as though, even when contemplating suicide, he was not willing to antagonize the one person on whom his future well-being – if he were to have a being at all – would depend.

For a suicide note it is a curiously exuberant performance; it reads as though he were enjoying himself. His own death, which he forecast for the following evening, seems far less important than his need to show everyone how sharply and unforgivingly he had seen through their pretensions. Once again he left the papers lying prominently around, once again they were promptly found. Lambert and his wife were horrified at the prospect of a suicide on their respectable premises and released Chatterton on the spot from his indentures. It was as though his most childishly omnipotent fantasies of a revenge suicide had come true. The threat of taking his own life had given him something which, before, only genuine suicide seemed to make possible: his freedom.

About a week later he left for London, confident that he would make his fortune as a writer. He had every reason to believe in his chances, since he had already published widely in metropolitan magazines whose editors had encouraged him and made vague, expansive promises. He visited them all as soon as he arrived in town and seems to have impressed them, as he impressed everybody, with his strangely impassioned, intense presence. They accepted his manuscripts and made even larger promises than before. The rich imagination which had invented Rowley transformed these hints into the visions of grandeur and success which he outlined enthusiastically in his letters to his mother and sister. For their benefit he also spun fantasies in which doors flew open at his touch and celebrities clamoured for his company.

In reality, he was living with a distant cousin of his mother's in a Shoreditch slum and, as always, was sharing his bedroom. This time his room-mate was the son of the house, who was greatly put out by Chatterton's habit of writing most of the night and then, before going to bed, strewing the floor with tiny fragments of the poems he had destroyed. Although he was publishing everywhere, churning out satiric verse, political essays and pamphlets with startling facility, he was also being systematically exploited. The editors grossly underpaid him, when they paid him at all. All his labours for the month of May brought him in only £4 15s. 9d., and even by the middle of that month, less than four weeks since his arrival in London, his luck was already running out. Two of the editors who encouraged him most were imprisoned for political reasons. The others read this, rightly, as an omen of a Government clamp-down on the Opposition press; they became proportionately cautious. Chatterton's tiny sources of income began to dry up.

Yet within another month his luck seemed to have turned again. He had written a letter championing William Beckford, the Lord Mayor of London and one of the political heroes of the day. Beckford approved of the work and consented to have another, similar letter addressed to him. Chatterton, using all his energy and charm, persuaded William Bingley to publish it in the *North Briton*, the most distinguished of all the current weeklies. Bingley was so impressed by the boy that he agreed to devote a whole issue of the paper to Chatterton's piece. Then, when the article was already set up in print, Beckford caught a cold which turned into rheumatic fever; on 21 June he died. Chatterton's great chance was gone. According to his Shoreditch relative, Mrs Ballance, 'He was perfectly frantic, out of his mind, and declared he was ruined.'

He had one final stroke of luck: a chance acquaintance in the pit of Drury Lane Theatre had introduced him to a musician, Dr Samuel Arnold. At Arnold's suggestion, Chatterton revamped an operetta he had written in Bristol a year before and sold it, early in July, to the owner of the pleasure-gardens at Marylebone. He was paid five guineas for the work, the largest fee he ever received, and probably the last.

Elated, he sent off presents to his mother and sister, but the accompanying letter made none of the usual golden predictions for the future. It was enough that he could finally make them the grand gesture he had been promising since he arrived in London three months before. The money also enabled him to make another gesture he had probably been promising himself for far longer: he rented a room of his own, a garret in Brooke Street, Holborn. It was the only room he ever had to himself.

At that point his meagre sources of income dried up entirely. Lord North's Government cracked down once more on the press, imprisoning more editors and wholly eliminating the market for Chatterton's political satires and pamphlets. Then, as the summer lengthened and the fashionable 'world' moved out of London to the country and the seaside, there was no more market for anything. He wrote one of his last and best poems, 'An Excelente Balade of Charitie'. Appropriately enough, it was the parable of the Good Samaritan updated into Rowleyese. He sent it to the one editor who had previously published a Rowley poem, but it was rejected. In Chatterton's case, neither Samaritan nor patron nor even Grub Street came to his rescue.

His Shoreditch cousin had shared the house with the family of a plasterer called Walmsley. After Chatterton died, Walmsley's niece said of him, 'He never touched meat, and drank only water, and seemed to live on the air.'

Her younger brother added, 'He lived chiefly on a bit of bread, or a tart, and some water.' By August even bread was almost beyond his means.

There was one vague hope: while he was in Bristol Chatterton, with the appetite and ease which marked his whole intellectual development, had picked up the elements of medicine from Barrett, who was a surgeon. In the eighteenth century that rudimentary training was enough to qualify him as a ship's doctor, provided Barrett would vouch for him. At the end of a letter to Catcott on 12 August he wrote: 'I intend going abroad as a Surgeon, Mr Barrett has it in his Power to assist me greatly by giving me a physical Character: I hope he will.' That the last sentence was as near a cry for help as Chatterton ever allowed himself. But it did no good. Mean-minded to the last, Barrett failed to oblige.

The August issue of the *Town and Country Magazine* was not, as he had hoped, filled with his work and none of the editors who owed him for contributions would pay up. His 'damn'd, native, unconquerable Pride' would not allow him to take whatever menial alternatives there may have been to starvation. So he hung on, 'living on the air', until 24 August. There is a story that on that day his landlady, Mrs Angel, 'as she knew Chatterton had not eaten anything for two or three days ... begged him ... to have some dinner with her. He was offended at her request, which seemed to hint to him that he was in want, and assured her he was not hungry.'[22] The story fits his character but is probably untrue; survivors of a suicide usually try to cheer themselves up after the event by showing that they, at least, were not to blame.

That night his neighbours in the lodging-house said they heard him pacing restlessly to and fro until the small hours. When he failed to appear in the morning they thought he was sleeping late. By the afternoon they were alarmed and finally forced his door. They found him, said Barrett, lying on his bed, 'a horrid spectacle, with features distorted, as if from convulsions'. He had swallowed arsenic. As always, his floor was littered with manuscripts torn into fragments no bigger than a sixpence.

No one came to identify his body at the inquest, and in the Register of Deaths they got his Christian name wrong, putting him down as 'William Chatterton'. He was buried in a pauper's grave in the Shoe Lane workhouse. He was still three months short of his eighteenth birthday.

Chatterton's tragedy is one of waste, a terrible waste of talent, vitality and promise. But it is also a peculiarly eighteenth-century tragedy of stinginess and snobbery and exploitation, a product of the high Tory, port-steeped arrogance of a time which was willing to squander any talent for the sake of its prejudices. Yet, in a way, Chatterton's abounding gifts themselves made his suicide more likely. Out of them he built a last line of defence: that pride which enabled him, as a final gesture, to destroy contemptuously all those gifts which those around him so conspicuously lacked. William James once wrote:

Mankind's common instinct for reality ... has always held the world to be essentially a theatre for heroism. In heroism, we feel, life's supreme mystery is hidden. We tolerate no one who has no capacity whatever for it in any direction. On the other hand, no matter what a man's frailties otherwise may be, if he be willing to risk death, and still more if he suffer it heroically, in the service he has chosen, the fact consecrates him forever. Inferior to ourselves in this way or that, if yet we cling to life, and he is able 'to fling it away like a flower' as caring nothing for it, we account him in the deepest way our born superior. Each of us in his own person feels that a high-hearted indifference to life would expiate all his short-comings.[23]

On these terms, Chatterton may have taken his own life ambitiously, to vindicate himself and cancel out his failure. That, certainly, accounts for the hold he has had over the imaginations of succeeding generations, despite the fact that his poetry, for good reasons, is not much read. He is the supreme illustration of the belief that those with most life and passion go soon, while those with little to lose hang on.

Yet the basic questions remain: why did he turn so readily to suicide – even if only as a gesture – when his life in Bristol became impossible? Why, pride apart, did he do it in the end? After all, pride is a superficial motive, an excuse you offer yourself for impulses you do not care to examine too closely. My own guess is that, even if his luck had been better and social prejudices less impossibly loaded against him, suicide would still not have been too far away. Certainly, what we now know of the mechanics of the act suggests most of the elements were present in Chatterton from the start. His father had died before he was born. I do not know if he was buried in the graveyard of St Mary Redcliffe but he and generations of his family had been associated with the church and had their graves there. What is sure is that, apart from a book on necromancy which the young Chatterton valued highly and kept with him until his sudden departure for London, the boy's only patrimony was a pile of old parchments his father had taken from the Muniment Room of the church, where they had been left scattered over the floor. Since some came from 'Mr Canynge's Cofre', a number of them must have concerned that wise, magnanimous patron – almost patron-saint – of the Rowley poems. In time they assumed a great emotional importance for the boy.

Despite his vast precocity, he was a slow starter. According to his sister, 'My brother was dull at learning, not knowing many letters at four years old.'[24] The master of the local infant school sent him home as unteachable, Then one day, when his mother was tearing up an old folio music book which had belonged to his father, his eye was caught by the large illuminated letters and, said his mother, 'he fell in love with them'. From then on he learned quickly. But he objected to small books, so his mother taught him to read in a big black-letter medieval bible. In other words, he was soaked from the start in a medieval world which was directly associated with his dead father.

Later, when he came to write the Rowley poems, he was not satisfied simply with writing the verse, he also took huge pains to make the calligraphy, spelling and vocabulary resemble the parchments his father had left him. The results seemed authentic enough to convince many of the amateur antiquarians of his day. Add to that the poems' framework of a benign, father-like Canynge who encouraged and cared for his devoted poet and admirer Thomas Rowley as a kind of insurance against oblivion, and who built, as his other monument for posterity, St Mary Redcliffe, the Chatterton family church. The whole extraordinary effort seems to me like an attempt to recreate an idealized image of his dead father for himself and exclusively on terms of his own making. It may even have been fantasies of this kind which possessed him when those weird fits of abstraction came over him, particularly when he was writing the Rowley poems. His friend William Smith, whose brother later committed suicide, remarked: 'There was one spot in particular, full in view of the church, in which he seemed always to take a particular delight. He would frequently lay himself down, fix his eyes upon the church, and seem as if he were in a kind of ecstasy or trance.'[25]

Chatterton was a genius – in precociousness, if not in

actual achievement – and there is never any simple mechanical explanation for that. All I am suggesting is that the need to resurrect his dead father – to set him up, as the psycho-analysts would say, in his ego – might account for some of the urgency and forwardness of his creative drive, just as it accounts more obviously for the over-all plan of the Rowley poems. It may also have made the idea of suicide, when the going got rough, more than usually tempting. As with Sylvia Plath, death might have seemed less terrible if it meant rejoining someone loved and already dead.

Yet no shadow of this gets into his poetry, except at a considerable remove of abstraction. His Rowley poems are part of the Gothic Revival, as eighteenth-century in their way as his political pamphleteering. So, too, were his reasons for suicide. They had nothing to do with imagination or poetic vulnerability or extremism. Instead, suicide was a solution to a practical problem, altogether more obvious and nasty: Grub Street failure and starvation. Arsenic merely forestalled by a few days an ending that was already inevitable.

4. The Romantic Agony

To that eminently eighteenth century figure, Dr Johnson, Chatterton was the object of a grudging, amiably condescending admiration: 'This is the most extraordinary young man that has encountered my knowledge. It is wonderful how the whelp has written such things.' The signs are that had Chatterton lived he would have developed into the kind of writer whom the Doctor found easy to praise and the nineteenth-century Romantics detested; the days of his Gothic Rowley poems were more or less over before he died, and his tastes had turned towards satire, politics and the stage.

Yet within a generation Chatterton had become the supreme symbol of the Romantic poet. Even Wordsworth, whose absorption in the 'egotistical sublime' would presumably have made him chronicly antipathetic to Chatterton's whole style of life, interests and talent, called him 'the marvellous Boy, The sleepless Soul that perished in his pride'. Coleridge wrote a 'Monody' on his death, Keats composed a lame sonnet on him, de Vigny a vastly successful and influential play, and Shelley invoked him beautifully in 'Adonais', his elegy on Keats:

> The inheritors of unfulfilled renown
> Rose from their thrones, built beyond mortal thought,
> Far in the Unapparent. Chatterton
> Rose pale, – his solemn agony had not
> Yet faded from him . . .

But of all the Romantics, only Keats seems to have used and understood Chatterton's poetry in itself. Two days after he composed the ode 'To Autumn', he wrote a letter to his friend John Reynolds:

I always somehow associate Chatterton with autumn. He is the purest writer in the English Language. He has no French idiom, or particles like Chaucer – 'tis genuine English Idiom in English Words. I have given up Hyperion – there were too many Miltonic inversions in it – Miltonic verse cannot be written but in an artful or rather artist's humour. I wish to give myself up to other sensations. English ought to be kept up.[26]

For Keats, then, the example of Chatterton's poetry itself was crucial to the development of his last, great poems. For the others, the boy's verse seems to have been largely by the way. What mattered was his way of life: the brilliant, untutored creative gift appearing out of nowhere, and his stirring combination of pride and precocity. More important still was his way of death. Although the exact circumstances and grinding financial reasons were not quite the Romantics' style, the broad outline was their ideal: the untimeliness, waste, pathos, the lack of recognition, the rejection and prematurity. For the Romantics, Chatterton became the first example of death by alienation.

The traditional combination of genius and melancholy, which had so preoccupied the Renaissance, was transformed by the Romantics into the Siamese twins of genius and premature death. 'Cover his face: mine eyes dazzle: he died young.' Given the ideal of lyric spontaneity and a unity with nature so exquisite and complete that the poet flourishes and fades like, in Shelley's words, a 'sensitive plant', it could scarcely have been otherwise.[27] Youth and poetry became synonymous. Thus Keats died in 1821 at the age of twenty-five, Shelley the next year at twenty-nine, and when Byron died two years later at thirty-six his brain and heart, according to the post-mortem, already showed symptoms of old-age: '. . . the intense atom glows A moment, then is quenched in a most cold repose.' That is from 'Adonais', the fullest and most emphatic statement of the Romantic belief that, for the poet, life itself is the real corruption, and only 'the white radiance of eternity' is pure enough for his fine sensibilities:

> Peace, peace! he is not dead, he doth not sleep –
> He hath awakened from the dream of life –
> 'Tis we, who lost in stormy visions, keep
> With phantoms an unprofitable strife,
> And in mad trance, strike with our spirit's knife
> Invulnerable nothings. – *We* decay
> Like corpses in a charnel; fear and grief
> Convulse us and consume us day by day,
> And cold hopes swarm like worms within our living clay.

What Keats – with his appetites, vigour, nerve, relish of life, and canny, restless intelligence – would have thought of all this is beside the point. Like Chatterton, he had become part of the myth. His savage treatment at the hands of the reviewers, the heart-break with Fanny Brawne may, like his early death, have been as irrelevant to his gifts as Severn's sickly posthumous portraits were to his vitality. But they were essential to the Romantic image. Keats famous, honoured, married and middle-aged would have been, for the nineteenth century, an altogether unsatisfactory figure, even if he had fulfilled every last hint of his creative genius:

> From the contagion of the world's slow stain
> He is secure, and now can never mourn
> A heart grown cold, a head grown gray in vain;
> Nor, when the spirit's self has ceased to burn,
> With sparkless ashes load an unlamented urn.

It was a Romantic dogma that the intense, true life of feeling does not and cannot survive into middle-age. Balzac defined the alternatives in *La Peau de Chagrin*: 'To kill the emotions and so live on to old age, or to accept the martyrdom of our passions and die young, is our fate.' Even Coleridge, who lived on into his prosaic sixties, seems to have subscribed to this. But where the other Romantics believed that 'the visionary powers' vanished inexorably, like youth and with youth, Coleridge alone recognized the death of his creativity as a kind of suicide. That, in fact, is the theme of his masterpiece, 'Dejection: An Ode':

> But now afflictions bow me down to earth:
> Nor care I that they rob me of my mirth:
>   But oh! each visitation
> Suspends what nature gave me at my birth,
>   My shaping spirit of Imagination.
> For not to think of what I needs must feel,
>   But to be still and patient, all I can;
> And haply by abstruse research to steal
>   From my own nature all the natural man –
>   This was my sole resource, my only plan:
> Till that which suits a part infects the whole,
> And now is almost grown the habit of my soul.
>
> Hence, viper thoughts . . .

Part of the genius of the poem is in the curious, plangent realism with which Coleridge faces the complexities of his situation, the responsibilities of dejection. If afflictions bow him down now as they could not before, it is not simply because they are more powerful and he is older, but because he himself has co-operated in his own betrayal.

That he recognized this as a form of suicide is, I think, certain, if for no other reason than that the passage reworks a theme from his 'Monody on the Death of Chatterton', a poem which was apparently on his mind for years. He had written the first, utterly undistinguished version while he was still a sixteen-year-old schoolboy at Christ's Hospital. At that stage the only hint of his own commitment to Chatterton's final solution was in the ambiguous last few lines, which no one would ever have suspected of being suicidal without an embarrassed footnote added later by someone other than Coleridge. Over the years he continued to tinker with the poem, rewriting and adding to it until it was almost twice its original length. Only in the final additions to the final version did he admit his own temptation to suicide, though still with more rhetoric than conviction:

> . . . [I] dare no longer on the sad theme muse,
> Lest kindred woes persuade a kindred doom :
> For oh ! big gall-drops, shook from Folly's wing,
> Have blacken'd the fair promise of my spring;
> And the stern Fate transpierc'd with viewless dart
> The last pale Hope that shiver'd at my heart !
> Hence, gloomy thoughts . . .

Six years later, in 1802, when he wrote his great ode 'Dejection', the same theme and echoes of the same language reappeared. Thus by the beginning of the nineteenth century the example of Chatterton haunted the imagination of the poets in their moments of crisis; he was the standard by which they measured their despair. Just as he had swallowed arsenic, so Coleridge deliberately poisoned his creative gifts by an overdose of Kant and Fichte, because to survive as a poet demanded an effort, sensitivity and continual exposure to feeling which were too painful for him. Subsequently, opium finished what metaphysics had begun. Although he went on writing verse until his death in 1834, it was, as he himself called it, 'Work Without Hope',

Poetically speaking, the last thirty odd years of his life were a posthumous existence.

Coleridge's symbolic suicide – <u>creative death by opium</u> – was to become one of the Romantic alternatives for those fated not to die prematurely: Baudelaire also had the opium habit and systematically immersed himself in *les bas fonds*; Rimbaud, who called himself a '*littératuricide*', had abandoned poetry by the age of twenty, and finished his life as a trader in Ethiopia. And so on, through a host of lesser figures. I shall return to this. For the moment, all that matters is that the image of the poet changed radically with the Romantics. He became a doomed figure; his public expected it of him.

The ground had already been prepared, within four years of the death of Chatterton, by Goethe's novel, *The Sorrows of Young Werther*. That martyr of unrequited love and excessive sensibility created a new international style of suffering:

There was a *Werther* epidemic: *Werther* fever, a *Werther* fashion – young men dressed in blue tail coats and yellow waistcoats – *Werther* caricatures, *Werther* suicides. His memory was solemnly commemorated at the grave of the young Jerusalem, his original, while the clergy preached sermons against the shameful book. And all this continued, not for a year, but for decades; and not only in Germany but in England, France, Holland and Scandinavia as well. Goethe himself noted with pride that even the Chinese had painted Lotte and Werther on porcelain; his greatest personal triumph was when Napoleon told him at their meeting, that he had read the book seven times . . .

. . . When the epidemic was at its height some officer said: 'A fellow who shoots himself for the sake of a girl he cannot sleep with is a fool, and one fool, more or less, in the world is of no consequence.' There were many such fools. One 'new Werther' shot himself with particular éclat: having carefully shaved, plaited his pigtail, put on fresh clothes, opened *Werther* at page 218 and laid it on the table, he opened the door, revolver in hand, to attract an audience and, having looked round to make sure they were paying sufficient attention, raised the weapon to his right eye and pulled the trigger.[28]

Before the craze for *Werther*, suicide for reasons more high-minded than money was thought to be a lapse of taste; now it was more than exonerated, it was fashionable. The great burst of spontaneous high feeling, which erupted like a genie from a bottle at the close of the eighteenth century, was vindicated by its very excesses. It was precisely these that demonstrated the new freedom from the rational, gossipy, powdered restrictions of the classical period. Two suicides – Werther and, in a slightly different way, Chatterton – were models of the new style of genius:

The word genius in those days was used frequently and indiscriminately, and it had a derisive secondary meaning: a 'genius' was a rather bizarre, haughty young man who made great claims for himself without having proved whether or not such claims were mere arrogance.

It follows that real geniuses, who produced as well as posed, had to live at a certain dramatic pitch – at least, in the imagination of their adoring public. At the height of the Romantic fever this personal intensity became almost more important than the work itself. Certainly, the life and work began to seem inseparable. However strenuously the poets insisted on the impersonality of art, the audience was reluctant to read them in any way except that by which Keats's tuberculosis, Coleridge's opium and Byron's incest became an intrinsic part of their work – almost an art in themselves, equal and not at all separate.

Again, *Werther* is the first and best paradigm:

In those days the public had a very personal attitude towards an author, and towards the characters of a novel too . . . The

originals of famous fictional characters were tracked down
with the utmost zeal, and, once found, their private lives were
subjected to the most unrestrained and shameless intrusions. As
Lotte, Frau Hofrat Kestner was the first victim of this treatment, to her sorrow and satisfaction; next came her husband,
who entered into the game and complained in all sincerity that,
as 'Albert', Goethe had not given him sufficient integrity and
dignity. The grave of the unhappy Jerusalem became a place of
pilgrimage. The pilgrims cursed the parson who had denied him
an honest burial, put flowers on the grave, sang sentimental
songs and wrote home about their moving experience.

An essential part of the Romantic revolution was to make
literature not so much an accessory of life – a pleasure and
recreation for gentlemen of means and leisure, as Walpole
had primly told the struggling Chatterton – but a way of
life in itself. Thus for the reading public Werther was no
longer a character in a novel, he was a model for living
who set a whole style of high feeling and despair. The rationalists of the previous generations had vindicated the act
of suicide, they had helped to change the laws and moder-
ate the primitive churchly taboos, but it was Werther who
made the act seem positively desirable to the young
Romantics all over Europe. Chatterton did much the same
for the British poets; his considerable reputation depended
not on his writing but on his death.

The Romantic stance, then, was suicidal. Byron, the most
selfconsciously doomed and dramatic of them all, remarked that 'no man ever took a razor into his hand who
did not at the same time think how easily he might sever
the silver cord of life'. Goethe, on the other hand, despite
the vast success of Young Werther's tragedy, remained
sceptical about the whole enterprise. He recounts how, in
his youth, he had so admired the Emperor Otto, who had
stabbed himself, that he finally decided that if he were not

brave enough to die in the same manner, he wasn't brave enough to die at all :

> By this conviction, I saved myself from the purpose, or indeed, more properly speaking, from the whim of suicide. Among a considerable collection of arms, I possessed a costly well-ground dagger. This I laid down nightly by my side, and, before extinguishing the light, I tried whether I could succeed in sending the sharp point an inch or two deep into my heart. But as I truly never could succeed, I at last took to laughing at myself, threw away these hypochondriacal crotchets, and determined to live.[29]

However laughable the whim may have seemed to Goethe in his maturity, the fact remains that the Romantics thought of suicide when they went to bed at night, and thought of it again in the morning when they shaved.

William Empson once remarked that the first line of Keats's 'Ode to Melancholy' – 'No, no, go not to Lethe; neither twist . . .' – 'tells you that somebody, or some force in the poet's mind, must have wanted to go to Lethe very much, if it took four negatives in the first line to stop them'.[30] In varying degrees, this was true of all the Romantics. Death was, literally, their fatal Cleopatra. But they conceived of death and suicide childishly : not as an end of everything but as the supreme, dramatic gesture of contempt towards a dull bourgeois world. *Werther's* progress was like that of the Indian Juggernaut; its triumph was measured by the number of suicides in its wake. It was the same with de Vigny's *Chatterton*, which was credited with doubling the annual suicide-rate in France between 1830 and 1840. But these epidemics of suicide *à la mode* had one belief in common: that the suicide himself would be present to witness the drama created by his death. 'Our unconscious,' said Freud, '. . . does not believe in its own death; it behaves as if it were immortal.' Thus suicide as a gesture enhances a personality which magically survives. It is as much a literary affectation as was the fashion for Werther's blue tail coat and yellow waistcoat. Freud again :

It is an inevitable result of [our complex denial of death] that we should seek in the world of fiction, in literature and the theatre compensation for what has been lost in life. There we still find people who know how to die – who, indeed, even manage to kill someone else. There alone too the condition can be fulfilled which makes it possible for us to reconcile ourselves with death; namely, that behind all the vicissitudes of life we should still be able to preserve a life intact. For it is really too sad that in life it should be as it is in chess, where one false move may force us to resign the game, but with the difference that we can start no second game, no return-match. In the realm of fiction we find the plurality of lives which we need. We die with the hero with whom we have identified ourselves; yet we survive him, and are ready to die again just as safely with another hero.[31]

At the high point of Romanticism, life itself was lived as though it were fiction and suicide became a literary act, a hysterical gesture of solidarity with whichever imaginative hero was, at that moment, the rage. 'The one desire,' said Sainte-Beuve, '. . . of all the Renés and all the Chattertons of our time is to be a great poet and to die.' When Alfred de Musset, aged twenty, was shown a particularly lovely view, he cried with pleasure, 'Ah! It would be a beautiful place to kill oneself in!' Gérard de Nerval said much the same thing on an evening walk by the Danube. Years later Nerval hanged himself – with an apron-string which, in his madness, he thought was 'the girdle Mme de Maintenon wore when she acted at Saint Cyr in *Esther*'.[32] But he was one of the very few writers who finally acted out the romantic agony to its logical end. The rest contented them-

selves with writing about it. Even Flaubert, who graduated
swiftly to far cooler things, confessed in his letters that as a
youth 'I dreamed of suicide'. He and his group of young
provincial friends, he wrote nostalgically, 'lived in a
strange world, I assure you; we swung between madness
and suicide; some of them killed themselves ... another
strangled himself with his tie, several died of debauchery in
order to escape boredom; it was beautiful!'[33]

For the young Romantics who had the attitudes but not
the gifts of their heroes, death was 'the great inspirer' and
'great consoler'. It was they who made suicide fashionable
and, during the epidemic in France in the 1830s, 'practised
it as one of the most elegant of sports'.[34] One man, when
charged with pushing his pregnant mistress into the Seine,
defended himself by saying, 'We live in an age of suicide;
this woman gave herself to death.' For the young would-be
poets, novelists, dramatists, painters, great lovers and members of countless Suicide Clubs, to die by one's own hand
was a short and sure way to fame. In the words of the hero
of a contemporary satirical novel, *Jérôme Paturot à
la recherche d'une position sociale* (1844), 'A suicide estab-
lishes a man. Alive one is nothing; dead one becomes a
hero ... All suicides are successful; the papers take them up;
people feel for them. I must decidedly make my preparations.' Jérôme may have been an object of derision but
dozens of young people had already done as he said. From
1833 to 1836, says Maigron, the papers were full of their
deaths by suicide; every morning, over coffee, *'le lecteur
peut s'en donner, avec un petit frisson, l'émotion délicieuse'*.

In England the epidemic never properly took hold. The
suicide-rate mounted, but the causes were thought to be
characteristically sturdier and more practical than literary
excess. Writing in 1840, a surgeon, Forbes Winslow,
blamed the rising figures on socialism; there was, he said, a

sudden increase after the publication of Tom Paine's *Age of Reason*. He also attributed it to 'atmospherical moisture' and, of course, masturbation – 'a certain secret vice which, we were afraid, is practised to an enormous extent in our public schools'. As a cure for the French fever of suicide he recommended cold showers and laxatives – the Public-School answer to the ultimate question.

As the nineteenth century wore on and Romanticism degenerated, the ideal of death degenerated also. In *The Romantic Agony* Mario Praz has shown how fatalism gradually came to mean fatal sex; the *femme fatale* replaced death as the supreme inspiration. *Le satanisme a gagné,*' said Baudelaire, '*Satan s'est fait ingénu.*' Homosexuality, incest and sado-masochism took over where suicide left off, if only because they seemed at the time far more shocking. As the social, religious and legal taboos against suicide lost their power, sexual taboos intensified. Fatal sex also had the added advantage of being safer and slower than suicide, an enhancement rather than the contradiction of a life dedicated to art.

5. Tomorrow's Zero:
The Transition to the
Twentieth Century

Suicide did not disappear from the arts; instead, it became part of their fabric. In their heyday the Romantics established in the popular mind the idea that suicide was one of the many prices to be paid for genius. Although that idea faded, nothing has been the same since. Suicide has permeated western culture like a dye that cannot be washed out. It is as though the Romantic epidemics in Germany and France created throughout Europe a general tolerance for the act. 'Tolerance' in both the ordinary and medical senses of the word: the public attitude became more forbearing – the suicide was no longer thought of as a criminal, whatever the outdated laws decreed – and, at the same time, the cultural system acquired a tolerance for suicide, as for a drug or a poison. It survived not merely despite the high level of suicides, it flourished because of them, rather in the way Poe and Berlioz swallowed near-lethal doses of opium during the course of unhappy love-affairs and, instead of dying, were inspired.

Once suicide was accepted as a common fact of society – not as a noble Roman alternative, nor as the mortal sin it had been in the Middle Ages, nor as a special cause to be pleaded or warned against – but simply as something people did, often and without much hesitation, like committing adultery, then it automatically became a common property of art. And because it threw a sharp, narrow, intensely dramatic light on life at its extreme moments, suicide became the preoccupation of certain kinds of post-Romantic writers, like Dostoievsky, who were the fore-runners of twentieth-century art.

At the core of the Romantic Revolution was the acceptance of a new responsibility. When, for example, the Augustans spoke of 'the World' they meant their audience, polite society; 'the World' flourished in certain salons in London and Paris, Bath and Versailles. For the Romantics, on the other hand, the world usually meant Nature – probably mountainous, certainly untamed – through which the poet moved in isolation, justified by the intensity of his unpremeditated responses – to the nightingale and the lark, the primrose and the rainbow. At first it was enough that these responses should be pure, fresh and his own, that the artist should be free from the iron conventions of classicism that had fettered him for more than a hundred years. But as the initial enthusiasm wore off it became clear that the revolution was more profound than it had first appeared. A radical reorientation had taken place: the artist was no longer responsible to polite society – on the contrary, he was often at open war with it. Instead, his prime responsibility was towards his own consciousness.

The arts of the twentieth century have inherited this responsibility and gone on from it, just as we have inherited political responsibilities – principles of democracy and self-government – laid down in the French and American revolutions. But since the discovery, or rediscovery, of the self as the arena of the arts was also concurrent with the collapse of the whole framework of values by which experience was traditionally ordered and judged – religion, politics, national cultural tradition and, finally, reason itself[35] – it follows that the new, permanent condition of the arts was depression. Kierkegaard put this first and clearest in his *Journals*:

The whole age can be divided into those who write and those who do not write. Those who write represent despair, and those who read disapprove of it and believe that they have a superior wisdom – and yet, if they were able to write, they would write the same thing. Basically they are all equally despairing, but when one does not have the opportunity to become important with his despair, then it is hardly worth the trouble to despair and show it. Is this what it is to have conquered despair?[36]

Despair was for Kierkegaard what grace was for the Puritans: a sign, if not of election, at least of spiritual potentiality. For Dostoievsky and most of the important artists since him, it is the one common quality that defines their whole creative effort. Although it seemed limiting, it became finally a way through to new areas, new norms and new ways of looking from which the traditional concepts of art – as a social grace and ornament, as an instrument of religion or even of Romantic humanitarian optimism – themselves appeared narrow and bounded. If the new concern of art was the self, then the ultimate concern of art was, inevitably, the end of self – that is, death.

Obviously, this was nothing new; perhaps half the literature of the world is about death. What was new was the emphasis and the perspective. In the Middle Ages, for example, men were preoccupied with death to the point of obsession. But for them death was an entrance to the afterlife; consequently, life itself seemed unimportant, devalued. The modern preoccupation – which began in the nineteenth century and has steadily intensified since – is with death without an after-life. Thus how you die no longer decides how you will spend eternity; instead, it sums up and somehow passes judgement on how you have lived:

From the dark horizon of my future a sort of slow, persistent breeze had been blowing towards me, all my life long, from the years that were to come. And on its way that breeze levelled out all the ideas that people had tried to foist on me in the equally unreal years I then was living through.

Meursault, the hero of Camus's *The Outsider*, achieves this bleak and thankless revelation in his great tirade against the priest who comes to solace him in the condemned cell. The closeness of death reduces to nothing all the pieties on which social morality rests. Significantly, it is a priest who helps the Outsider to this overwhelming insight, since as the power of religion weakened the power of suicide grew. It was no longer merely accepted and unshocking, it was also a logical necessity :

> I am bound to express my unbelief ... No higher idea than that there is no God exists for me ... All man did was to invent God so as to live without killing himself. That's the essence of universal history till now. I am the only man in universal history who for the first time refused to invent God.

So Kirilov in *The Possessed*, who then shoots himself. He commits what Dostoievsky calls a 'logical suicide'. Camus in *The Myth of Sisyphus* calls it 'a metaphysical crime' of which the logic, inevitably, is absurd. Camus, that is, transforms Kirilov into a twentieth-century figure. And this makes perfect sense of the depth and variety with which Dostoievsky endows the character, his mixture of seriousness and irritability, obsession, method, energy and tenderness. Yet it may be that Dostoievsky's intentions were narrower than his art. Five years after he wrote *The Possessed*, he returned to the theme of logical suicide in that extraordinary monthly document, *The Diary of a Writer*. Without the creative impersonality of a novel to qualify and thicken his responses, his involvement seems at once more urgent and, at the same time, more traditional.

On and off throughout 1876 he worried at the question of

suicide like a terrier, and would not let it be. He ransacked the newspapers, official reports, the gossip of friends, and came up with suicides because of pride, 'swinishness', even faith. He based a short story on one of them, for another he invented an elaborate speech of self-justification. And continually he returned to the one idea that suicide is inextricably entwined with the belief in immortality. In particular, he was fascinated and appalled by the suicide note of a seventeen-year-old girl: 'I am undertaking a long journey. If I should not succeed, let people gather to celebrate my resurrection with a bottle of Cliquot. If I should succeed, I ask that I be interred only after I am altogether dead, since it is very disagreeable to awake in a coffin in the earth. It is not *chic*!'[37]

It is clear why Dostoievsky should have found this irresistible: that mixture of perversity and despair was precisely the style of the heroes and heroines of his own novels. But the perversity, as he sees it, is not simple:

> She wrote about champagne from the desire, when dying, to perpetrate some cynicism as abominable and filthy as possible ... in order to insult, with this filth, everything she was forsaking on earth, to damn earth and her whole earthly life ... the boundless exasperation of that twist ... bears witness to the suffering and painful mood of her spirit, to her despair in the last moment of her life.

The level of the girl's flippancy and cynicism is directly proportional to her spiritual anguish. It is the measure of her revolt 'against the simplicity of the visible, against the meaninglessness of life'.

Dostoievsky devotes pages to this case, and keeps returning to it. But why this intensity, this need to nag away at the problem like a man enraged by a bad tooth? It may be that he found suicide a greater temptation than he would have wished to acknowledge; but that is impossible to tell.

What is certain is that the girl's elegant contempt for those who, she feels, survive stupidly, as unfeeling as oxen, is like Kirilov's desire to adorn his suicide note with a face sticking its tongue out at *them*. Both are gestures challenging the accepted order of things. By implication, they also call into question Dostoievsky's whole painful effort as a writer, for if the soul is not immortal, if the visible *is* simple and death puts a stop to everything, then life is without meaning and even his work is pointless.

Inspired, or exacerbated, by this terrible possibility, he postulated a 'logical suicide' whose arguments make the point once and for all:

I will not and cannot be happy on the condition of being threatened with tomorrow's zero.... [It] is profoundly insulting ... Now, therefore, in my unmistakable role of a plaintiff and of a defendant, of a judge and of an accused, I sentence this nature, which has so unceremoniously and impudently brought me into existence for suffering, to annihilation, together with myself.... And because I am unable to destroy nature, I am destroying only myself, weary of enduring a tyranny in which there is no guilty one.

This is Kirilov's argument stripped to its essentials. But there is also a difference: Kirilov, being a created character who exists *out there*, can follow his logic beyond the point where Dostoievsky, in the *Diary*, stops short. So where Kirilov's suicide makes him seem somehow richer and more human, that of the 'logical suicide' is petulant, faintly ridiculous, because in the end Dostoievsky will not allow himself to endorse it. 'All man did was to invent God so as to live without killing himself,' says Kirilov. That is, if you believe that everything you do is God's will, to forestall that will and take your own life is a crime against God. This is the classic argument by which Aquinas proved that suicide is a mortal sin. If, however, there is no God,

then man's will, like man's life, is his own. He therefore
becomes a god, not in any posing Nietzschean sense, but
flatly, unflatteringly; there is nothing beyond him, or
higher. Therefore the supreme assertion of his self-will is to
assume God's function and allot to himself his own death.

It was Wittgenstein who later pointed out that suicide
was the pivot on which every ethical system turns:

If suicide is allowed then everything is allowed.
If anything is not allowed then suicide is not allowed.
This throws a light on the nature of ethics, for suicide is, so to
speak, the elementary sin. And when one investigates it is like
investigating mercury vapour in order to comprehend the
nature of vapours.
Or is even suicide in itself neither good nor evil?[38]

This argument had already been acted out dramatically by
Kirilov. By his suicide he endorsed everything Camus later
came to call 'the Absurd': the belief that there are no ultimate solutions, only the world as it is in its contradictions,
flux and contrariness.

In the *Diary* Dostoievsky will not accept the perspective
of 'tomorrow's zero'. The terrible anguish he projects into
the young girl's cynicism and the 'logical suicide's' refusal
to be insulted by the meaninglessness of life is a measure of
the strain and intensity with which he himself insisted on
inventing God, almost against his instincts as an artist. 'It is
clear, then,' he writes in the *Diary*, 'that suicide – when the
idea of immortality has been lost – becomes an utter and
inevitable necessity for any man who, by his mental development, has even slightly lifted himself above the level of
cattle.' The necessity is of his own making and the tone is
strident, as though by threatening suicide he could force
God to reveal himself.

It is finally, I suspect, as much a question of his work
as of his soul. If there is nothing beyond this life and

tomorrow's terminal zero, then all that effort might as well not have been, and all those books are brought down to the level of passing gratification and vanity, along with 'the love of fish-pies, beautiful trotters, debauch, ranks, bureaucratic power, the adoration of . . . subordinates and hall porters'. Dostoievsky's ambivalent Christianity – a belief so edgy that he seemed at every moment likely to cut himself on it – was the spiritual parallel of his conservative politics. It relieved his despair by endowing it with an ultimate coherence, without which his unredeemed vision as an artist would have seemed to him insupportable.

It is, then, on the question of suicide that Dostoievsky acts as a bridge between the nineteenth century and our own. As a novelist he can create characters who act out the drama of the spiritual life when it has gone beyond religion: so Kirilov, in full consciousness and by his own inescapable logic, kills himself triumphantly. But as an individual Dostoievsky himself refuses the logic and will not let go of his traditional beliefs. Christianity was, as it were, the excuse he gave himself for writing, for continuing to celebrate the life that swarms in his books. But at the same time it was also the measure of his despair. Thus in his novels the greater the Christian love and charity, the more intense the guilt and duplicity. When the saintly Father Zosima dies, his body begins immediately to stink. It is as though somewhere Dostoievsky felt that his Christian yearnings stank in his own nostrils.*

---

*Even Tolstoy, whose acceptance of life as a supreme value in itself seems unwavering, passed through a similar suicidal crises before his religious conversion: 'The truth lay in this – that life had no meaning for me. Every day of life, every step in it, brought me nearer the edge of a precipice, whence I saw clearly the final ruin before me. To stop, to go back, were alike impossible; nor could I shut my eyes so as not to see the suffering that alone awaited me, the death of all in me even to annihilation. Thus I, a healthy and happy man, was brought to feel that I could live no longer, that an irresistible force was dragging me down into the grave. I do not mean that I had an intention of committing suicide. The force that drew me away from life was stronger, fuller, and concerned with far wider consequences than any mere wish; it was a force like that of my previous attachment to life, only in a contrary direction. The idea of suicide came as naturally to me as formerly that of bettering my life. It had so much attraction for me that I was compelled to practise a species of self-deception, in order to avoid carrying it out too hastily. I was unwilling to act hastily, only because I had determined first to clear away the confusion of my thoughts, and, that once done, I could always kill myself. I was happy, yet I hid away a cord, to avoid being tempted to hang myself by it to one of the pegs between the cupboards of my study, where I undressed alone every evening, and ceased carrying a gun because it offered too easy a way of getting rid of life. I knew not what I wanted; I was afraid of life, and yet there *was* something I hoped for from it.' That is from the long description of the crisis through which he went about the age of fifty, and described in remorseless detail in *My Confession*. He used the whole episode again, in a rather different way, in one of the most beautiful of all short stories, 'The Death of Ivan Illych'.

6. Dada: Suicide as an Art

Faced with a mid-life crisis in which the prospect of death called into question the value of their whole life and work, both Tolstoy and Dostoievsky managed to perform an *auto da fé* which enabled them to go on writing. But with the exception of T. S. Eliot, they were the last of the great writers to take what Kierkegaard called 'the leap of Faith' into orthodox religion. Lawrence and Yeats – in very different ways – invented pseudo-religions for themselves; Pasternak clung to Christianity as to a life-raft, in order to survive Stalin's terror. For the rest, whatever the social, church-going habits of the artists, Christianity was no longer integral to the fabric of their art.

'What is it to me whether God exists,' wrote Miguel Unamuno, 'unless I can live forever?' But if God does not exist, then the very shape of death changes too. It ceases to be a human, or even superhuman, presence – macabre or god-like or seductive. It is neither the dancing skeleton of the Middle Ages, nor the shrewd, powerful adversary with whom John Donne fought, nor the fatal lover of the Romantics. It ceases even to be an extension of the dying man's personality: an entry into the after-life, or a moment of revelation which, hopefully, will explain everything. Without God, death becomes simply the end: brief, flat, final. The heart stops, the body decays, life continues elsewhere. This is 'tomorrow's zero', which made Tolstoy, before his conversion, inveigh against 'the meaningless absurdity of life'. Camus saw this absurdity, this blank sense of there being nothing more to life than life itself, as the foundation on which all modern art rests. And he elaborated his theory of the Absurd in his book on the problem of suicide, *The Myth of Sisyphus*.

But Camus's conception of the Absurd was, in fact, not so much a programme for work to be done as a theory to explain an art already powerfully thriving since before the turn of the century: W. B. Yeats sensed the new and alien presence as early as 1896 when he attended the first performance of Jarry's *Ubu Roi*: 'After Stéphane Mallarmé, after Paul Verlaine, after Gustave Moreau, after Puvis de Chavannes, after my own verse, after all our subtle colour and nervous rhythm, after the faint mixed tints of Conder, what more is possible? After us the Savage God.'[39] In a sense, the whole of twentieth-century art has been dedicated to the service of this earthbound Savage God who, like the rest of his kind, has thrived on blood-sacrifice. As with modern warfare, enormous sophistication of theory and technique has gone into producing an art which is more extreme, more violent and, finally, more self-destructive than ever before.

The clearest example of the whole movement is Dada, whose reign in Paris began with a suicide, ended with one, and included others in its progress. Admittedly, Dada matters relatively little in modern literature; the serious figures associated with it were all visual artists – Arp, Schwitters, Picabia, Duchamp. But in its vague aims – they were too dispersed and anarchic to be called a programme – Dada was a caricature of the twentiety-century inheritance, magnifying and distorting most of the pressures that finer, more sophisticated and also more retiring artists were subjected to.

The aim of the Dadaists was destructive agitation against *everything*: not simply against the establishment and the bourgeoisie which made up their audience, but also against art, even against Dada itself:

> No more painters, no more writers, no more musicians, no more sculptors, no more religions, no more republicans, no more royalists, no more imperialists, no more anarchists, no more socialists, no more Bolsheviks, no more politicians, no more proletarians, no more democrats, no more armies, no more police, no more nations, no more of these idiocies, no more, no more, NOTHING, NOTHING, NOTHING.
>
> Thus we hope that the novelty which will be the same thing as what we no longer want will come into being less rotten, less immediately GROTESQUE.[40]

The raw excesses of Dada and its total rejection of all values were precipitated by the sense of universal moral bankruptcy which followed the First World War. But this was merely a speeding up of the processes of doubt and disillusion which had begun far earlier. Almost fifty years before, Rimbaud – aged seventeen but already far into a career that was to be the paradigm of the whole rejecting, contemptuous, exploratory spirit of the modern arts – had called himself a *littératuricide*. Now, after four years of pointless slaughter which changed nothing but a few boundaries, the Savage God was no longer a vague threat on the horizon; he was a looming, ubiquitous presence, blocking every view. Even Lenin seemed to have sensed him. During his exile in Zurich, he occasionally visited the Cabaret Voltaire where Dada began in 1916: 'I don't know how radical you are.' he said to a young Rumanian Dadaist, 'or how radical I am. I am certainly not radical enough. One can never be radical enough; that is, one must always be as radical as reality itself.'[41]

The central belief of Dada was that in the face of a radical reality art mattered less than outrage. Richard Huelsenbeck, the German poet and medical student who founded the movement with another German poet, Hugo Ball,* used to recite his nonsense sound-poems accompanying himself *fortissimo* on a tomtom. According to Ball, 'He wanted the [Negro] rhythm *reinforced*: he would have liked to drum literature into the ground.'[42] As it was, he and his colleagues did their best, bombarding their audiences with insults, noise and nonsense on the principle that, in the words of one of their immediate descendants, Antonin Artaud, 'All writing is garbage'.

But when art is against itself, destructive and self-defeating, it follows that suicide is a matter of course, Doubly so, since when art is confused with gesture, then the life or, at least, the behaviour of the artist *is* his work. If one is useless and worthless, so is the other. Since Dada arose as a response to the collapse of European culture during the First World War, angrily asserting by its meaninglessness the meaninglessness of traditional values, then for the pure Dadaist suicide was inevitable, almost a duty, the ultimate work of art. This is Kirilov's logic, but stripped of its redeeming despair and guilt and passion. For the Dadaists suicide would have been simply a logical joke, had they believed in logic. Since they didn't, they preferred the joke to be merely psychopathic.

The model for them all was Jacques Vaché, who was the decisive influence on André Breton, later the founder of Surrealism. Vaché was in many ways remote from the noise and abusiveness of Dada. In appearance he was a *fin de siècle* figure, a tall young man with auburn hair, elegant, exquisite, eccentric: he failed to recognize his best friends in the street, never answered letters, never said hullo or

* The story is that Ball and Huelsenbeck found the word *dada* in a French-German dictionary whilst looking for a stage name for a singer at their Cabaret Voltaire. *Dada* is French baby-talk for anything to do with horses.

good-bye. 'He lived with a young woman,' said Emile Bouvier, 'whom he obliged to remain motionless and silent in a corner while he was entertaining a friend, and whose hand he merely kissed with ineffable dignity, when she served the tea.' Although he had been an art student and was prodigiously well read, he devoted his life to systematic idleness. When Breton met him in 1916 – in a military hospital in Nantes where Vaché was recovering from a leg wound – 'he entertained himself by drawing and painting a series of postcards for which he invented strange captions. Men's fashions provided almost the only substance that nourished his imagination . . . Every morning he spent a good hour arranging one or two photographs, some saucers, a few violets on a little lace-top table within reach of his hand.'[43] Later, when he was better, he amused himself by parading the streets of Nantes dressed up as a hussar, an airman or a doctor. When Breton met him again, one year later, he was threatening the first-night audience of Apollinaire's *Les Mamelles de Tirésias* with a loaded revolver.

Vaché was at once a dandy, an exquisite and *un immoral violent* who shaped his life as a savage Ubuesque comedy. He claimed that his guiding principle was '*umore* (pronounce: umoree)', by which he meant that at a certain stage of enlightenment the futility of life becomes comic. But his particular style of comedy bristled with menace, since the humorist – or 'umorist' – like Père Ubu wilfully cultivated a kind of malignant, destructive stupidity. It was the comedy of despair gone full circle into nonsense. Vaché died according to his principles, comically and malignantly. 'I object to being killed in the war,' he had written from the front, '. . . I shall die when I want to die, and then I shall die with somebody else. To die alone is boring; I should prefer to die with one of my best friends.'[44] He did precisely that. In 1919, when he was twenty-three years old, he took an overdose of opium; at the same time, he administered the same lethal dose to two friends who had come along merely for the trip and had no suicidal intentions. It was the supreme Dada gesture, the ultimate psychopathic joke: suicide and double murder.

For the young Romantics at the height of the epidemic, to kill oneself was the next best thing to being a great artist. But for the pure Dadaist, his life and his death *were* his art. Hence Vaché's extraordinary influence on those who came after him, although almost nothing survives him except their memoirs and a volume of his letters. What he was mattered more than what he produced. Like his dandified *fin de siècle* predecessors, he treated his life as an art-object; but, as a true Dadaist, he also treated art itself as worthless. In the last analysis, Tingueley's auto-destructive sculptures and the disposable art from the wilder shores of Pop descend directly from Vaché's suicide.

It was the same with Arthur Cravan, poet, art-critic and specialist in insult, who died the year before Vaché. His works amount to little more than a few slaughter-house reviews but his legend places him securely in the Dada pantheon. According to a fighting autobiographical note he published in 1914 in his own magazine, *Maintenant*, he was 'Confidence man – sailor in the Pacific – muleteer – orange-picker in California – snake-charmer – hotel thief – nephew of Oscar Wilde – lumberjack – ex-boxing champion of France, grandson of the Queen's Chancellor, chauffeur in Berlin – etc.' No doubt much of this was untrue – that, after all, would have been in the proper spirit of Dada – like his boast that he had brought off the perfect robbery in a Swiss jewellery store. But his authenticated exploits were extraordinary enough in themselves. He travelled clear across Europe on a forged passport at the height of the First World War, then repeated this achievement in the United

States, Canada and Mexico in order to avoid conscription. (It is curious that the most violent literary figure on record should have gone to such lengths to avoid fighting in the war; perhaps legalized murder offended his sense of artistic independence.) He challenged and fought the Negro boxer Jack Johnson, the most formidable of all world heavy-weight champions – although he was realistic enough about his chances to arrive in the ring reeling drunk and be knocked out in the first round. When invited to lecture at the Exhibition of Independent Painters in New York in 1917, he turned up drunk as usual, proceeded to belch and swear at the audience of Fifth Avenue hostesses, started to strip off his clothes, and was finally dragged away, hand-cuffed, by the police. 'What a wonderful lecture,' said Marcel Duchamp, whose own contribution to the show was a signed urinal. When Cravan finally disappeared in the Gulf of Mexico, in a small boat he was sailing to Buenos Aires to meet his wife, she searched for him in all the mouldering jails of Central America. Although she never found him, she clearly knew the appropriate places to look. Another Dada work of art was complete: missing, presumed suicide.

Violence, shock, psychopathic humour and suicide, these are the rhythms of Dada. 'Suicide is a vocation,' said Jacques Rigaut, whose own suicide in 1929 is said to have marked the end of the Dada epoch. Although the evidence is that the movement had effectively expired five years earlier, when Breton broke with Tristan Tzara and set up the rival firm of Surrealism, Rigaut lived on briefly as its last, perfect flowering. Like Vaché, he was an elegant figure of self-conscious high style – so high, in fact, that he was concerned lest a prospective employer should think him *trop gigolo*. The employer was Jacques-Emile Blanche, a sedate academic painter and critic, for whom Rigaut worked as a secretary for several years. After his death, Blanche wrote of the odd contrast between Rigaut's stylishness and the shabby company he kept: 'When he would bring his Dadaistic comrades to my house, and when I would compare Rigaut's Latin face and American getup with theirs, I became conscious of the fact that the path he had chosen to follow was not his by instinct. Which would get him, Dada or the Ritz?'

The answer, as it turned out, was Dada. A friend once called Rigaut 'an empty suitcase', meaning that his baggage in life was unencumbered by any faith. In its place, as Dostoievsky had predicted, was the 'vocation' of suicide, and Rigaut fashioned his life accordingly with un-Dada-like thoroughness. As a writer, he destroyed almost everything he wrote as soon as he finished it. According to Blanche, even his affectation of accepting a life of the most conventional and futile sort was suicidal: 'The only way left to us of showing our contempt of life,' he wrote in one of the few pieces that survive him, 'is to accept it. Life is not worth the trouble it takes to leave it . . . A man who is spared worries and boredom, achieves perhaps in suicide the most disinterested of all gestures, provided he is not curious about death!'[45] His own disinterestedness was as profound as his suicide was methodical. His admirer and friend, Drieu de Rochelle, described both with a suitable elegance:

This ridiculous act, not absurd (too big a word which might have scared them off), but flat, indifferent, this is how it becomes possible. 'Going to bed one morning, instead of pressing the electric light switch, without paying attention, I make a mistake, I pull the trigger.'

This enraptured Gonzague [Rigaut] and his friends. For a brief time he had lived in a state of grace, of intimate glory. He had overcome suicide. He no longer knew if he was dead or alive, if he had fired a shot or if he had made a fire-log crack in the night.[46]

Four years before Rigaut's death the fugitive arts magazine, *La Révolution Surréaliste*, published a symposium on
the question 'Is Suicide a Solution?'. The majority of the
answers were as emphatically 'yes' as they would have
been in Paris ninety years before, although the tone was far
less effusive than that of the Romantics: 'Sir, allow me to
reply to your question by copying out the notice on my
bedroom wall: "Enter without knocking but you are re-
quested to commit suicide before leaving."' The implications of the symposium are clear: to accept suicide, in
however joky a way, was to accept the new arts, to align
oneself with the *avant garde*. But to accept it was not the
same as to do it. Of those in the symposium, only René
Crevel, 'the most beautiful of the Surrealists', who contributed one of the subtlest answers, actually went all the way.
Earlier in the same year he had described the perfect death
in his book *Détours*: 'A pot of tea on the gas stove; the
window tightly closed, I turn on the gas; I forget to light
the match. Reputation safe and the time to say one's
confiteor. . . .'[47] Eleven years later he killed himself in precisely this way. But Crevel was an exception who, as he
explained in his answer to the symposium, had been profoundly influenced as a child by the suicide of someone he
loved. So for him suicide was something more than an
article of artistic faith. Furthermore, he was not a Dadaist
but a Surrealist, and although the Surrealists, like the modern arts in general, accepted the Dada principle of attack,
continual attack on all the pieties, conventions and received, unquestioned principles on which society was established, they were already seeking, in the words of Georges
Hugnet, Surrealist and historian of Dada, 'a less anarchistic,
less offhand systematization of a struggle to be joined'. For
Dada was knowingly a dead end; its aims were incom-
patible with art in essence, not by accident. It could

scarcely have been otherwise, since it was founded not on any aesthetic but on a perverse concept of humour which viewed life as a joke in bad taste against oneself. The despair and unease which underlay this view may have been 'as radical as reality itself' but the Dada manner forbade any acknowledgement of this. Even those who were mad – and, to judge from the memoirs, Vaché, Cravan and Rigaut all seemed to have had their share of schizophrenic symptoms – did not, apparently, allow themselves to *suffer* from their madness. So they turned their anguish into jokes – ultimately suicidal perhaps, but jokes all the same. The others, more canny both in their self-preservation and their impact upon the public, merely imitated madness as it suited them. Like suicide, it was a fashionable thing to do.

'Dada is ageless', wrote Hugnet, '. . . Dada is not a *mal de siècle*, but a *mal du monde*.' It seems a vast claim for a minor movement yet, in some paradoxical way, it is true. The achievement of Dada may have been negligible in terms of work produced but in terms of artistic liberation it was disproportionately large. It helped, in its chaotic way, to open up new areas for those who followed. By treating suicide, madness and the psychopathology of everyday art as casual shock troops in their contemptuous assault on the public, they also helped to a voice those for whom despair was not an amusing alternative but a fate. Thus the grotesqueness of Dada's caricature of the modernist movement did not affect its essential accuracy. Instead, the differences were merely a matter of emphasis: all modernists assume from the start the destruction of traditional values but, unlike Dada, the others do not say so out loud. And this is neither a matter of cowardice nor of good taste but of practical survival. Twentieth-century art may start with nothing but it flourishes by virtue of its belief in itself, in the possibility of control over what seems essentially uncontrollable, in the coherence of the inchoate, and in its ability to create its own values.

The arts, that is, survive because artists continue to believe in the possibility of art in the teeth of everything that is anti-art. Dada on the other hand began by being anti-everything, including art, and ended, by the logic of caricature, by being anti-itself. Like so many of the Dadaists, Dada died by its own hand.

There was a man of double deed
Sowed his garden full of seed.
When the seed began to grow
'Twas like a garden full of snow.
When the snow began to melt
'Twas like a ship without a belt.
When the ship began to sail
'Twas like a bird without a tail.
When the bird began to fly
'Twas like an eagle in the sky.
When the sky began to roar
'Twas like a lion at the door.
When the door began to crack
'Twas like a stick across my back.
When my back began to smart
'Twas like a penknife in my heart.
When my heart began to bleed
'Twas death and death and death indeed.

— TRADITIONAL NURSERY RHYME

7. The Savage God

In talking of the collapse of values and the alienation which invariably goes with it, it is easy to strike a false note of crisis and despair which has little to do with experience and a great deal to do with theory. Life, after all, goes on, empirically and as rationally as possible, whatever the ultimate insecurities. For the artist, unlike the metaphysician, chaos is not a condition to be faced in qualified agony hourly or daily or even yearly. Rather, it is felt as an absence far back and a proportionately urgent need to create some new order for himself and from scratch; that is, it is more likely to inspire work than to frustrate it.

This, I think, was the impetus behind the first great period of modernism which followed the First World War. In this spirit, for example, T. S. Eliot wrote *The Waste Land* in Zurich, when convalescing from some kind of breakdown and, possibly, while in psychotherapy. In that poem inner chaos is projected outward on to society as the collapse of all traditional forms and values; but to express this sense of universal disintegration the poet created out of chaos itself a new style of formal order – detached, knowledgeable, subtle.

Whereas the Dadaists responded to the piercing sense of deliquescence and outrage like spoiled children – if their suitcases were empty of beliefs, then they would throw out art also – more creative figures reacted with a kind of formal passion: the greater the insecurities, the greater

their artistic effort. But at the same time, the greater their
effort to make art true to experience, the greater the risks
involved.

To put it most simply: one of the most remarkable features of the arts in this century has been the sudden, sharp
rise in the casualty-rate among the artists. Of the great pre-
modernists, Rimbaud abandoned poetry at the age of
twenty, Van Gogh killed himself, Strindberg went mad.
Since then the toll has mounted steadily. In the first great
flowering of modernism, Kafka wanted to turn his premature natural death from tuberculosis into artistic suicide by
having all his writings destroyed. Virginia Woolf drowned
herself, a victim of her own excessive sensitivity. Hart
Crane devoted prodigious energy to aestheticizing his
chaotic life – a desperate compound of homsexuality and
alcoholism – and finally, thinking himself a failure, jumped
overboard from a steamer in the Caribbean. Dylan Thomas
and Brendan Behan drank themselves to death. Artaud
spent years in lunatic asylums. Delmore Schwartz was
found dead in a run-down Manhattan hotel. Malcolm Lowry
and John Berryman were alcoholics who finally committed suicide. Cesare Pavese and Paul Celan, Randall Jar-
rell, and Sylvia Plath, Mayakovsky, Yesenin and Tsvetayeva
killed themselves. Among the painters, the suicides include
Modigliani, Arshile Gorki, Mark Gertler, Jackson Pollock
and Mark Rothko. Spanning the generations was Hemingway, whose prose was modelled on a kind of physical ethic
of courage and the control necessary at the limits of endur-
ance. He stripped his style to the bone in order to achieve
the aesthetic corollary of physical grace – a matter of great
economy, great precision, great tension under the appearance of ease. In such a perspective, the natural erosions of
age – weakness, uncertainty, clumsiness, imprecision, an
overall slackening of what had once been a highly tuned

machine – would have seemed as unbearable as losing the ability to write. In the end, he followed the example of his father and shot himself.

Each of these deaths has its own inner logic and un-repeatable despair, and to do them justice would require a degree of detail beyond my purposes here. But a simple point emerges: before the twentieth century it is possible to discuss cases individually, since the artists who killed themselves or were even seriously suicidal were rare excep-tions. In the twentieth century the balance suddenly shifts: the better the artist the more vulnerable he seems to be. Obviously, this is in no way a firm rule. The Grand Old Men of literature have been both numerous and very grand: Eliot, Joyce, Valéry, Pound, Mann, Forster, Frost, Stevens, Ungaretti, Montale, Marianne Moore. Even so, the casualty-rate among the gifted seems out of all proportion, as though the nature of the artistic undertaking itself and the demands it makes had altered radically.

There are, I think, a number of reasons. The first is the continuous, restless urge to experiment, the constant need to change, to innovate, to destroy the accepted styles. 'If it works,' says Marshall McLuhan, 'it's obsolete.' But experi-ment has a logic of its own which leads it unceasingly away from questions of formal technique into a realm where the role of the artist himself alters. Since art changes when the forms available are no longer adequate to what has to be expressed, it follows that every genuine technical revolution is parallel to a profound internal shift. (The superficial changes need not concern us since they are a matter merely of fashion and, as such, are dictated not by any inner necessities but by the economics of the art in-dustry and the demands of art-consumers.) Thus for the Romantic poets, a major gesture of their new emotional freedom was to abandon the straitjacket of the classical rhymed couplet. Similarly, the first modernists jettisoned traditional rhymes and metres in favour of a free verse which would allow them to follow precisely and without deflection the movement of their sensibilities. Technical exploration, in short, implies a degree of psychic exploration; the more radical the experiments, the deeper the responses tapped. That, presumably, is why the urge to experiment faded in the 1930s when it seemed that left-wing politics would provide all the answers, and again in England in the 1950s, when the Movement poets were busy immortalizing the securities and complacencies of life in the suburbs. Not that an experimental, *avant garde* appearance guarantees anything; it can be as easily assumed as any other fancy dress and, more easily than most, becomes an embarrassment to the timid and conventional, since its see-through design effortlessly reveals the user's lack of originality: witness the drab followers of Ezra Pound and William Carlos Williams, on both sides of the Atlantic.

But for the more serious artist experiment has not been a matter of merely tinkering with the machinery. Instead, it has provided a context in which he explores the perennial question, 'What am I?', without benefit of moral, cultural or even technical securities. Since part of his gift is also a weird knack of sensing and expressing the strains of his time in advance of other people, the movement of the modern arts has been, with continual minor diversions, towards a progressively more inward response to a progressively more intolerable sense of disaster. It is as though, by taking to its limits Conrad's dictum, 'In the destructive element immerse', his whole role in society has changed; instead of being a Romantic hero and liberator, he has become a victim, a scapegoat.

One of the most beautiful, and certainly the saddest statement of this new fate is by Wilfred Owen, who was dead before the great modernist change had properly begun. On New Year's Eve, 1917–18, he wrote to his mother:

I am not dissatisfied with my years. Everything has been done in bouts :

Bouts of awful labour at Shrewsbury and Bordeaux; bouts of amazing pleasure in the Pyrenees, and play at Craiglockhart; bouts of religion at Dunsden; bouts of horrible danger on the Somme; bouts of poetry always; of your affection always; of sympathy for the oppressed always.

I go out of this year a Poet, my dear Mother, as which I did not enter it. I am held peer by the Georgians; I am a poet's poet.

I am started. The tugs have left me; I feel the great swelling of the open sea taking my galleon.

Last year, at this time, (it is just midnight, and now is the intolerable instant of the Change) last year I lay awake in a windy tent in the middle of a vast, dreadful encampment. It seemed neither France nor England, but a kind of paddock where the beasts are kept a few days before the shambles. I heard the revelling of the Scotch troops, who are now dead, and who knew they would be dead. I thought of this present night, and whether I should indeed – whether we should indeed – whether you would indeed – but I thought neither long nor deeply, for I am a master of elision.

But chiefly I thought of the very strange look on all the faces in that camp; an incomprehensible look, which a man will never see in England, though wars should be in England; nor can it be seen in any battle. But only in Étaples.

It was not despair, or terror, it was more terrible than terror, for it was a blindfold look, and without expression, like a dead rabbit's.

It will never be painted, and no actor will ever seize it. And to describe it, I think I must go back and be with them.[48]

Nine months later Owen was back in France. Two months after that he was killed in action, exactly one week before the war ended.

There are two forces at work in this letter, each pulling in the opposite direction: nurture and nature, training and instinct, or, in Eliot's phrase, 'tradition and the individual talent'. Both are personal yet both also correspond to vital elements in his poetry. The first is traditional, which is inevitable since Owen was, in many ways, still at one with the comfortable Georgians who had no truck with the poetic changes already beginning around them. As such, he was responding in the heroic tradition of Sir Philip Sidney and, say, Captain Oates, as 'a brave man and an English gentleman'. He was going back to France because he had to do his duty as a soldier; since duty invariably means sacrifice, even the chance of the ultimate sacrifice must be accepted without fuss.

But even more strongly, there is an anti-heroic force at work which corresponds to all those elements in his writing which went to make him one of the British forerunners of modernism; it corresponds, that is, to his poems' harsh, disabused vision of the war and, technically, to their subtle, decisive use of half-rhymes which helped effectively to dispose of the chiming sweetness of much Georgian verse. It was this second force which impelled him to return to France not as 'an officer and a genteman' but as a writer. The letter is, after all, about his coming-of-age as a poet, and it was in the context of this newly matured power that he made his decision to return to the front. It seems, literally to have been a decision: he had already seen a great deal of active service and, as a result, had been hospitalized with shell-shock. Moreover, his poetry had brought him powerful friends, one of whom, Proust's translator Scott-Moncrieff, worked in the War Office and had been using his influence to get Owen a safe posting in England. It may, then, have taken as much effort and organization to return to the fighting as to stay away. What drew him back, I think, had nothing to do with heroism and everything to do with poetry. The new powers he felt in himself seem to have been inextricably linked with the strange unprecedented vision he had had in France :

> But chiefly I thought of the very strange look on all the faces in that camp; an incomprehensible look, which a man will never see in England, though wars should be in England; nor can it be seen in any battle. But only in Etaples.
>
> It was not despair, or terror, it was more terrible than terror, for it was a blindfold look, and without expression, like a dead rabbit's.
>
> It will never be painted, and no actor will ever seize it. And to describe it, I think I must go back and be with them.

That numbness – beyond hope, despair, terror and, certainly, beyond heroics – is, I think, the final quantum to which all the modish forms of twentieth-century alienation are reduced. Under the energy, appetite, and constant diversity of the modern arts is this obdurate core of blankness and insentience which no amount of creative optimism and effort can wholly break down or remove. It is like, for a believer, the final, unbudgeable illumination that God is not good. A psychiatrist has defined it, in more contemporary terms, as that 'psychic numbing' which occurs in an overwhelming encounter with death. That is, when death is everywhere and on such a vast scale that it becomes indifferent, impersonal, inevitable and, finally, without meaning, the only way to survive, however briefly, is by shutting oneself off utterly from every feeling, so that one becomes invulnerable, not like an armoured animal but like a stone :

> ... psychic closing-off can serve a highly adaptive function. It does so partly through a process of denial (If I feel nothing, then death is not taking place) ... Further, it protects the survivor from a sense of complete helplessness, from feeling him-

self totally inactivated by the force invading his environment. By closing himself off, he resists being 'acted upon' or altered ... We may thus say that the survivor initially undergoes a radical but temporary diminution of his sense of actuality in order to avoid losing this sense completely and permanently; he undergoes a reversible form of symbolic death in order to avoid a permanent physical or psychic death.[49]

Dr Lifton is, as it happens, describing the defence mechanisms brought into play by the survivors of the Hiroshima atom bomb and the Nazi concentration camps. But that awareness of a ubiquitous, arbitrary death – which descends like a medieval plague on the just and unjust alike, without warning or reason – is, I think, central to our experience of the twentieth century. It began with the pointless slaughters of the First World War, continued through Nazi and Stalinist extermination camps, through a Second World War which culminated in two atomic explosions, and has survived with genocide in Tibet and Biafra, a senseless war in Vietnam, atomic testing which poisons the atmosphere, and the development of biological weapons which kill haphazardly and more or less without control; it ends with the possibility of the globe itself shadowed by nuclear weapons orbiting in outer space.

It is important not to exaggerate; after all, this sense of disaster is, for the moment, mercifully peripheral to the lives most of us lead. To harp on it like Cassandra is as foolish, and ultimately as boring, as to ignore it completely. Yet the fact remains that the context in which our arts, morals and securities are created has changed radically:

After Hiroshima [says Dr Lifton] we can envisage no war-linked chivalry, certainly no glory. Indeed, we can see no relationship – not even a distinction – between victimizer and victim – only the sharing in species annihilation ... In every age man faces a pervasive theme which defies his engagement and yet must be engaged. In Freud's day it was sexuality and moralism. Now it is unlimited technological violence and absurd death.

In other words, that sense of chaos which, I suggested, is the driving force behind the restless experimentalism of the twentieth-century arts has two sources – one developing directly from the period before 1914, the other emerging for the first time during the First World War and growing increasingly stronger and more unavoidable as the century has gone on. Both, perhaps, are consequences of industrialism: the first is connected with the destruction of the old social relationships and the related structures of belief during the Industrial Revolution; the second is produced by the technology itself which, in the process of creating the wherewithal to make life easier than ever before, has perfected, as a kind of lunatic spin-off, instruments to destroy life completely. More simply, just as the decay of religious authority in the nineteenth century made life seem absurd by depriving it of any ultimate coherence, so the growth of modern technology has made death itself absurd by reducing it to a random happening totally unconnected with the inner rhythms and logic of the lives destroyed.

This, then, is the Savage God whom Yeats foresaw and whose intolerable, demanding presence Wilfred Owen sensed at the front. To be true to his vocation as a poet Owen felt he must describe that 'blindfold look, and without expression, like a dead rabbit's'; which meant he had to return to France and risk his life. This double duty – to forge a language which will somehow absolve from or validate absurd death, and to accept the existential risks involved in doing so – is, I think, the model for everything that was to follow. 'There exist no words, in any human language,' wrote a Hiroshima survivor, 'which can comfort guinea pigs who do not know the cause of their death.'[50] It

is precisely the pressure to discover a language adequate to
this apparently impossible task which is behind the curious
sense of strain characteristic of nearly all the best and most
ambitious work of this century.

There are, of course, other more obvious pressures, some
of which I have already touched on: the collapse of traditional values, impatience with worn-out conventions, the
minor pleasures of iconoclasm and experiment for their
own sakes. There is also the impact of what Marshall
McLuhan calls the 'electronic culture', which has so effortlessly usurped both the audience and many of the functions
of the 'formal' highbrow arts. But beyond all these, and
becoming continually more insistent as the atrocities have
grown in size and frequency, has been the absolute need to
find an artistic language with which to grasp in the imagination the historical facts of this century; a language, that is,
for 'the destructive element', the dimension of unnatural,
premature death.

Inevitably, it is the language of mourning. Or rather, the
arts take on the function of mourning, breaking down that
'psychic numbness' which follows any massive immersion
in death:

The books we need [wrote Kafka in a letter to his friend
Oscar Pollack] are the kind that act upon us like a misfortune,
that make us suffer like the death of someone we love more
than ourselves, that make us feel as though we were on the
verge of suicide, or lost in a forest remote from all human
habitation – a book should serve as the axe for the frozen sea
within us.[51]

Clearly, books of this order will not be written simply by
invoking the atrocities – a gesture which usually guarantees
nothing but rhetoric and the cheapening of all those millions of deaths. What is required is something a good deal
more difficult and individual: the creative act itself, which

gives shape, coherence and some kind of gratuitous beauty to all those vague depressions and paranoias art is heir to. Freud responded to the First World War by positing a death instinct beyond the pleasure principle; for the artist, the problem is to create a language which is both beyond the pleasure principle and, at the same time, pleasurable.

This ultimately is the pressure forcing the artist into the role of scapegoat. In order to evolve a language of mourning which will release all those backed-up guilts and obscure hostilities he shares with his audience, he puts himself at risk and explores his own vulnerability. It is as though he were testing out his own death in his imagination – symbolically, tentatively and with every escape hatch open. 'Suicide,' said Camus, 'is prepared within the silence of the heart, as is a great work of art.' Increasingly, the corollary also seems to be true: under certain conditions of stress, a great work of art is a kind of suicide.

There are two opposite ways into this dimension of death. The first is through what might be called 'Totalitarian Art' – which is, incidentally, different in kind from traditional art in a totalitarian society. It tackles the historical situation frontally, more or less brutally, in order to create a human perspective for a dehumanizing process. The second is what I have called elsewhere 'Extremist Art': the destruction is all turned inwards and the artist deliberately explores in himself that narrow, violent area between the viable and the impossible, the tolerable and the intolerable. Both approaches involve certain changes in the relationship of the artist to his material.

For Totalitarian Art the changes are both inevitable and unwilling. The simple reason is that a police state and its politics of terror produce conditions in which the intense individualism on which art is traditionally based – its absolute trust in the validity of the unique personal insight – is no longer possible. When the artist is valued, like an engineer or factory worker or bureaucrat, only to the extent to which he serves the policies of the State, then his art is reduced to propaganda – sometimes sophisticated, more often not. The artist who refuses the role refuses everything; he becomes superfluous. In these circumstances the price of art in the traditional sense and with its traditional values is suicide – or silence, which amounts to the same thing.

Perhaps this explains the phenomenal casualty-rate among the generation of Russian poets who had begun to work before the convulsions of 1917 and refused the Joycean alternative of 'silence, exile and cunning'. In 1926, after Sergei Yesenin hanged himself, first cutting his wrists and then, as a last great aesthetic gesture, writing a farewell poem in his own blood, Mayakovsky wrote, condemning him:

> In this life it is not difficult to die
> It is more difficult to live.

Yet less than five years later Mayakovsky himself, poetic hero of the Revolution and inveterate gambler who had twice already played Russian roulette with a loaded revolver, came to the conclusion that his political principles were poisoning his poetry at its source. He played Russian roulette for the last time and lost. In his suicide note he wrote laconically, 'I don't recommend it for others'. Yet several others did, in fact, follow him, apart from all those who, like Mandelstam and Babel, disappeared in the purges. Boris Pasternak wrote an epitaph on them all:

To start with what is most important: we have no conception of the inner torture which precedes suicide. People who are physically tortured on the rack keep losing consciousness, their suffering is so great that its unendurable intensity shortens the end. But a man who is thus at the mercy of the executioner is not annihilated when he faints from pain, for he is present at his own end, his past belongs to him, his memories are his and, if he chooses, he can make use of them, they can help him before his death.

But a man who decides to commit suicide puts a full stop to his being, he turns his back on his past, he declares himself a bankrupt and his memories to be unreal. They can no longer help or save him, he has put himself beyond their reach. The continuity of his inner life is broken, his personality is at an end. And perhaps what finally makes him kill himself is not the firmness of his resolve but the unbearable quality of this anguish which belongs to no one, of this suffering in the absence of the sufferer, of this waiting which is empty because life has stopped and can no longer fill it.

It seems to me that Mayakovsky shot himself out of pride, because he condemned something in himself, or close to him, to which his self-respect could not submit. That Yesenin hanged himself without having properly thought out the consequences of his act, still saying in his inmost heart: 'Who knows? Perhaps this isn't yet the end. Nothing is yet decided.' That Maria Tsvetayeva had always held her work between herself and the reality of daily life; and when she found this luxury beyond her means, when she felt that for her son's sake she must, for a time, give up her passionate absorption in poetry and look round her soberly, she saw chaos, no longer screened by art, fixed, unfamiliar, motionless, and, not knowing where to run for terror, she hid in death, putting her head into the noose as she might have hidden her head under her pillow. It seems to me that Paolo Yashvili was utterly confused, spellbound by the Shigalyovshchina of 1937 as by witchcraft; and that he watched his daughter as she slept at night and, imagining himself unworthy to look at her, went out in the morning to his friends' house and blasted his head with grapeshot from his double-barrelled gun. And it seems to me that Fadeyev, still with the apologetic smile which had somehow stayed with him through all the crafty ins and outs of politics, told himself just before he pulled the trigger: 'Well, now it's over. Goodbye, Sasha.'

What is certain is that they all suffered beyond description, to the point where suffering has become a mental sickness. And, as we bow in homage to their gifts and to their bright memory, we should bow compassionately before their suffering.[52]

Pasternak writes, I think, with the poignancy of a man who has been there himself. This is not, in any way, to imply that he had considered taking his own life – a question which is none of our business – but simply that he had endured those conditions in which suicide becomes an unavoidable fact of society. As he describes them, they are precisely the same as those which obtain, according to Hannah Arendt, when a totalitarian system achieves full power: like the victim of the totalitarian state, the suicide assists passively at the cancellation of his own history, his work, his memories, his whole inner life – in short, of everything that defines him as an individual:

> The concentration camps, by making death itself anonymous (making it impossible to find out whether a prisoner is dead or alive), robbed death of its meaning as the end of a fulfilled life. In a sense they took away the individual's own death, proving that henceforth nothing belonged to him and he belonged to no one. His death merely set a seal on the fact that he had never existed.[53]

For both the exterminated millions whom Miss Arendt writes about and for Pasternak's suicides the conditions of terror were the same: 'chaos, no longer screened by art, fixed, unfamiliar, motionless'. But the suicides retained at least one last shred of freedom: they took their own lives. In part this is a political act, both a gesture of defiance and a condemnation of the set-up – like the self-immolation of the student, Jan Palach, in Prague in 1969. It is also an act of affirmation; the artist values life and his own truths too much to be able to tolerate their utter perversion. Thus the totalitarian state presents its artists with suicide as though with a gift, a final work of art validating all his others.

It was part of Pasternak's own genius and uniqueness that he refused to be cancelled in this way and continued, by some political miracle, to write his poems and his novel as though all those improbable personal values still survived. No doubt he paid for his understanding in isolation and depression, but few others got out so cleanly. Yet neither those who survived contaminated nor those who went under ever managed to hold up the mirror to that complete corruption of nature which is the totalitarian system in action. Not necessarily for lack of trying. But despite the hundreds of attempts, police terror and the concentration camps have proved to be more or less impossible subjects for the artist; since what happened to them was beyond the imagination, it was therefore also beyond art and all those human values on which art is traditionally based.

The most powerful exception is the Pole, Tadeusz Borowski. Where the Russian poets to whom Pasternak paid his homage continued to write up to the point where they felt their whole life and work had been cancelled by history, Borowski was unique in beginning with that cancellation. In one of his Auschwitz stories, 'Nazis', he remarks sardonically: 'True, I could also lie, employing the age-old methods which literature has accustomed itself to using in pretending to express the truth – but I lack the imagination.' Lacking the imagination, he avoided all the tricks of melodrama, self-pity and propaganda which elsewhere are the conventional literary means of avoiding the intolerable facts of life in the camps. Instead, he perfected a curt, icy style, as stripped of feeling as of ornament, in which the monstrous lunacies of life in Auschwitz were allowed to speak for themselves, without comment and therefore without disguise: 'Between two throw-ins in a soccer game, right behind my back, three thousand people had been put to death.'[54] Following an almost idyllic, almost pastoral description of a lazy game of football in a setting for the moment as peaceful as an English village cricket green, the sentence explodes like a bomb. Borowski's art is one of reduction; his prose and his stories are as bare and deprived as the lives described in them. A Polish critic has pointed out that his notion of tragedy 'has nothing to do with the classical conception based on the necessity of choice between two systems of value. The hero of Borowski's stories is a hero *deprived of all choice*. He finds himself in a situation without choice because every choice is base.' Because death in the ovens came to all, regardless of their innocence or their crimes, 'the de-individualization of the hero was accompanied by a *de-individualization of the situation*'.[55] Borowski himself called his stories 'a journey to the utmost limit of a certain kind of morality'. It is a morality created out of the absence of all morality, a skilful, minimal yet eloquent language for the most extreme form of what Lifton called 'psychic numbing'. By reducing his prose to the facts and images of camp life and refusing to intrude his own comments, Borowski also contrived to define, as though by his omissions and silences, precisely that state of mind in which the prisoners lived: brutal, depersonalized, rapacious, deadly. Morally speaking, it is a posthumous existence, like that of the suicide, as Pasternak described him, who 'puts a full stop to his being . . . turns his back on his past . . . declares himself a bankrupt and his memories to be unreal'.

This, then, is Totalitarian Art; it is as much an art of

successful suicides as Extremist Art is that of the attempt. And in order to achieve it, Borowski himself underwent a progressive, triple suicide. Although he had behaved with great courage in Auschwitz, voluntarily giving up the relatively easy post of a hospital orderly in order to share the lot of the common prisoners, his first person singular narrator is callous, corrupt, well placed in the camp hierarchy, a survival artist who hates his fellow victims more than the guards because their weakness illuminates his, and each new death means a further effort of denial and a sharper guilt. Thus his first self-destruction was moral: he assuaged his guilt for surviving when so many others had gone under by identifying with the evil he described. The second suicide came after his concentration camp stories were written: he abandoned literature altogether and sank himself into Stalinist politics. Finally, having escaped the Zyklon B of Auschwitz for so long, he gassed himself at home in 1951, when he was twenty-seven years old.

The politicians and economists of disaster may talk glibly of 'thinking about the unthinkable', but for the writers the problem is sharper, closer and considerably more difficult. Like the Hiroshima survivor I mentioned earlier, Borowski seems to have despaired of ever communicating adequately what he knew: 'I wished to describe what I have experienced, but who in the world will believe a writer using an unknown language? It's like trying to persuade trees or stones.' The key to the language turned out to be deprivation, a Totalitarian Art of facts and images, without frills or comments, as depersonalized and deprived as the lives of the victims themselves. In the same way, when Peter Weiss created his documentary tragedy, *The Investigation*, he invented nothing and added nothing; he simply used a blank stage, unnamed, anonymously dressed actors, and skilfully edited fragments of the

Auschwitz trials in Frankfurt. The result was a great deal more shocking than any 'imaginative' re-creation of the camps could ever have been.

Similarly, Samuel Beckett began at the other end of the spectrum with an Irish genius for words, words, words and finished by creating a world of what Coleridge called 'Life-in-Death'. His people lead posthumous, immobile lives, stripped of all personal qualities, appetites, possessions and hope. All that remains to them is language; they palliate their present sterility by dim, ritual invocations of a time when things still happened and their emotions still stirred. The fact that Beckett's detachment and impeccable timing produce comedy out of this universal impotence only serves, in the end, to make the desolation more complete. By refusing even the temptation to tragedy and by stylizing his language to the point of minimal survival, he makes his world impregnable. He is creating a world which God has abandoned, as life might abandon some burnt-out star. To express this terminal morality he uses a minimal art, stripped of all artifact. It is the complement of Borowski's concentration camp stories, and equally deprived: the totalitarianism of the inner world.

It is here that Totalitarian and Extremist Art meet. When Norman Mailer calls the modern, statistical democracies of the West 'totalitarian', he is not implying that the artist is bound and muzzled and circumscribed as he would be in a dictatorship – a vision not even the most strenuous paranoia could justify. But he is implying that mass democracy, mass morality and the mass media thrive independently of the individual, who joins them only at the cost of at least a partial perversion of his instincts and insights. He pays for his social ease with what used to be called his soul – his discriminations, his uniqueness, his psychic energy, his self. Add to that the ubiquitous sense of violence erupting con-

tinually at the edges of perception: local wars, riots, dem-
onstrations and political assassinations, each seen, as it
were, out of the corner of the eye as just another news
feature on the television screen. Add, finally, the submerged
but never quite avoidable knowledge of the possibility of
ultimate violence, known hopefully as the balance of terror. The result is totalitarianism not as a political phenomenon but as a state of mind.

'To extreme sickness, extreme remedies,' said Montaigne.
In this instance the remedy has been an artistic revolution
as radical and profound as that which took place after
Wordsworth and Coleridge published the *Lyrical Ballads* or
Eliot brought out *The Waste Land*. In a sense it completes
the revolution which began with the first Romantics' insistence on the primacy of their subjective vision. The implied
ideal of spontaneity was acceptable in principle but not
wholly in practice since it seemed to deny what was self-
evidently undeniable: the intelligence of the artist – his
realistic understanding of the value and practical uses of his
inspiration – and the whole drab, boring labour of creativity. Hence the excesses of Romanticism were continually
counterbalanced by the criterion which Matthew Arnold,
Flaubert, James, Eliot and Joyce made so much of: that of
the artist as a disembodied, utterly detached creator whose
work is objective, autonomous, 'containing in itself', in
Coleridge's words, 'the reason why it is so and not otherwise'. These Arnoldian concepts acted as a substitute
classicism which defended the best nineteenth- and
twentieth-century artists against the weaknesses, conceit
and often downright silliness inherent in their beliefs, from
that split between feeling and intelligence which has bedev-
illed decadent Romanticism from Shelley to Ginsberg.

The opposite of all this is the post-Arnold, post-Eliot art
we have now, where the work is not set off on its own, a law

unto itself, but is, instead, in a continual, cross-fertilizing relationship with the artist's life. The existence of the work of art, that is, is contingent, provisional; it fixes the energy, appetites, moods and confusions of experience in the most lucid possible terms so as to create a temporary clearing of calm, and then moves on, or back, into auto-biography. Camus first hinted at this in *The Myth of Sisyphus* when he suggested that a man's works 'derive their definitive significance' only from his death: 'They receive their most obvious light from the very life of their author. At the moment of death, the succession of his works is but a collection of failures. But if those failures all have the same resonance, the creator has managed to repeat the image of his own condition, to make the air echo with the sterile secret he possesses.' This idea was taken up by the American poet Hayden Carruth, and applied eloquently to the situation of the arts now:

In its authenticity [life] is our own interpretation and re-organization of experience, structured metaphorically. It is the result of successive imaginative acts – it is a work of art! By conversion, a work of art is life, *provided it be true to the experiential core*. Thus in a century artists had moved from an Arnoldian criticism of life to an Existential creation of life, and both the gains and the losses were immense.

The biggest loss perhaps was a large part of what we thought we had known about art. For now we saw in exactly what way art is limitless. It is limitless because it is free and responsible: it is a life. Its only end is the adventitious cutting off that comes when a heart bursts, or a sun. Still, the individual 'piece' of art must be objective in some sense; it lies on the page, on the canvas. Practically speaking, what is a limitless object? It is a fragment; a random fragment; a fragment without intrinsic form, shading off in all directions into whatever lies beyond. And this is what our art has become in the past two decades: random, fragmentary, and open-ended.

Hence in literature any particular 'work' is linear rather than circular in structure, extensible rather than terminal in intent, and at any given point inclusive rather than associative in substance; at least these are its tendencies. And it is auto-biographical, that goes without saying. It is an act of self-creation by an artist within the tumult of experience.[56]

The break with classicism has produced, then, not a new form of Romanticism – which remains too cosy, self-indulgent and uncritical to be adequate to the realities of the period – but an existential art, as tense and stringent as its classical forebears but far less restricted, since its subject is precisely those violent confusions from which both the Augustans and the neo-classicists of the last hundred years withdrew nervously and with distaste.

For example, a poem by T. S. Eliot is opaque; it gathers the light into itself and gives back only the image of its own perfection. In contrast, a poem by Robert Lowell, though no less carefully constructed, is like a transparent filter; you look through it to see the man as he is. Similarly, in *The Armies of the Night*, Norman Mailer takes a fragment of contemporary history in which he played a part (the march on the Pentagon in October 1967), presents it, like a good journalist, in all its attendant farce, muddle and political jostling, and yet at the same time transforms it into an internal scenario in which all the conflicting, deadening facts take on a sharpened coherence as reflections in the somewhat bloodshot eye of his own developing consciousness as an artist. The politics of power are replaced by the politics of experience.

None of this absolves the artist from the labour of art – which is one reason, among many, why the confessional poets who follow Ginsberg seem so sad. On the contrary, the more directly an artist confronts the confusions of experience, the greater the demands on his intelligence, control and a certain watchfulness; the greater, too, the imaginative reserves he must tap so as not to weaken or falsify what he knows. But the intelligence required is essentially different from that of classical art. It is provisional, dissatisfied, restless. As D. H. Lawrence said of his own free verse: 'It has no finish. It has no satisfying stability, satisfying for those who like the immutable. None of this. It is the instant; the quick.'[57] What is involved, then, is an artistic intelligence working at full pitch to produce not settled classical harmonies but the tentative, flowing, continually improvised balance of life itself. But because such a balance is always precarious, work of this kind entails a good deal of risk. And because the artist is committed to truths of his inner life often to the point of acute discomfort, it becomes riskier still.

It is here that post-Arnoldian art joins with what I have called the dimension of absurd death: the artistic revolution of the last decade and a half has occurred, I think, as a response to totalitarianism in Mailer's sense of the word: not as so many isolated facts out there in another country and another political system for which somebody else is responsible, but as part of the insidious atmosphere we breathe. The nihilism and destructiveness of the self – of which psycho-analysis has made us sharply and progressively more aware – turns out to be an accurate reflection of the nihilism of our own violent societies. Since we can't, apparently, control it on the outside, politically, we can at least try to control it in ourselves, artistically.

The operative word is 'control'. The Extremist poets are committed to psychic exploration out along that friable edge which divides the tolerable from the intolerable; but they are equally committed to lucidity, precision and a certain vigilant directness of expression. In this, they have more in common with the taxingly high standards set by

Eliot and the other grand-masters of the 1920s than with the Surrealists, who were concerned with the wit, or whimsicality, of the unconscious. Out of the haphazard, baroque connections of the mind running without restraints the Surrealists created what is, essentially, a landscape art. In comparison, the Extremist artists are committed to the stage below this, a stage before what Freud called 'the dream-work' begins. That is, they are committed to the raw materials of dreams; all the griefs and guilts and hostility which dreams express only elliptically, by displacement and disguise, they seek to express directly, poignantly, skilfully and in full consciousness. Extremism, in short, has more in common with psycho-analysis than with Surrealism.

In poetry, the four leading English-language exponents of the style are Robert Lowell, John Berryman, Ted Hughes and Sylvia Plath, all of whom are highly disciplined and highly aware of formal demands and possibilities. All begin with a thickly textured, wary, tensely intelligent style they inherited ultimately from Eliot, and progress, in their different ways, towards a poetry in which the means, though no less demanding, are subordinate to a certain inner urgency which makes them push continually at the limits of what poetry can be made to bear. Inevitably so, since each of them is knowingly salvaging his verse from the edge of some kind of personal abyss. The crucial work was Lowell's *Life Studies*, in which he turned away from the highly wrought Roman Catholic symbolism of his earlier poetry in order to face – without benefit of clergy, and in a translucent, seemingly more casual style – his own private chaos as a man subject to periodic breakdowns. By some odd creative logic, compounded partly of his great natural gifts and partly of some hitherto unrecognized need in his audience – an impatience, perhaps, with strictly aesthetic criteria which took no account of the confusions and depressions of a life unredeemed by art – the more simply and personally he wrote, the more authentic and authoritative his work became. He transformed the seemingly private into a poetry central to all our anxieties.

In much the same way, John Berryman turned from the public, literary world of *Homage to Mistress Bradstreet* to the still stylized but far more intimate cycle of *Dream Songs*. These began as a quirky poetic journal of misdemeanours, gripes, hangovers and morning-after despair, then gradually clarified and deepened into an extended act of poetic mourning for the suicide of a father, the premature deaths of friends and his own suicidal despair. Berryman had always been a poet of bristling nervous energy; now his sense of grief and loss added an extra, urgent dimension to his work, impelling it through the whole process of mourning – guilt, hostility, expiation – which ends with the beautifully lucid acceptance of his own mortality. He ends, that is, by writing his own epitaph.

Ted Hughes and Sylvia Plath, belonging to a younger generation, began further along the road and explored further into the hinterland of nihilism. Thus Hughes starts with a series of extraordinary animal poems, full of sharp details and unexpected shifts of focus, in which he elegantly projects on to a whole zooful of creatures whatever unpredictable violence he senses in himself. Then gradually, as in a case of demonic possession, the animals begin to take over; the portraits turn into soliloquies in which murder is no longer disguised or excused; the poet himself becomes both predator and prey of his own inner violence. Following the example of the Yugoslav poet Vasco Popa, Hughes exercises strict control over his private monsters by making them subject to arbitrary rules, as in some psychotic child's game, but he also carries the hunt on into the darkness with exceptional single-mindedness. The result so far has been the creation of Crow, anti-hero of an anti-epic, whose one distinction is survival. Jaunty and murderous, he bobs up irrepressibly from every disaster, as unkillable as hope. But he is unkillable precisely because he is without hope. He has a beady eye only for destructiveness and his pessimism is unwavering. Hughes's other animals were all redeemed, in their different ways, by a certain instinctive grace. In comparison, Crow is irredeemable: pure death instinct.

But it is with Sylvia Plath that the Extremist impulse becomes total and, literally, final. To repeat briefly: her dissatisfaction with the elegant, rather arty style of her early poems more or less coincided with the appearance of *Life Studies*. Lowell proved that it was possible to write about these things without sinking into the witless morass of 'confessional' verse. And this was the excuse she had been waiting for, the key to unlock the reserves of pain which had built up steadily since her father's premature death when she was a child and her own suicide attempt at the age of twenty. In the mass of brilliant poems which poured out in the last few months of her life she took Lowell's example to its logical conclusion, systematically exploring the nexus of anger, guilt, rejection, love and destructiveness which made her finally take her own life. It is as though she had decided that, for her poetry to be valid, it must tackle head-on nothing less serious than her own death, bringing to it a greater wealth of invention and sardonic energy than most poets manage in a lifetime of so-called affirmation.

If the road had seemed impassable, she proved that it wasn't. It was, however, one-way, and she went too far along it to be able, in the end, to turn back. Yet her actual suicide, like Berryman's or like Lowell's breakdowns or the private horrors of Hughes, is by the way; it adds nothing to her work and proves nothing about it. It was simply a risk she took in handling such volatile material. Indeed, what the Extremists have in common is not a style but a belief in the value, even the necessity, of risk. They do not deny it like our latter day aesthetes, nor drown it in the benign, warm but profoundly muddied ocean of hippy love and inarticulateness. This determination to confront the intimations not of immortality but of mortality itself, using every imaginative resource and technical skill to bring it close, understand it, accept it, control it, is finally what distinguishes genuinely advanced art from the fashionable crowd of pseudo-*avant gardes*. On these terms, an artist could live to be as old as Robert Frost or Ezra Pound and yet, in his work, still be a suicide of the imagination.

I am suggesting, in short, that the best modern artists have in fact done what that Hiroshima survivor thought impossible: out of their private tribulations they have invented a public 'language which can comfort guinea pigs who do not know the cause of their death'. That, I think, is the ultimate justification of the highbrow arts in an era in which they themselves seem less and less convinced of their claims to attention and even existence. They survive morally by becoming, in one way or another, an imitation of death in which their audience can share. To achieve this the artist, in his role of scapegoat, finds himself testing out his own death and vulnerability for and on himself.

It may be objected that the arts are also about many other things, often belligerently so; for example, that they are preoccupied as never before with sex. But I wonder if sexual explicitness isn't a diversion, almost a form of conservatism. After all, that particular battle was fought and won by Freud and Lawrence in the first quarter of this century. The old guard may grumble and occasionally sue, but in a society where *Portnoy's Complaint* is a record-breaking best-seller sexual permissiveness is no longer an issue. The real resistance now is to an art which forces its audience to recognize and accept imaginatively, in their nerve-ends, not the facts of life but the facts of death and violence: absurd, random, gratuitous, unjustified, and inescapably part of the society we have created. 'There is only one liberty,' wrote Camus in his *Notebooks*, 'to come to terms with death. After which, everything is possible.'

The whole world can be divided into those who write and those who do not write. Those who write represent despair, and those who read disapprove of it and believe that they have a superior wisdom – and yet, if they were able to write, they would write the same thing. Basically they are all equally despairing, but when one does not have the opportunity to become important with his despair, then it is hardly worth the trouble to despair and show it. Is this what it is to have conquered despair?

– SOREN KIERKEGAARD

Life is impoverished, it loses in interest, when the highest stake in the game of living, life itself, may not be risked. It becomes as shallow and empty as, let us say, an American flirtation . . . It is evident that war is bound to sweep away [the] conventional treatment of death. Death will no longer be denied; we are forced to believe in it. People really die; and no longer one by one, but many, often tens of thousands, in a single day . . . Life has, indeed, become interesting again; it has recovered its full content.

– SIGMUND FREUD

Every battle with death is lost before it begins. The splendour of the battle cannot lie in its outcome, but only in the dignity of the act.

— PAUL-LOUIS LANDSBERG

> I balanced all, brought all to mind,
> The years to come seemed waste of breath,
> A waste of breath the years behind
> In balance with this life, this death.

— W. B. YEATS

The private terror of the liberal spirit is invariably suicide, not murder.

— NORMAN MAILER

It is the duty of the intellectuals to commit suicide as a class.

— CHE GUEVARA

The thing most feared in secret always happens...
All it needs is a little courage. The more the pain grows clear and definite, the more the instinct for life asserts itself and the thought of suicide recedes. It seemed easy when I thought of it. Weak women have done it. It needs humility not pride. I am sickened by all this. Not words. Action. I shall write no more.

— CESARE PAVESE'S last diary entry

Part 5
Epilogue: Letting Go

After great pain, a formal feeling comes –
The Nerves sit ceremonious, like Tombs –
The stiff Heart questions was it He, that bore,
And Yesterday, or Centuries before?

The Feet, mechanical, go round –
Of Ground, or Air, or Ought –
A Wooden way
Regardless grown,
A quartz contentment, like a stone –

This is the Hour of Lead –
Remembered, if outlived,
As Freezing persons, recollect the Snow –
First – Chill – then Stupor – then the letting go –

– EMILY DICKINSON

After all this, I have to admit that I am a failed suicide. It is a dismal confession to make, since nothing, really, would seem to be easier than to take your own life. Seneca, the final authority on the subject, pointed out disdainfully that the exits are everywhere: each precipice and river, each branch of each tree, every vein in your body will set you free. But in the event, this isn't so. No one is promiscuous in his way of dying. A man who has decided to hang himself will never jump in front of a train. And the more sophisticated and painless the method, the greater the chance of failure. I can vouch, at least, for that. I built up to the act carefully and for a long time, with a kind of blank pertinacity. It was the one constant focus of my life, making everything else irrelevant, a diversion. Each sporadic burst of work, each minor success and disappointment, each moment of calm and relaxation, seemed merely a temporary halt on my steady descent through layer after layer of depression, like a lift stopping for a moment on the way down to the basement. At no point was there any question of getting off or of changing the direction of the journey. Yet, despite all that, I never quite made it.

I see now that I had been incubating this death far longer than I recognized at the time. When I was a child, both my parents had half-heartedly put their heads in the gas-oven. Or so they claimed. It seemed to me then a rather splendid gesture, though shrouded in mystery, a little area of veiled intensity, revealed only by hints and unexplained, swiftly suppressed outbursts. It was something hidden, attractive and not for the children, like sex. But it was also something that undoubtedly did happen to grown-ups. However hysterical or comic the behaviour involved – and to a child it seemed more ludicrous than tragic to lay your head in the greasy gas-oven, like the Sunday joint – suicide was a fact, a subject that couldn't be denied; it was something, however awful, that people did. When my own time came, I did not have to discover it for myself.

Maybe that is why, when I grew up and things went particularly badly, I used to say to myself, over and over, like some latter-day Mariana in the Moated Grange, 'I wish I were dead.' It was an echo from the past, joining me to my tempestuous childhood. I muttered it unthinkingly, as automatically as a Catholic priest tells his rosary. It was my special magic ritual for warding off devils, a verbal nervous tic. Dwight Macdonald once said that when you don't know what to do with your hands you light a cigarette, and when you don't know what to do with your mind you read *Time* Magazine. My equivalent was this one sentence repeated until it seemingly lost all meaning: 'Iwishiweredead. Iwishiweredead. Iwishiweredead . . .' Then one day I understood what I was saying. I was walking along the edge of Hampstead Heath after some standard domestic squabble, and suddenly I heard the phrase as though for the first time. I stood still to attend to the words. I repeated them slowly, listening. And realized that I meant it. It seemed so obvious, an answer I had known for years and never allowed myself to acknowledge. I couldn't understand how I could have been so obtuse for so long.

After that, there was only one way out, although it took a long time – many months, in fact – to get there. We moved to America – wife, child, *au pair* girl, myself, and trunk-upon-trunk-load of luggage. I had a term's appointment at a New England university and had rented a great professorial mansion in a respectably dead suburb, ten miles from the campus, two from the nearest shop. It was Germanic, gloomy and far too expensive. For my wife, who didn't drive, it was also as lonely as Siberia. The neighbours were mostly twice her age, the university mostly ignored us, the action was nil. There wasn't even a television set in the house. So I rented one and she sat disconsolately in front of it for two months. Then she gave up, packed her bags, and took the child back to England. I didn't even blame her. But I stayed on in a daze of misery. The last slide down the ice-slope had begun and there was no way of stopping it.

My wife was not to blame. The hostility and despair that poor girl provoked in me – and I in her – came from some pure, infantile source, as any disinterested outsider could have told me. I even recognized this for myself in my clear moments. I was using her as an excuse for troubles that had their roots deep in the past. But mere intellectual recognition did no good and, anyway, my clear moments were few. My life felt so cluttered and obstructed that I could hardly breathe. I inhabited a closed, concentrated world, airless and without exits. I doubt if any of this was noticeable socially : I was simply tenser, more nervous than usual, and I drank more. But underneath I was going a bit mad. I had entered the closed world of suicide and my life was being lived for me by forces I couldn't control.

When the Christmas break came at the university, I decided to spend the fortnight in London. Maybe, I told myself, things would be easier, at least I would see the child. So I loaded myself up with presents and climbed on a jet, dead drunk. I passed out as soon as I reached my seat and woke to a brilliant sunrise. There were dark islands below – the Hebrides, I suppose – and the eastern sea was on fire.

From that altitude, the world looked calm and vivid and possible. But by the time we landed at Prestwick the clouds were down like the black cap on a hanging judge. We waited and waited hopelessly on the runway, the rain drumming on the fuselage, until the soaking fog lifted at London Airport.

When I finally got home, hours late, no one was there. The fires were blazing, the clocks were ticking, the telephone was still. I wandered round the empty house touching things, frightened, expectant. Fifteen minutes later, there was a noise at the front door and my child plunged shouting up the stairs into my arms. Over his shoulder I could see my wife standing tentatively in the hall. She, too, looked scared.

'We thought you were lost,' she said. 'We went down to the terminal and you didn't come.'

'I got a lift straight from the airport. I phoned but you must have left. I'm sorry.'

Chilly and uncertain, she presented her cheek to be kissed. I obliged, holding my son in my arms. There was still a week until Christmas.

We didn't stand a chance. Within hours we were at each other again, and that night I started drinking. Mostly, I'm a social drinker. Like everyone else, I've been drunk in my time but it's not really my style; I value my control too highly. This time, however, I went at the bottle with a pure need, as though parched. I drank before I got out of bed, almost before my eyes were open. I continued steadily throughout the morning until, by lunch-time, I had half a bottle of whisky inside me and was beginning to feel human. Not drunk: the first half-bottle simply brought me to that point of calm where I usually began. Which was not particularly calm. Around lunch-time a friend – also depressed, also drinking – joined me at the pub and we boozed until closing time. Back home with our wives, we kept at it steadily through the afternoon and evening, late into the night. The important thing was not to stop. In this way, I got through a bottle of whisky a day, and a good deal of wine and beer. Yet it had little effect. Towards evening, when the child was in bed, I suppose I was a little tipsy, but the drinking was merely part of a more jagged frenzy which possessed us all. We kept the hi-fi booming pop, we danced, we had trials of strength: one-arm press-ups, handstands, somersaults; we balanced pint pots of beer on our foreheads, and tried to lie down and stand up again without spilling them. Anything not to stop, think, feel. The tension was so great that, without the booze, we would have splintered into sharp fragments.

On Christmas Eve, the other couple went off on a skiing holiday. My wife and I were left staring at each other. Silently and meticulously, we decorated the Christmas tree and piled the presents, waiting. There was nothing left to say.

Late that afternoon I had sneaked off and phoned the psychotherapist whom I had been seeing, on and off, before I left for the States.

'I'm feeling pretty bad,' I said. 'Could I possibly see you?'

There was a pause. 'It's rather difficult,' he said at last. 'Are you really desperate, or could you wait till Boxing Day?'

Poor bastard, I thought, he's got his Christmas, too. Let it go. 'I can wait.'

'Are you sure?' He sounded relieved. 'You could come round at 6.30, if it's urgent.'

That was the child's bed-time; I wanted to be there. 'It's all right,' I said, 'I'll phone later. Happy Christmas.' What did it matter? I went back downstairs.

All my life I have hated Christmas: the unnecessary presents and obligatory cheerfulness, the grinding expense, the
anti-climax. It is a day to be negotiated with infinite care,
like a minefield. So I fortified myself with a stiff shot of
whisky before I got up. It combined with my child's excitement to put a glow of hope on the day. The boy sat among
the gaudy wrapping-paper, ribbons and bows, positively
crowing with delight. At three years old, Christmas can still
be a pleasure. Maybe, I began to feel, this thing could be
survived. After all, hadn't I flown all the way from the
States to pull my marriage from the fire? Or had I? Perhaps
I knew it was unsavable and didn't want it to be otherwise.
Perhaps I was merely seeking a plausible excuse for doing
myself in. Perhaps that was why, even before all the presents were unwrapped, I had started it all up again: silent
rages (not in front of the child), muted recriminations,
withdrawals. The marriage was just one aspect of a whole
life I had decided, months before, to have done with.

I remember little of what happened later. There was the
usual family turkey for the child and my parents-in-law. In
the evening we went out to a smart and subdued dinner-
party, and on from there, I think, to something wilder. But
I'm not sure. I recall only two trivial but vivid scenes. The
first is very late at night. We are back home with another
couple whom I know only slightly. He is small, dapper,
cheerful, an unsuccessful poet turned successful journalist.
His wife is faceless now but him I still see sometimes on
television, reporting expertly from the more elegant foreign
capitals. I remember him sitting at our old piano, playing
1930's dance tunes; his wife stands behind him, singing
the words: I lean on the piano, humming tunelessly; my
wife is stretched, glowering, on the sofa. We are all very
drunk.

Later still, I remember standing at the front door, joking

with them as they negotiate the icy steps. As they go through the gate, they turn and wave. I wave back. 'Happy Christmas,' we call to each other. I close the door and turn back to my wife.

After that, I remember nothing at all until I woke up in the hospital and saw my wife's face swimming vaguely towards me through a yellowish fog. She was crying. But that was three days later, three days of oblivion, a hole in my head.

It happened ten years ago now, and only gradually have I been able to piece together the facts from hints and snippets, recalled reluctantly and with apologies. Nobody wants to remind an attempted suicide of his folly, or to be reminded of it. Tact and taste forbid. Or is it the failure itself which is embarrassing? Certainly, a successful suicide inspires no delicacy at all; everybody is in on the act at once with his own exclusive inside story. In my own case, my knowledge of what happened is partial and second-hand; the only accurate details are in the gloomy shorthand of the medical reports. Not that it matters, since none of it now means much to me personally. It is as though it had all happened to another person in another world.

It seems that when the poet-journalist left with his wife, we had one final, terrible quarrel, more bitter than anything we had managed before, and savage enough to be heard through his sleep by whoever it was who was staying the night in the guest-room above. At the end of it, my wife marched out. When she had returned prematurely from the States, our own house was still let out to temporary tenants. So she had rented a dingy flat in a florid but battered Victorian mansion nearby. Since she still had the key to the place, she went to spend the night there. In my sodden despair, I suppose her departure seemed like the final nail. More likely, it was the unequivocal excuse I had been waiting for. I went upstairs to the bathroom and swallowed forty-five sleeping pills.

I had been collecting the things for months obsessionally, like Green Shield Stamps, from doctors on both sides of the Atlantic. This was an almost legitimate activity since, in all that time, I rarely got more than two consecutive hours of sleep a night. But I had always made sure of having more than I needed. Weeks before I left America, I stopped taking the things and began hoarding them in preparation for the time I knew was coming. When it finally arrived, a box was waiting stuffed with pills of all colours, like Smarties. I gobbled the lot.

The following morning the guest brought me a cup of tea. The bedroom curtains were drawn, so he could not see me properly in the gloom. He heard me breathing in an odd way but thought it was probably a hangover. So he left me alone. My wife got back at noon, took one look and called the ambulance. When they got me to hospital I was, the report says, 'deeply unconscious, slightly cyanosed, vomit in mouth, pulse rapid, poor volume'. I looked up 'cyanosis' in the dictionary: 'A morbid condition in which the surface of the body becomes blue because of insufficient aeration of the blood.' Apparently, I had vomited in my coma and swallowed the stuff; it was now blocking my right lung, turning my face blue. As they say, a morbid condition. When they pumped the barbiturates out of my stomach, I vomited again, much more heavily, and again the muck went down to my lungs, blocking them badly. At that point I became – that word again – 'deeply cyanosed'; I turned Tory blue. They tried to suck the stuff out, and gave me oxygen and an injection, but neither had much effect. I suppose it was about this time that they told my wife there wasn't much hope. This was all she ever told me of the whole incident; it was a source of great bitterness to her. Since my lungs were still blocked, they performed a bronchoscopy. This time they sucked out a 'large amount of mucus'. They stuck an airpipe down my throat and I began to breathe more deeply. The crisis, for the moment, was over.

This was on Boxing Day, 26 December. I was still unconscious the next day and most of the day after that, though all the time less and less deeply. Since my lungs remained obstructed, they continued to give me air through a pipe; they fed me intravenously through a drip-tube. The shallower my coma, the more restless I became. On the evening of the third day, 28 December, I came to. I felt them pull a tube from my arm. In a fog I saw my wife smiling hesitantly and in tears. It was all very vague. I slept.

I spent most of the next day weeping quietly and seeing everything double. Two women doctors gently cross-questioned me. Two chunky physiotherapists, with beautiful, blooming, double complexions, put me through exercises – it seems my lungs were still in a bad state. I got two trays of uneatable food at a time and tried, on and off and unsuccessfully, to do two crossword puzzles. The ward was thronged with elderly twins.

At some point, the police came, since in those days suicide was still a criminal offence. They sat heavily but rather sympathetically by my bed and asked me questions they clearly didn't want me to answer. When I tried to explain, they shushed me politely. 'It was an accident, wasn't it, sir?' Dimly, I agreed. They went away.

I woke during the night and heard someone cry out weakly. A nurse bustled down the aisle in the obscure light. From the other side of the ward came more weak moaning. It was taken up faintly from somewhere else in the dimness. None of it was desperate with the pain and sharpness you hear after operations or accidents. Instead, the note was enervated, wan, beyond feeling. And then I understood why, even to my double vision, the patients had all seemed so old: I was in a terminal ward. All around me, old men were trying feebly not to die; I was thirty-one years old, and, despite everything, still alive. When I stirred in bed I felt, for the first time, a rubber sheet beneath me. I must have peed myself, like a small child, while I was unconscious. My whole world was shamed.

The following morning my double vision had gone. The ward was filthy yellow and seemed foggy in the corners. I tottered to the lavatory; it, too, was filthy and evil-smelling. I tottered back to bed, rested a little and then phoned my wife. Since the pills and the booze hadn't killed me, nothing would. I told her I was coming home. I wasn't dead, so I wasn't going to die. There was no point in staying.

The doctors didn't see it that way. I was scarcely off the danger-list; my lungs were in a bad state; I had a temperature; I could relapse at any time; it was dangerous; it was stupid; they would not be responsible. I lay there dumbly, as weak as a new-born infant, and let the arguments flow over me. Finally, I signed a sheaf of forms acknowledging that I left against advice, and absolving them from responsibility. A friend drove me home.

It took all my strength and concentration to climb the one flight of stairs to the bedroom. I felt fragile and almost transparent, as though I were made of tissue paper. But when I got into pyjamas and settled into bed, I found I smelled bad to myself: of illness, urine and a thin, sour death-sweat. So I rested for a while and then took a bath. Meanwhile my wife, on orders from the hospital, phoned our National Health doctor. He listened to her explanation without a word and then refused, point blank, to come. Clearly, he thought I was going to die and didn't want me added to his, no doubt, already prodigious score. She banged down the receiver on him in a rage, but my green face and utter debility frightened her. Someone had to be sent for. Finally, the friend who had driven me home from the hospital called in his private family doctor. Authoritative, distinguished, unflappable, he came immediately and soothed everyone down.

This was on the evening of Thursday the 29th. All Friday and Saturday I lay vaguely in bed. Occasionally, I raised myself to perform the exercises which were supposed to help my lungs. I talked a little to my child, tried to read, dozed. But mostly, I did nothing. My mind was blank. At times I listened to my breath coming and going; at times I was dimly aware of my heart beating. It filled me with distaste. I did not want to be alive.

On Friday night I had a terrible dream. I was dancing a savage, stamping dance with my wife, full of anger and mutual threat. Gradually, the movements became more and more frenzied, until every nerve and muscle in my body was stretched taut and vibrating, as though on some fierce, ungoverned electrical machine which, fraction by fraction, was pulling me apart. When I woke, I was wet with sweat but my teeth were chattering as if I were freezing. I dozed off almost at once and again went through a similar dream: this time I was being hunted down; when the creature, whatever it was, caught me, it shook me as a dog shakes a rat, and once again every joint and nerve and muscle seemed to be rattling apart. Finally, I came awake completely and lay staring at the curtains. I was wide-eyed and shuddering with fear. I felt I had tasted in my dreams the death which had been denied me in my coma. My wife was sleeping in the same bed with me, yet she was utterly beyond my reach. I lay there for a long time, sweating and trembling. I have never felt so lonely.

Saturday night was New Year's Eve. Before I even

arrived back from the States, we had arranged a party; there seemed no point now, despite everything, in calling it off. I had promised the doctor to spend it in bed, so for a while I held court regally in pyjamas and dressing-gown. But this was an irritating, self-important posture. Friends came up to see me out of a sense of duty – they had been told I had had pneumonia. Obviously, they were bored. The music and voices below were enticing and, anyway, I had nothing now to lose. At 10.30 I got up, just to see in the New Year, I said. I got back to bed at six the following morning. At 10 a.m. I was up again and went down to help clean the house while my wife slept on. The debris of that New Year's binge seemed to me like the debris of the monstrous life I had been leading. I set to work cheerfully and with a will, mopping up, polishing, throwing things away. At lunch-time, when my wife staggered down hung over, the house was sparkling.

A week later, I returned to the States to finish the university term. While I was packing, I found, in the ticket-pocket of my favourite jacket, a large, bright yellow, torpedo-shaped pill, which I had conned off a heavily insomniac American the day I left. I stared at the thing, turning it over and over on my palm, wondering how I'd missed it on the night. It looked lethal. I had survived forty-five pills. Would forty-six have done it? I flushed the thing down the lavatory.

And that was that. Of course, my marriage was finished. We hung on a few months more for decency's sake, but neither of us could continue in the shadow of such blackmail. By the time we parted, there was nothing left. Inevitably, I went through the expected motions of distress. But in my heart, I no longer cared.

The truth is, in some way I *had* died. The over-intensity, the tiresome excess of sensitivity and self-consciousness, of arrogance and idealism, which came in adolescence and stayed on and on beyond their due time, like some visiting bore, had not survived the coma. It was as though I had finally, and sadly late in the day, lost my innocence. Like all young people, I had been high-minded and apologetic, full of enthusiasms I didn't quite mean and guilts I didn't understand. Because of them, I had forced my poor wife, who was far too young to know what was happening, into a spoiling, destructive role she had never sought. We had spent five years thrashing around in confusion, as drowning men pull each other under. Then I had lain for three days in abeyance, and woken to feel nothing but a faint revulsion from everything and everyone. My weakened body, my thin breath, the slightest flicker of emotion filled me with distaste. I wanted only to be left to myself. Then, as the months passed, I began gradually to stir into another style of life, less theoretical, less optimistic, less vulnerable. I was ready for an insentient middle age.

Above all, I was disappointed. Somehow, I felt, death had let me down; I had expected more of it. I had looked for something overwhelming, an experience which would clarify all my confusions. But it turned out to be simply a denial of experience. All I knew of death was the terrifying dreams which came later. Blame it, perhaps, on my delayed adolescence: adolescents always expect too much; they want solutions to be immediate and neat, instead of gradual and incomplete. Or blame it on the cinema: secretly, I had thought death would be like the last reel of one of those old Hitchcock thrillers, when the hero relives as an adult that traumatic moment in childhood when the horror and splitting-off took place; and thereby becomes free and at peace with himself. It is a well-established, much imitated and persuasive formula. Hitchcock does it best but he himself did not invent it; he was simply popularizing a new tradition of half-digested psycho-analytic talk about 'abreaction', that crucial moment of cathartic truth when the complex is removed. Behind that is the old belief in last-moment revelations, death-bed conversions, and all those old wives' tales of the drowning man reliving his life as he goes down for the last time. Behind that again is an older tradition still: that of the Last Judgement and the after-life. We all expect something of death, even if it's only damnation.

But all I had got was oblivion. To all intents and purposes, I had died: my face had been blue, my pulse erratic, my breathing ineffectual; the doctors had given me up. I went to the edge and most of the way over; then gradually, unwillingly and despite everything, I inched my way back. And now I knew nothing at all about it. I felt cheated.

Why had I been so sure of finding some kind of answer? There are always special reasons why a man should choose to die in one way rather than in another, and my own reasons for taking barbiturates were cogent enough, although I did not recognize them at the time. As a small baby, I had been given a general anaesthetic when a major operation was performed on my ankle. The surgery had not been a great success and regularly throughout my childhood the thing gave me trouble. Always the attacks were heralded by the same dream: I had to work out a complicated mathematical problem which involved my whole family; their well-being depended on my finding the right answer. The sum changed as I grew, becoming more sophisticated as I learned more mathematics, always keeping one step ahead of me, like the carrot and the donkey. Yet I knew that however complex the problem, the answer would be simple. It merely eluded me. Then, when I was fourteen, my appendix was removed and I was once again put under a general anaesthetic. The dream, by then, had not recurred for a year or two. But as I began to breathe in the ether, the whole thing happened again. When the first sharp draught of gas entered my lungs, I saw the problem, this time in calculus, glowing like a neon sign, with all my family crowding around, dangling, as it were, from the terms. I breathed out and then, as I drew in the next lungful of ether, the figures whirred like the circuits of a computer, the stages of the equation raced in front of me, and I had the answer: a simple two-figure number. I had known it all along. For three days after I came round, I still knew that simple solution, and why and how it was so. I didn't have a care in the world. Then gradually it faded. But the dream never returned.

I thought death would be like that: a synoptic vision of life, crisis by crisis, all suddenly explained, justified, redeemed, a Last Judgement in the coils and circuits of the brain. Instead, all I got was a hole in the head, a round zero, nothing. I'd been swindled.

Months later, i began to understand that I had had my answer, after all. The despair that had led me to try to kill myself had been pure and unadulterated, like the final, unanswerable despair a child feels, with no before or after. And, childishly, I had expected death not merely to end it but also to explain it. Then, when death let me down, I gradually saw that I had been using the wrong language; I had translated the thing into Americanese. Too many movies, too many novels, too many trips to the States had switched my understanding into a hopeful, alien tongue. I no longer thought of myself as unhappy; instead, I had 'problems'. Which is an optimistic way of putting it, since problems imply solutions, whereas unhappiness is merely a condition of life which you must live with, like the weather. Once I had accepted that there weren't ever going to be any answers, even in death, I found to my surprise that I didn't much care whether I was happy or unhappy; 'problems' and 'the problem of problems' no longer existed. And that in itself is already the beginning of happiness.

It seems ludicrous now to have learned something so obvious in such a hard way, to have had to go almost the whole way into death in order to grow up. Somewhere, I still feel cheated and aggrieved, and also ashamed of my stupidity. Yet, in the end, even oblivion was an experience of a kind. Certainly, nothing has been quite the same since I discovered for myself, in my own body and on my own nerves, that death is simply an end, a dead end, no more, no less. And I wonder if that piece of knowledge isn't in itself a form of death. After all, the youth who swallowed the sleeping pills and the man who survived are so utterly different that someone or something must have died. Before the pills was another life, another person altogether, whom I scarcely recognize and don't much like – although I suspect that he was, in his priggish way, far more likeable than I could ever be. Meanwhile, his fury and despair seem improbable now, sad and oddly diminished.

The hole in my head lasted a long time. For five years after the event I had periods of sheer blankness, as though some vital centre had been knocked out of action. For days on end I went round like a zombie, a walking corpse. And I used to wonder, in a vague, numb way, if maybe I had died, after all. But if so, how could I ever tell?

In time, even that passed. Years later, when the house where it had happened was finally sold, I felt a sharp pang of regret for all the exorbitant pain and waste. After that, the episode lost its power. It became just so much dead history, a gossipy, mildly interesting anecdote about someone half-forgotten. As Coriolanus said, 'There is a world elsewhere.'

As for suicide: the sociologists and psychologists who

talk of it as a disease puzzle me now as much as the Catholics and Muslims who call it the most deadly of mortal sins. It seems to me to be somehow as much beyond social or psychic prophylaxis as it is beyond morality, a terrible but utterly natural reaction to the strained, narrow, unnatural necessities we sometimes create for ourselves. And it is not for me. Perhaps I am no longer optimistic enough. I assume now that death, when it finally comes, will probably be nastier than suicide, and certainly a great deal less convenient.

Life *is*, in fact, a battle. Evil is insolent and strong; beauty enchanting but rare; goodness very apt to be weak; folly very apt to be defiant; wickedness to carry the day; imbeciles to be in great places, people of sense in small, and mankind generally unhappy. But the world as it stands is no illusion, no phantasm, no evil dream of a night; we wake up to it again for ever and ever; we can neither forget it nor deny it nor dispense with it.

— HENRY JAMES

Dieu a tout fait de rien. Mais le rien perce.

— PAUL VALÉRY

Notes

2. THE BACKGROUND

1 Quoted by E. H. Carr, *The Romantic Exiles*, Harmondsworth, 1949, p. 389.

2 Both quotations from Glanville Williams, *The Sanctity of Life and the Criminal Law*, New York, 1957, and London, 1958, p. 233.

3 See Emile Durkheim, *Suicide*, trans. J. A. Spaulding and G. Simpson, New York, 1951, and London, 1952, pp. 327–30.

4 Quoted by Giles Romilly Fedden, *Suicide*, London and Toronto, 1938, p. 224. In this section I have leaned heavily and gratefully on this learned but unusually readable book.

5 Fedden, op. cit., p. 223.

6 *The Connoisseur*, quoted in Charles More, *A Full Enquiry into the Subject of Suicide*, 2 vols., London, 1790, 1, pp. 323–4.

7 See Fedden, op. cit., pp. 27–48, who gives many other examples.

8 Glanville Williams, op. cit., p. 233.

9 *The Times*, 21 January, 1970. See also 26 and 27 January, 1970.

10 John Donne, *Biathanatos*, Part 1, Distinction 3, Section 2, Facsimile Text Society, New York, 1930, p 58.

11 See Freud, 'Totem and Taboo', *Complete Psychological Works*, ed. James Strachey *et al.*, Vol. XIII, London, 1962, especially pp. 18–74.

12 J. G. Frazer, *The Golden Bough*, abridged edition. New York, 1959, and London, 1960, p. 467.

13 See More, op. cit., 1, p. 147.

14 Rapin's *Introduction to the History of England*, quoted by More, op. cit., 1, p. 149 fn.

15 Gregory Zilboorg, 'Suicide Among Civilized and Primitive Races', *American Journal of Psychiatry*, Vol. 92, 1936, p. 1,362.

16 See Durkheim, op. cit., p. 218.

17 op. cit., p. 1,368.

18 J. Wisse, *Selbstmord und Todesfurcht bei den Naturvolkern*, Zutphen, 1933, pp. 207–8, quoted by Zilboorg, op. cit., pp. 1,352–3.

19 See Fedden, op. cit., pp. 55, 59.

20 Libanius, quoted by Durkheim, op. cit., p. 330.

21 Fedden, op. cit., p. 83.

22 Both these quotations are taken from Fedden, op. cit., pp. 79–80.

23 Fedden, op. cit., p. 50.

24 Quoted by Helen Silving, 'Suicide and Law', in *Clues to Suicide*, ed. Edwin S. Shneidman and Norman L. Farberow, New York, 1957, and Maidenhead, 1963, pp. 80–1.

25 See Fedden, op. cit., p. 93.

26 Donne, op. cit., p. 54.

27 Quoted by Fedden, op. cit., p. 84.

28 See Donne, op. cit., pp. 64–5.

29 ibid., p. 66.

30 ibid., p. 60.

31 ibid., pp. 63, 65.

32 Gibbon, *Decline and Fall of the Roman Empire*, III, p. 401, quoted by More, op. cit., I, p. 290.

33 Helen Silving, loc. cit., p. 81–2.

34 Glanville Williams, op. cit., p. 226, quoting Perlson and Karpman, 'Psychopathologic and Psycopathetic Reaction in Dogs', *Quarterly Journal of Criminal Psychopathology*, 1943, pp. 514–5.

35 Henry Morselli, *Suicide*, London, 1881, p. 3.

3. THE CLOSED WORLD OF SUICIDE

1 K. R. Eissler, *The Psychiatrist and the Dying Patient*, New York and Folkestone, 1955, p. 67.

2 Erwin Stengel, *Suicide and Attempted Suicide*, revised edition, Harmondsworth, 1969, p. 37.

3 Muralt's *Letters on the French and English Nations*, quoted in Charles More, *A Full Enquiry into the Subject of Suicide*, 2 vols., London, 1790, 1, p. 377.

4 *The Spirit of the Laws*, translated by Mr Nugent, London, 1752, Book xiv, ch. xii, pp. 330–31.

5 See Stengel, op. cit., p. 22.

6 Cesare Pavese, *This Business of Living*, translated by A. E. Murch, London and Toronto, 1961, p. 59. All subsequent quotations from Pavese are from this volume.

7 Forbes Winslow, *The Anatomy of Suicide*, London, 1840, p. 202.

8 Jack D. Douglas, *The Social Meanings of Suicide*, Princeton, 1967, and London, 1968, p. 275.

9 Stengel, op. cit., p. 14.

10 Margarethe von Andics, *Suicide and the Meaning of Life*, London and Washington, 1947, p. 94 *et seq.*

11 J. Tas, 'Psychical Disorders Among Inmates of Concentration Camps and Repatriates', *Psychiatric Quarterly*, Vol. 25, 1951, pp. 683–4, 687.

12 Robert E. Litman, 'Sigmund Freud on Suicide', in *Essays in Self-Destruction*, ed. Edwin S. Shneidman, New York, 1967, pp. 324 ff. This is a lucid, illuminating and exceptionally helpful essay.

13 Ludwig Binswanger, 'The Case of Ellen West', in *Existence*, ed. Rollo May, *et al*, New York, 1958, p. 295.

14 Paul Friedman (ed.), *On Suicide – With Particular Reference to Suicide Among Young Students*, New York and Folkestone, 1967.

15 Sigmund Freud, 'Mourning and Melancholia', *Complete Psychological Works*, ed. James Strachey *et al.*, xiv, London, 1964, p. 252.

16 Leonard M. Moss and Donald M. Hamilton, 'Psychotherapy of the Suicidal Patient', in *Clues to Suicide*, ed. Edwin S. Shneidman and Norman L. Farberow, New York, 1957, and Maidenhead, 1963, pp. 99–110.

17 Freud, op. cit., XIV, p. 247.

18 Freud, 'The Ego and the Id', *Complete Psychological Works*, XIX, London, 1964, p. 53.

19 ibid., p. 58.

20 See S. A. K. Strahan, *Suicide and Insanity*, London, 1893, p. 108.

21 See Fedden, op. cit., p. 305.

22 Hannah Arendt, *The Human Condition*, Chicago, 1958, and London, 1959, p. 319.

23 Nadezhda Mandelstam, *Hope Against Hope*, New York, 1970, and London, 1971, p. 261.

24 *Artaud Anthology*, ed. Jack Hirschman, San Francisco, 1965, and Great Horwood, 1967, p. 56.

25 Paul Valéry, *Oeuvres*, Paris, 1962, II, pp. 610–11.

26 Neil Kessel, 'Self-Poisoning', in *Essays in Self-Destruction*, (see note 12 above), p. 35.

4. SUICIDE AND LITERATURE

1 Elliott Jaques, 'Death and the Mid-Life Crisis', *International Journal of Psycho-Analysis*, Vol. 46, 1965, pp. 502–14.

2 *The Divine Comedy of Dante Alighieri*, with translation and comment by John D. Sinclair, London and New York, 1948, I, p. 177.

3 J. Huizinga, *The Waning of the Middle Ages*, New York, 1954, p. 147.

4 *The Essayes of Michael Lord of Montaigne*, trans. John Florio, Oxford, 1929, II, p. 25.

5 See M. D. Faber, 'Shakespeare's Suicides', in *Essays in Self-Destruction*, ed. Edwin S. Shneidman, New York, 1967, pp. 31–7.

6 *The Complete Poetry and Selected Prose of John Donne*, ed. Charles M. Coffin, New York, 1952, pp. 387–8.

7 *Biathanatos*, New York, 1930, pp. 17, 18.

8 Donald Ramsay Roberts, 'The Death Wish of John Donne', *Publications of the Modern Language Society of America*, LXII, 1947, pp. 958–76.

9 Izaak Walton, 'The Life of John Donne', in *Walton's Lives*, London and New York, 1951, p. 56.

10 ibid., p. 62.

11 Coffin, op. cit., pp. 375–6.

12 Lawrence Babb, *The Elizabethan Malady*, East Lansing, 1951, p. 184. See also Babb's *Sanity in Bedlam*, East Lansing, 1959.

13 *The Anatomy of Melancholy*, Part 1, Section 4, Mem. 1; sixteenth ed., 1838, p. 285. The other quotations are from the same section.

14 Bergen Evans, *The Psychiatry of Robert Burton*, London and New York, 1944, p. vii.

15 S. E. Sprott, *The English Debate on Suicide from Donne to Hume*, La Salle, Illinois, 1961, pp. 121–2.

16 David Hume, *Essays Moral, Political and Literary*, London, 1898, 2 vols, II, pp. 410, 411–12.

17 Horace Walpole, *Correspondence*, ed. W. S. Lewis, vol. 31, London and New Haven, 1961, p. 337.

18 Robert Southey, *The Life and Works of William Cowper*, London, 1836, I, p. 7.

19 ibid., pp. 120–31.

20 Unless otherwise noted, all Chatterton quotations are from John Cranstoun Nevill, *Thomas Chatterton*, London and Toronto, 1948.

21 See Sigmund Freud, 'Fragment of an Analysis of a Case of Hysteria' (1905), *Complete Psychological Works*, VII, London, 1964, p. 23 et seq.

22 John H. Ingram, *The True Chatterton*, London, 1910, p. 280.

23 William James, *The Varieties of Religious Experience*, London, 1902, p. 364.

24 *Cit.* Ingram, op. cit., p. 31.

25 ibid., p. 112.

26 *The Letters of John Keats*, ed. by Maurice Buxton Forman, third ed., London and New York, 1948, p. 384.

27 See one of the earliest documents of English Romanticism, Edward Young's *Conjectures on Original Composition*, 1759: 'An Original may be said to be of a *vegetable* nature; it rises spontaneously from the vital root of genius; it *grows*, it is not *made* ...' *Cit.* Raymond Williams, *Culture and Society 1780–1950*, London, 1958, p. 37.

28 This and the following two quotations are from Richard

Friedenthal, *Goethe: His Life and Times*, London and New York, 1965, pp. 128, 130, 219

29 *Cit*. Forbes Winslow, *The Anatomy of Suicide*, London, 1840, p. 118.

30 *Seven Types of Ambiguity*, London, 1930, and New York, 1931, p. 205.

31 'Thoughts for the Times on War and Death' (1915), in *Complete Psychological Works*, XIV, London, 1964, p. 296.

32 Maxime Du Camp, *Literary Recollections*, London, 1893, I, p. 112; II, p. 122.

33 *Correspondance*, Paris, 1887–93, II, pp. 191, 58.

34 All the quotations in this paragraph are from Louis Maigron, *Romanticism et les Moeurs*, Paris, 1910. He has a particularly fascinating and informative chapter called 'Romanticism and Suicide'.

35 This is a large statement to stand unsupported. I have discussed this theme in detail in the title essay of *Beyond All This Fiddle*, London, 1968, and New York, 1969, pp. 7–11.

36 *Soren Kierkegaard's Journals and Papers*, ed. and trans H. V. and E. H. Kong, Bloomington, Indiana, 1967, and London, 1968, p. 345.

37 This and the two following quotations are from *The Diary of a Writer*, translated by Boris Brasol, London and New York, 1949, pp. 469, 472–3, 546.

38 Ludwig Wittgenstein, *Notebooks, 1914–16*, ed. Anscombe, Rhees and Von Wright, Oxford and New York, 1961, p. 91e. Entry dated 10.1.17.

39 *Autobiographies*, New York, 1953, and London 1955, pp. 348–9.

40 Manifesto by Louis Aragon at the second Dada manifestation, 5 February 1920, at the *Salon des Indépendants*. Quoted by Maurice Nadeau, *The History of Surrealism*, trans. Richard Howard, London, 1968, p. 62.

41 See *The Dada Painters and Poets: An Anthology*, ed. Robert Motherwell, New York, 1951. Unless otherwise indicated, all the quotations in this chapter are from this book which gathers together all the essential histories, manifestos and memoirs.

42 Hans Richter, *Dada*, London and New York, 1965, p. 20.

43 André Breton, 'La Confession dédaigneúse', *cit.* Nadeau, op. cit., p. 54.

44 See Richter, op. cit., p. 172.

45 *La Révolution Surréaliste*, no. 12, December 1929.

46 ibid.

47 See Nadeau, op. cit., p. 102.

48 Wilfred Owen, *Collected Letters*, ed. Harold Owen and John Bell, London and New York, 1967, p. 521.

49 Robert Jay Lifton, *Death in Life. The Survivors of Hiroshima*, London and New York, 1968, p. 500. And see pp. 479–541, 'The Survivor'.

50 Keisuke Harada, cit. Lifton, op. cit., p. 528.

51 Used by Anne Sexton as epitaph to her *Selected Poems*, London, 1964, p. ix.

52 Boris Pasternak, *An Essay in Autobiography*, trans. Manya Harari, London and New York, 1959, pp. 91–3. '*Shigalyov-shchina*' means, according to Mrs Harari's notes, '"Shigalyov methods". Shigalyov is a conspirator in Dostoievski's *The Possessed* who "sets out from boundless freedom and arrives at boundless despotism". According to another member of the conspiracy he says, "everyone must spy and inform on everyone else . . . All are slaves and equal in their slavery . . ."'

53 Hannah Arendt, *The Origins of Totalitarianism*, New York, 1951, pp. 423–4. See also the whole section 'Totalitarianism in Power', pp. 376–428.

54 *This Way for the Gas, Ladies and Gentlemen*, London and New York, 1967, p. 64. I have discussed Borowski and the general problems of writing about the concentration camps in 'The Literature of the Holocaust', op. cit., pp. 22–33.

55 Andrzej Wirth, 'A Discovery of Tragedy', *The Polish Review*, Vol. 12, 1967, pp. 43–52.

56 Hayden Carruth, 'A Meaning of Robert Lowell', *The Hudson Review*, Autumn 1967, pp. 429–47.

57 Introduction to *New Poems*, in *Phoenix*, London, 1961, p. 221.

Index